Hitchcock and Herrmann

Hitchcock and Herrmann

The Friendship and Film Scores That Changed Cinema

STEVEN C. SMITH

OXFORD
UNIVERSITY PRESS

Oxford University Press is a department of the University of Oxford.
It furthers the University's objective of excellence in research, scholarship,
and education by publishing worldwide. Oxford is a registered trade mark of
Oxford University Press in the UK and certain other countries.

Published in the United States of America by Oxford University Press
198 Madison Avenue, New York, NY 10016, United States of America.

© Oxford University Press 2025

All rights reserved. No part of this publication may be reproduced, stored in a retrieval system, transmitted, used for text and data mining, or used for training artificial intelligence, in any form or by any means, without the prior permission in writing of Oxford University Press, or as expressly permitted by law, by license or under terms agreed with the appropriate reprographics rights organization. Inquiries concerning reproduction outside the scope of the above should be sent to the Rights Department, Oxford University Press, at the address above.

You must not circulate this work in any other form
and you must impose this same condition on any acquirer.

Library of Congress Cataloging-in-Publication Data
Names: Smith, Steven C., author.
Title: Hitchcock and Herrmann : the friendship and film scores
that changed cinema / Steven C. Smith.
Description: [1.] | New York : Oxford University Press, 2025. |
Includes bibliographical references and index.
Identifiers: LCCN 2025004953 (print) | LCCN 2025004954 (ebook) |
ISBN 9780197681282 (hardback) | ISBN 9780197681305 (epub) |
ISBN 9780197681299 | ISBN 9780197681312
Subjects: LCSH: Herrmann, Bernard, 1911–1975. | Hitchcock, Alfred, 1899–1980. |
Composers—United States—Biography. | Motion picture producers and
directors—United States—Biography. | Motion picture
music—United States—20th century—History and criticism. |
Motion pictures and music—United States—History—20th century. |
Male friendship. | LCGFT: Biographies.
Classification: LCC ML410.H562 S6 2025 (print) |
LCC ML410.H562 (ebook) |
DDC 781.5/42092 [B]—dc23/eng/20250211
LC record available at https://lccn.loc.gov/2025004953
LC ebook record available at https://lccn.loc.gov/2025004954

DOI: 10.1093/oso/9780197681282.001.0001

Printed by Sheridan Books, Inc., United States of America

The manufacturer's authorized representative in the EU for product safety is
Oxford University Press España S.A., Parque Empresarial San Fernando de Henares,
Avenida de Castilla, 2 – 28830 Madrid (www.oup.es/en).

*For Wayne Bryan and Patt Morrison
who put me on the path*

In each man, of course, a demon lies hidden.
—Fyodor Dostoevsky, *The Brothers Karamazov*

I'd like to have lived here then. The color and the excitement . . . the power . . . the freedom.
—*Vertigo*, final screenplay draft by Samuel Taylor

Contents

List of Illustrations	ix
Prelude	1
1. Shadows of Doubt	12
2. Troubles with Harry	32
3. The Team That Knew So Much	55
4. Wronged Men	76
5. I Want You So to Love Me: *Vertigo*, Part 1	94
6. We'll Just Have the Camera and You: *Vertigo*, Part 2	115
7. On the Rocks	132
8. Something Terrible Is Going to Happen: *Psycho*, Part 1	148
9. The Real *Psycho* Theme: *Psycho*, Part 2	164
10. Electronic Assassins	180
11. Murder by Television	197
12. Torture the Women: *Marnie*	212
13. The Curtain Falls: Part 1	228
14. The Curtain Falls: Part 2	244
15. Coda: Hitchcock's Secret	258
Acknowledgments	271
Notes	275
Selected Bibliography	289
Index	291

Illustrations

P.1	Bernard Herrmann, c. 1974.	3
P.2	Bernard Herrmann, early 1940s.	4
P.3	Alfred Hitchcock, c. 1955.	6
P.4	Lew Wasserman.	9
1.1	James Stewart, Grace Kelly, and Hitchcock on the set of *Rear Window*, 1953.	13
1.2	Hitchcock directs *The Pleasure Garden* (1925), Alma Reville behind him.	16
1.3	Hitch and Alma marry on December 2, 1926.	17
1.4	During the 1955 filming of *The Man Who Knew Too Much*.	20
1.5	Bernard Herrmann, mid-1940s.	23
1.6	Ida Herrmann with (from left) her children, Louis, Rose, and Benny.	25
1.7	Benny and Orson Welles during the filming of *Citizen Kane*, 1940.	29
2.1	Jerry Mathers makes a discovery in *The Trouble with Harry* (1955).	33
2.2	Hitch, John Forsythe, and Shirley MacLaine in Vermont, 1954.	35
2.3	Benny at home with mother Ida, Lucy Anderson, and his daughters from his first marriage, Dorothy (Taffy) and Wendy.	41
2.4	Benny poolside with one of Bluebell Avenue's feline family members.	41
2.5	Benny works at home, late 1940s.	42
2.6	Herrmann conducts at CBS, 1940s.	50
2.7	Hitch and Benny in 1955—the first official photo of the pair.	53
3.1	Hitch during production of *The Man Who Knew Too Much* with (from left) art director Henry Bumstead, unit production manager C. O. "Doc" Erickson, and associate producer Herbert Coleman.	57
3.2	The assassin (Reggie Nalder) prepares.	60
3.3	Sheet music for *Man*'s Oscar-winning song, 1956.	62
3.4	Hitch directs Benny at the Albert Hall, May 1955. © Academy of Motion Picture Arts & Sciences.	68
3.5	*Storm Clouds* composer Arthur Benjamin sits between Hitch and Benny. © Academy of Motion Picture Arts & Sciences.	69
3.6	Herrmann onscreen in *The Man Who Knew Too Much*.	73
4.1	Herrmann rehearsing the Glendale Symphony, 1957.	78

x ILLUSTRATIONS

4.2	Hitch and Robert Burks capture Henry Fonda on a New York subway, 1956.	82
4.3	*The Wrong Man* publicity still.	89
5.1	Benny with first wife Lucille Fletcher, Wendy (left), and Dorothy, 1946.	96
5.2	Hitchcock's smile belies the challenge of filming *Vertigo* (1958).	103
5.3	James Stewart and Kim Novak, *Vertigo* (1958).	103
5.4	Herrmann's pencil score for *Vertigo*'s "Prelude." Courtesy of Norma Herrmann.	107
5.5	Visual innovation that finds a musical analogue: *Vertigo* (1958).	111
6.1	James Stewart, Kim Novak, and Fort Point, San Francisco, in *Vertigo* (1958).	116
6.2	A famous Herrmann portrait, c. 1958, here unretouched.	124
6.3	Jay Livingston and Ray Evans's title song was recorded only once. Signed by Livingston, courtesy of Paul Farrar.	128
6.4	Saul Bass and John Whitney's spiral design for the main title inspired the visuals of *Vertigo*'s ad campaign.	129
7.1	Benny poses his with his beloved dog Twi, c. 1960.	133
7.2	Hitch makes the most of limited time at Mount Rushmore, filming *North by Northwest* in 1958.	138
7.3	Cary Grant and Eva Marie Saint, publicity still.	140
7.4	A twenty-four-hour seduction is deepened by music in *North by Northwest*.	143
7.5	"Every good artist uses black at times": Herrmann stays silent during a legendary set piece.	144
7.6	Benny relaxes between takes in 1959 with bassoonist Don Christlieb. Courtesy of Don Christlieb.	145
8.1	Hitch as master of publicity: *Psycho* (1960).	151
8.2	Directing the shower scene, 1959.	154
8.3	Herrmann embraces the darkness, c. 1960.	157
8.4	Original pencil score for *Psycho*'s "Prelude." Courtesy of Norma Herrmann.	159
9.1	Herrmann, c. 1960.	165
9.2	"For the first time, movies weren't safe": *Psycho* (1960).	167
9.3	*Psycho* publicity still (1960).	170
9.4	An end without resolution: Norman, and a hint of the superimposed Mrs. Bates.	172
9.5	Hitch and Lew Wasserman confer outside the Bates Motel.	175
10.1	Herrmann, early 1960s.	181
10.2	The "only stars" of *The Birds*. Publicity still, 1963.	184
10.3	Assistant Peggy Robertson takes careful notes as usual, 1968.	186
10.4	The ultimate filmmaking course: Hitch and Tippi Hedren, c. 1962.	187

10.5	Filming *The Birds*' finale, 1962.	187
10.6	Benny experiments, with director William Dieterle, on *All That Money Can Buy* (1941).	190
10.7	Hitch and Oskar Sala find new sounds for *The Birds*, West Berlin, December 1962.	194
10.8	Hitch "prepares" moviegoers for the trautonium.	195
11.1	Hitch with Joan Harrison, chief producer of *Alfred Hitchcock Presents* and, with Norman Lloyd, *The Alfred Hitchcock Hour*.	200
11.2	Benny in the studio, 1960.	201
11.3	A Ray Bradbury nightmare comes to life: "The Jar" (1964).	206
11.4	Viewers felt Dana Wynter's fear in "An Unlocked Window" (1965).	209
12.1	Lucy Anderson, c. 1963.	213
12.2	A relationship sours on the set of *Marnie* (1964).	216
12.3	Benny shows the love he gave most freely, c. 1963.	222
12.4	*Marnie* poster (1964).	226
13.1	A glum assignment: Hitch, Julie Andrews, and Paul Newman on the set of *Torn Curtain*, 1965.	235
13.2	Hitch and Newman agree at least to shrug, 1965.	235
13.3	Two admirers and a wary director: Ray Bradbury, Hitchcock, and Herrmann on the set of *Torn Curtain*, 1965.	242
14.1	*Torn Curtain*'s highlight: the killing of Gromek.	245
14.2	Before the fall: December 1965.	249
14.3	Norman Lloyd, one of Herrmann's last supporters at Universal.	253
14.4	Sheet music for *Torn Curtain*'s attempt at a song hit.	256
15.1 and 15.2	1968 passport photos for Norma Herrmann and Benny.	259
15.3	Editor Paul Hirsch, Benny, director Brian De Palma, and producer George Litto recording *Obsession*, August 1975. Courtesy of Paul Hirsch.	264
15.4	Hitchcock receives the AFI Lifetime Achievement Award, 1979. © American Film Institute.	266

Prelude

> *FADE IN: A cloud of steam rising from the manhole covers on a street :00*
> *A taxi starts to come to camera from out of the cloud of steam :07*
> —*Taxi Driver* music timing notes, November 20, 1975[1]

The screen stretched across the studio wall more than twenty feet wide and eight feet tall. But few of the forty musicians who sat beneath it, inside Scoring Stage One of the Burbank Studios, could see—or wished to see—the movie scenes projected above them.

Some of the musicians caught glimpses: of hallucinatory shots of Times Square, a smoke-drenched purgatory of squalor and godlessness . . . of a twelve-year-old prostitute slow-dancing with her pimp . . . of leisure-suited hoods inside New York's filthiest tenement, their flesh ripped opened by the gunfire of an intruder. The killer is a pale man with a Mohawk dressed in camouflage, an arsenal of weapons strapped to his rail-thin body.

The studio musicians—first-chair freelancers, among Hollywood's busiest—faced a soundproof recording booth twenty yards away. Inside it, *Taxi Driver* producer Michael Phillips, director Martin Scorsese, and others watched through glass. During the two days it took to record his film's score, December 22 and 23, 1975, Scorsese's eyes shifted quickly between screen and orchestra.

The musicians' eyes remained on their conductor.

The silver-haired man on the podium was slouched. His posture reflected the fatigue of someone whose poor health—there were rumors of heart problems—was worsened by an eleven-hour flight from his home in London to Los Angeles. Near his leg was the walking stick he used to steady his gait, or knock offending objects out of his path. His tie was crooked, and his worn jacket hung open, framing a paunch. Only sixty-four years old, he looked a decade older.[2]

And yet... the impression conveyed by composer Bernard Herrmann was not weakness. It was intimidation. "We were all scared of Bernie," Michael Phillips later said. "There was a gooseneck lamp that he kept hitting with his baton, and he blamed the lamp." At one point "he quit, and threw his baton into the orchestra."[3] It wasn't his first outburst. Days earlier, after Herrmann's flight landed at Los Angeles International Airport, he reportedly marched to a counter and asked for a ticket back to London. Fortunately, his work ethic overrode his instinct to flee the city that had brought him so much misery.

The music he conducted added to the impression of Herrmann as simmering volcano, with its militaristic blasts of timpani and brass. Even the score's quiet passages—the steady, time-bomb tick of a snare drum, as Travis Bickle drove his taxi... the deceptively lovely jazz theme for saxophone that captured Travis's romantic obsession—even those cues unsettled, like whispers before a scream.

During the sessions, music might stop abruptly with a rap of the conductor's baton. Head tilted down, Herrmann would peer above spectacles resting low on his nose, and shoot a glare known to many in the orchestra after thirty-five years of collaboration and conflict. "You're playing the wrong notes," he told a group of instrumentalists. His voice was low, and still carried a New York City edge twenty-five years after leaving his place of his birth.

One musician politely countered: Was Mr. Herrmann sure? Although the score had them playing different notes, it seemed as if unison writing would be...

"Whaddya want—*LINOLEUM*?"

Another music cue, another baton rap. This time a single musician was targeted. "Hey you!" Herrmann snapped. "Play what's written." His voice dropped to an ominous rasp. "Unless you have a *better* idea."

In the booth, a wide-eyed Scorsese turned to production assistant Chris Soldo. "Holy shit!" Scorsese murmured.

With just two major films to his name, the thirty-three-year-old director had never worked with a composer as abrasive as Herrmann. But during their collaboration, Scorsese saw other sides of the man: His gift for concisely articulating his creative vision. His brilliant on-the-spot adjustments. An unexpected compliment to a musician. His knowledge of film, concert music, literature, and art—a knowledge that both friends and enemies labeled encyclopedic.

Then there were the surprising moments of sentimentality. At the end of a session, or with friends at his flat in London's Regent's Park, Herrmann would

Example P.1 Bernard Herrmann, c. 1974.

quietly share memories, of a life that transported him from Depression-era Second Avenue in New York, to international concert hall platforms, and most famously to Hollywood. There, his mastery at conveying character psychology in music found its ideal vessel in film scores. His first was for *Citizen Kane*. By 1975, many considered him the most brilliant composer working in cinema.

As Scorsese heard *Taxi Driver*'s music for the first time, conducted by Herrmann and Jack Hayes—Herrmann was too weak to lead some cues—the director felt validation. "The only man who could do the score would be Herrmann. There's no one else," Scorsese had told producer Phillips in 1974. "It has to have the feeling of *Marnie*, of *Vertigo*, of *Psycho*."[4]

He wasn't disappointed. The score "gave an immense amount of power to the picture. You see Bob [De Niro] looking left to right, but it's the music under it that provided the psychological basis throughout."

By Day Two of recording, there was less of Herrmann's irascibility. Sporting a blue beret he'd bought in Paris, he joked with the musicians,

Example P.2 Bernard Herrmann, early 1940s.

during his first L.A. session since the late 1960s. "It was an exciting event," assistant Chris Soldo recalled. "The musicians were excited, and there were autograph seekers."[5]

There were also more prominent fans. "You gotta get over here!" Scorsese told twenty-nine-year-old Steven Spielberg by phone. "You gotta meet Bernard Herrmann!" Spielberg, whose breakthrough feature *Jaws* was still packing theaters six months after opening, hung up and headed for Burbank.

Minutes later, the directing wunderkind was crouching before Herrmann, who sat holding his cane before him like a royal scepter. A lifelong soundtrack buff, Spielberg began to gush. "Mr. Herrmann—I'm such an admirer of your work..."

"*Yeah?* So why do you always use *Johnny Williams* for your pictures?!"

Herrmann was a friend and admirer of Williams. But the man who distrusted flattery couldn't resist putting Spielberg on the spot.[6]

Other industry players made the trek. Here in person was a legend—the man whose iconoclasm, and contempt for "empty-heads" who valued dollars over art, had led to his being crossed off Hollywood hiring lists a decade earlier. But his rediscovery in the early 1970s by a new generation of directors, including Scorsese and Brian De Palma, had restored him to the top rank of in-demand composers. His work calendar for the year ahead, 1976, was completely full.

It was clear to Scorsese that Herrmann was savoring his comeback. "He was so vibrant and alive, and so enjoying doing the music. We idolized him." But others who had known Herrmann longer were shocked by his appearance. "I could see he was deathly ill," recalled cellist Eleanor Slatkin. "There was no resemblance to the man I knew, who could be a tyrant. We chatted very amicably. I had empathy for the man, because he looked like a walking ghost."[7]

To twenty-five-year-old scoring coordinator Jill Meyers, Herrmann conveyed a different quality: urgency. An additional half-day on December 24 had been scheduled, "but Herrmann was pushing, pushing, pushing. He was like a steamroller. He wanted to finish on the 23rd. Normally a composer wants to have as much time as possible. It was almost as if he had a premonition."[8]

Thanks to the sight-reading skill of the musicians, and the quiet diplomacy of conductor Jack Hayes, Herrmann got his wish. The recording was completed by 5:30 P.M. on December 23. The composer warmly thanked Hayes and left to join a small party in his honor in an office near the stage. Guiding him through the well-wishers was his wife, Norma. A thirty-five-year-old BBC producer born in Yorkshire, England, Norma possessed a wit, unflappability, and beauty that had buoyed Herrmann's spirits through years of empty appointment diaries.

But before he could leave the studio, Scorsese had one more request. *Taxi Driver* ends with Travis Bickle hailed as a hero, for his vigilante killings of a pimp and other lowlifes. Our last sight of him is in his cab's rear-view mirror, as Travis's eyes dart up suddenly and see—what? "I wanted to get across the idea that it could start all over again," Scorsese recalled. "He could snap at any second. I needed a musical emphasis on that, and Herrmann said, 'You need a sting.' There was a man with xylophones.* The man did the sting [a sharp, accented note or chord] with the xylophone. I said, 'It's too direct, it's too obvious.' Herrmann said, 'Play it backwards!' and walked out. That was the last time I saw him."

---

* The instrument used was a vibraphone, played with hard mallets.

Herrmann left audiences with one more clue that Travis's homicidal rage would flare again. In the score's final seconds, the jazzy sax theme fades away. In its place, low woodwinds intone three notes—an irresolute phrase of menace.

It is the "Madhouse" theme from *Psycho*.

The specter of Alfred Hitchcock loomed over many aspects of *Taxi Driver*. It started with Scorsese's impulse to score his "New York Gothic horror" with music by the composer of *The Man Who Knew Too Much*, *Vertigo*, *North by Northwest*, *Psycho*, and other Hitchcock classics. He was the filmmaker Herrmann was most proud to have worked with . . . the man whose friendship he had cherished . . . and the source of much of his deepest pain. And on December 23, 1975, the last night of Bernard Herrmann's life, Hitchcock would in a sense be near his side.

Columbia had booked Benny and Norma into a hotel near the *Taxi Driver* sessions: the Sheraton Universal. From its top twentieth floor, a guest could see below the movie studio that gave the hotel its name. Within the lot was the office of Alfred Hitchcock, who had made Universal his production home since 1962.

Example P.3 Alfred Hitchcock, c. 1955.

The Master of Suspense was now seventy-six and increasingly infirm after a heart attack months earlier. He had spent much of the year slogging through what would be his final feature, *Family Plot*. By December 1975, its shooting was complete. Hitch had left L.A. to holiday in St. Moritz, Switzerland. As always, he was joined by his wife Alma, a former film editor and screenwriter who for half a century had been his closest creative partner. Hitchcock first visited St. Moritz as a lowly crew member on a British silent film in 1924. Two years later, he and Alma honeymooned there.

Their return in 1975 was shadowed by a depressing realization Hitch shared with his friend, actor Norman Lloyd.[9] Despite the director's usual process of detailed script meetings and months of planning, *Family Plot* fell short of its maker's standards. It was a passable comic thriller, from an artist whose greatest work was as transgressive as it was entertaining.

By 1975, Hitchcock knew that his chief value to Universal was not as a filmmaker, but as a brand. A reminder of past glory loomed on a hill a short walk from his office: the Bates mansion from 1960's *Psycho*. That iconic house of horrors was now among the most popular stops on the Universal Studios Tour. As buses carted movie fans past the Victorian-style façade, their photo op was embellished by audio blasting from the tram's speakers: shrill and shrieking strings. It triggered jumps and nervous laughter. They needed no explanation that it was the shower murder music from *Psycho*.

Well into the twenty-first century, the ubiquity of that music—the most imitated, most parodied in film—defies measurement. A Google search yields some eight million references. Even toddlers imitate its slashing "*Eeek eeek eeek*" without ever having seen *Psycho*. The sixth of nine Hitchcock-Herrmann collaborations—eight would see completion—*Psycho* was "the masterpiece that culminated the period in which Hitchcock and his public were in closest touch," author William Rothman observed.[10] The film had been a risky experiment, financed by Hitchcock himself. And it might only exist today in massively shortened form as a television program, if not for Herrmann. When Hitch lost faith in the film before its scoring, it was his composer who rescued it with a daring idea: "to complement the black-and-white photography of the film with a black-and-white sound,"[11] created entirely with strings.

Starting with the mordantly comic *The Trouble with Harry*, through 1964's *Marnie*, Hitch and Benny—their names for each other—forged an artistic bond rooted in emotions they both knew well. Fear. Anxiety. Hate. Desire. That teaming endured despite their disparate personalities and backgrounds: Hitchcock was a Catholic from London who loathed conflict. Herrmann was a volatile Jew from New York's East Side.

The drama of their collaboration played against a fast-changing industry backdrop. Independent film productions, television, and rock 'n' roll were rewriting the traditions of moviemaking that Hollywood studios had followed since the 1920s. A young generation of moviegoers, later known as baby boomers, weren't interested in glamour and happy endings. They wanted edge and reality, and stories that reflected the libidinous freedom and anti-authoritarianism of their own lives. And if Hollywood, still bowing to rules of censorship written in 1930, couldn't deliver, steamy European imports with stars like Brigitte Bardot could.

Watching these cultural shifts with the steady calculation of an abacus was a black-tied businessman who had more power behind the scenes than any studio chief. Lew Wasserman had helped build Music Corporation of America, better known as MCA, into the world's largest talent agency, handling over seven hundred of Hollywood and Broadway's finest. In the 1950s, with cofounder Jules Stein as chairman and Wasserman as president, MCA expanded into TV production. A decade later, MCA owned and operated Universal Studios.

In 1953, Wasserman's genius for deal-making made possible the most sustained period of greatness in the career of Alfred Hitchcock. It also played a role in the bitter final rupture between Hitchcock and Herrmann—an event now almost as famous as the films and scores that preceded it.

"Each of the three men had discovered that the other allowed him to realize his dreams," observed film historian R. Lee Procter. "But they worked in a volatile, ever-evolving art form. Hitchcock was an artist-businessman. Herrmann was driven by an absolute need to express himself, and to prove that his insights were correct. Lew Wasserman was inventing a new industry ecosystem. These three people, each a force of nature, merged out of self-interest. But the seeds of that merger's implosion were there from the beginning."[12]

Example P.4 Lew Wasserman.

October 16, 2022. The Alexandra Palace, London. On the stage of the 1873 theater, actors Toby Jones and Tim McInnerny stand before an audience of 700. Jones is portraying Alfred Hitchcock. McInnerny is Bernard Herrmann. Tonight is the premiere of Andrew McCaldon's drama "Benny & Hitch," which will air on BBC Radio 3 and later receive the BBC Audio Drama Award for writing. Behind the actors, the BBC Concert Orchestra will punctuate the dialogue—imagined by McCaldon, reflecting real events—with music from its characters' films. Skillfully blending fact and imagination, McCaldon places the two men in an afterlife, where they relive their triumphs and relitigate the conflict that tore them apart.

HITCH: *Might I at least set the scene?*
BENNY: *Set it! Not direct it.*
HITCH: *Very well. Wide shot. A recording studio. Los Angeles, 1966 ... and on the floor—a corpse.*

BENNY: *Metaphorical!*
HITCH: *A cadaver. The bloodied body on the parquet is all that remains of our professional collaboration.*
BENNY: *The greatest composer-director relationship in film history. Isn't that how it's always written up today?*
HITCH: *Yes, Benny. And that relationship lies dead on the floor as a result of your betrayal.*
BENNY: *The crime—the treachery—was against* me.... *Never did let fidelity to the facts get in the way of a good story, did you?*[13]

The breadth of Bernard Herrmann's career extended far beyond his work with Hitchcock. It included a symphony, an opera, and thousands of radio scores, many of them suffused with joy and optimism. But it is his scores for Hitchcock—hypnotic tone poems of anxiety, romance, horror, and dread—that have come to define his legacy. As our world becomes ever more frightening, its dangers more random, Herrmann's music is the soundtrack of our time.

To understand how that came to be, the reader must know not only the story's title characters but key supporting players—gifted men and women, whose essential roles often have been overlooked. We must also see beyond Hitchcock's oft-repeated claim that for him, shooting a movie was "boring," since he had already completed the project in his head. In 1966, the director confided his true feelings to a friend about the process of filming: "I go through hell."[14] Of the nine movies on which Hitch and Benny partnered, only two were shot without significant difficulties and changes.

"I've never met a producer who said to me, 'I've just finished a film and I don't need *you*!' " Herrmann once told a London audience, to appreciative laughter. "They say, 'You must come and see what you can do to *help* us. I wish it were possible historically to see some films the way they were given to the composer, and if they were given to the world that way, whether they would be regarded with the same esteem."[15]

In the pages that follow, the author's hope is to realize Herrmann's wish. You are invited to observe Hitchcock's filmmaking process from beginning to end. We will sit at his side during script meetings, and see the frustrations and compromises of a shoot day, as the director battles weather, a weak performance, and the mysterious *something* that keeps a scene from coming alive in front of the camera. From there, we will eavesdrop on discussions between director and composer, as they discuss a film's flaws that music may help. Then, under Herrmann's confident pen, a score is created. One that compresses or extends time for suspense . . . bolsters an awkward performance . . . and adds atmosphere so crucial it becomes a character in itself.

We will also travel to the present day, to see how music that was underappreciated when written is now celebrated, imitated, and exploited, in a range of media that would have amazed both director and composer. Herrmann's scores for Hitchcock have been reused in major theatrical features, including a Quentin Tarantino blockbuster and a Best Picture winner; in symphony and pop concerts; in a music video by Lady Gaga; and in everything else from mobile phone ringtones to hit Broadway musicals.

"*Sweeney [Todd]* is an homage to Bernard Herrmann," Stephen Sondheim said in 2003. "I even used a chord in the show that's what I call my Bernard Herrmann chord, and that is one of the basic building blocks of the whole piece."[16]

With help from insights by twenty-first-century musicians, filmmakers, and others, we will also unlock how Herrmann pulls us inexorably into the narrative of a nightmare, until the person we see onscreen is not James Stewart, or Kim Novak, or Anthony Perkins, or Janet Leigh.

Instead, we see ourselves.

1
Shadows of Doubt

From the beginning of the story, there was music.

Not just the popular tunes played on a piano inside Chasen's Restaurant, where Alfred and Alma Hitchcock relaxed on a cool August evening in 1954. Decades earlier, more aggressive music—the hot jazz of the 1920s—had played a role in the event the Hitchcocks were celebrating. For without '20s jazz, there would have been no MCA.

The Music Corporation of America had been formed in 1924 with the modest goal of booking dance bands. By 1954, it was one of Hollywood's most powerful corporations, negotiating multimillion-dollar deals for the industry's top figures. It was MCA that strategized the stunning financial win that Hitchcock and Alma reveled in that night in Beverly Hills.[1]

All Hollywood knew that Hitch's latest release, *Rear Window*, had opened spectacularly. But few were aware how greatly he would reap the rewards. *Rear Window* was the first movie made under a new contract the fifty-four-year-old director had signed with Paramount Pictures. Hitch was now one of the highest-paid and most creatively independent filmmakers in the history of cinema.

The deal marked a high point in a career that began over three decades earlier in the British film industry. From the start, Hitch's aim was to work in America—a dream he realized in 1938, by signing a Hollywood contract with producer David O. Selznick. His first US title, *Rebecca*, grossed the modern equivalent of $130 million, and won the Oscar for 1940's Best Picture. But Hitchcock soon chafed under Selznick's notorious micro-management. In 1947, he left Selznick to lead his own company, Transatlantic Pictures. But dreams of artistic control and sizable wealth quickly faded, after two commercial flops. Transatlantic was dissolved in 1953.[2]

The debts incurred by the company left Hitchcock creatively uncertain and financially insecure. Even at the best of times, he had a "highly neurotic preoccupation with money," according to colleague John Houseman.[3]

Fortunately, Hitchcock had a protector—an agent whose skill when it came to the art of the deal was precisely what the director needed.

Example 1.1 James Stewart, Grace Kelly, and Hitchcock on the set of *Rear Window*, 1953.

Six feet, two inches tall, as fit and trim as his client was corpulent, Lew Wasserman cut a figure of power. In 1945, the thirty-two-year-old agent began representing Hitch after Lew's employer, MCA, bought the clientele of the coveted Hayward-Deverich Agency. Swallowing other agencies was an MCA specialty. And after a federal judge dubbed MCA "the Octopus ... with tentacles reaching out to all phases and grasping everything in show business," the nickname stuck.[4]

In 1946, Lew became the Octopus's president; and despite his many duties, his involvement in Hitch's life grew. The director had few close friends, but Wasserman was among them. In January 1952, Lew cut a deal that placed Hitchcock at Warner Bros. There, he would produce and direct four films. His salary was a princely $999,000, plus some limited profit-sharing.[5] The deal was a win for director and studio, yielding hits like *Dial M for Murder*.

Lew counseled Hitch to invest in oil and livestock. Those moves netted his client wealth and security. Even a crisis led to opportunity. In March 1953,

Warner Bros. froze production costs. Jack Warner was distressed by falling box office, triggered in part by movies' biggest rival, television. Hitchcock urged Wasserman to find him another studio... and Lew knew exactly which company to call.

Since its founding in 1912, Paramount Pictures prided itself on both profit and sophistication. In the Depression-era 1930s, the antics of the Marx Brothers shared the screens of Paramount-owned theaters with the European polish of Marlene Dietrich and director Ernst Lubitsch. In the 1940s, Paramount gave audiences the rapid-patter comedies of Hope and Crosby, and director Preston Sturges, along with the work of Billy Wilder, a master of comedy *and* drama.

Then Hollywood underwent a tectonic change. In 1948, a government anti-monopoly ruling forced the studios to sell the theater chains they owned. Now there was no need for a flood of product, since the studios didn't own theaters to fill. Budgets were slashed, contract staff let go. It was the start of a new era—one in which actors and directors took charge of their own careers, working as freelancers and naming their own prices. The twenty-five-year era of the Hollywood studio system had begun its death rattle.

Paramount transitioned better than most. It convinced prestige directors like George Stevens and William Wyler to make Paramount their base, while retaining Billy Wilder and Cecil B. DeMille.

Another colossus was about to join them. Wasserman knew that Hitchcock had fans at Paramount: studio head Y. Frank Freeman and production chief Don Hartman. When Lew told the pair that Hitchcock was open to offers, the moguls did more than roll out a welcome mat. They agreed to a contract that only Wasserman could have orchestrated—one that would be a milestone in his client's career.

Hitchcock would produce and direct nine motion pictures for the studio. Four would be considered Paramount productions, the other five Alfred Hitchcock productions. For each Paramount production, the director would be paid $150,000 (or $250,000, depending on the source).[6] But he would also receive 10 percent of the gross profits, after twice the budget cost was recouped. Gross profits, based on straight box office take, were a rare concession by a studio, which preferred to award "net" profits that could be fiddled into nonexistence by accountants.

Hitch would receive no salary for his five Hitchcock productions. Instead, he got something more valuable. He would have *total ownership* of these five films, starting eight years after their premiere. He would also have control over story choice, screenwriters, casting, editing, and publicity, as long as his film cost $3 million or less. At the time, the average budget for an A-picture was $1.5 million.

Paramount had rarely if ever conceded so much to a filmmaker. But Hitchcock would repay their trust with the most consistently great work of his six-decade career.

The deal was a high point in the life of a man whose arrival in the world, fifty-four years earlier, promised little more than obscurity. Born on August 13, 1899, Alfred Joseph Hitchcock was a product of Britain's rigid caste system. The son of a middle-class greengrocer, Alfred lived above the family shop in London's unfashionable East End.

By his teens, he entertained fantasies of escape. His fascination with the visual drew him to study draftsmanship and advertising design. At London's Goldsmiths University, he studied art. In time, he would possess an infallible sense of composition and color.

He also rehearsed for the future he intended to have. Often alone—the unattractive, heavy-set boy did not make friends easily—he loved to don his best suit and dine in fine restaurants. (His greengrocer father instilled in him a love of quality food.) After dinner he headed for the cinema; and in the darkness of a movie palace, he studied both the film and audience reactions. Alfred's other love was theater, and at plays he took note of how a shift of colored lighting could electrify viewers. The intensity of some dramas, like J. M. Barrie's ghost story *Mary Rose*, gripped him so completely that decades later he could recall a specific lighting effect or the incidental music.

But film, not theater, became his focus. In 1920, Alfred submitted a portfolio of drawings to Famous Players-Lasky, a UK subsidiary of . . . Paramount Pictures. Shrewdly, he had drawn sample intertitles (dialogue cards) for an upcoming Lasky film. The movie was never made—but Hitchcock was.

As a jack-of-all-trades at Famous-Lasky, he found a new confidence. He exhibited an attitude of insolent, bawdy humor. And after tackling art direction, scriptwriting, and assistant direction, there was only one job he clamored for. He got it in May 1925, with *The Pleasure Garden*—the first motion picture directed by Alfred Hitchcock. Serving as his assistant was a petite twenty-five-year-old brunette born one day after him. Her name was Alma Reville.

Example 1.2 Hitchcock directs *The Pleasure Garden* (1925), Alma Reville behind him.

A respected film editor before Hitch set foot in a studio, Alma had versatility equal to his. After starting as a movie cutter, she graduated to supervising continuity on set, making sure that details like actors' wardrobes matched from shot to shot. She even acted. And by 1925, in the vital role of assistant director, Alma proved an agile problem solver.

For Hitch it was respect at first sight, followed by love. But not until he outranked her at the studio did the director feel it proper to (fumblingly) propose marriage.

The union that began on December 2, 1926, would last until Hitchcock's death. And despite the growing complexities of her husband's personality, their union remained a love match—for each other, and for the movies they made together. "The Hitchcock touch had four hands," critic Charles Champlin wrote in 1982, "and two of them were Alma's."[7]

Two months after marriage came Hitchcock's first success. *The Lodger*, a fog-shrouded variation on Jack the Ripper, was filled with startling camera angles and shock cuts. It starred stage heartthrob Ivor Novello as Hitchcock's first "wrong man," accused of killings he didn't commit. *The Lodger*'s story

Example 1.3 Hitch and Alma marry on December 2, 1926.

and themes would become Hitchcock signatures, as would its visual style. At one point, a group of apartment dwellers look up at the ceiling; a dissolve lets us see the footsteps pacing above them as if the floor had vanished.

Hitch's next decade was one of steady ascendance. As Alma stepped back from studio work—daughter Patricia was born in 1928—her husband helmed his first sound feature, *Blackmail* (1929). In 1934, he hit his stride with a string of thrillers that blended romance, humor, and sweat-wringing suspense: *The Man Who Knew Too Much*, *The 39 Steps*, *Sabotage*, *Young and Innocent*, *The Lady Vanishes*. At a time when few British titles played in America, Hitchcock's movies found favor abroad . . . and, by 1938, in the screening room of David O. Selznick.

Even under the thumb of his manic, pill-popping boss, Hitch managed to stretch his wings. When Selznick loaned him to other studios, the director took fuller charge of films like *Foreign Correspondent*, a sneakily pro-British propaganda tale, made before the United States entered World War II; *Shadow of a Doubt*, starring Joseph Cotten as an all-American serial killer; and *Notorious*, an espionage romance that flouted censors by making Ingrid Bergman's sex life—she's enlisted by US agents to bed and marry a Nazi—central to the plot. But even on these titles, Hitchcock worked within restrictions, imposed by the studio to which he was loaned.

Flash forward to 1954. *Rear Window*'s status as the year's third highest-grossing film—only *White Christmas* and *20,000 Leagues under the Sea* topped it[8]—meant that Hitchcock, with his percentage of the gross, would receive a bonus check larger than most of his past salaries.

Gross-point earnings were becoming a Wasserman specialty. Five years earlier, Lew negotiated a similar deal for James Stewart, on the western *Winchester '73*. That agreement "changed completely how Hollywood did business," Wasserman biographer Dennis McDougal wrote, "and hastened the funeral of the long-dying studio system. . . . *Winchester '73* was not the first ever gross profit deal, but it was the biggest."[9]

Like Hitchcock's, Wasserman's career had been a steady climb. It started in 1925, when twelve-year-old Lew sold candy in a Cleveland burlesque house. The film buff then got a job ushering at a movie house. And in 1935, Lew talked his way into becoming publicity director at Cleveland's red-hot Mayfair Casino. Its clientele included MCA agents, who took notice of the tall, handsome publicist, and offered him a job—in the mail room.

But Wasserman knew how to jump rungs ahead of rivals. Within months he was MCA's national publicity director. In 1938, MCA cofounder Jules Stein dispatched Lew and his wife Edie to California. There, Wasserman grew the agency's roster beyond musicians, to include Hollywood stars, producers, and directors. Bette Davis was the first, and by 1945 hundreds followed, including Henry Fonda, James Stewart, Katharine Hepburn, Laurence Olivier, Fred Astaire, Judy Garland, Barbara Stanwyck, Gregory Peck, Billy Wilder . . . and Alfred Hitchcock.

Key to Wasserman's success was his attention to detail, and a computer-like ability to calculate data. Recalled a friend, "He could walk into a theater and tell you how many kernels of corn were in a bag of popcorn, how many bags were sold, and whether the house was being cheated or not. He had that kind of mind."[10]

Like Hitchcock, he also knew the importance of outward show. "When I became a talent agent," Lew said, "the word 'agent' was synonymous with 'pimp.' Talent agents wore green suits and hung around street corners with big cigars in their mouths. I wanted to change the image."[11] Thus was born the bespoke black suit, white shirt, and black tie that became MCA's uniform. It was similar to Hitchcock's daily attire: a dark suit with white shirt, dark tie, and carefully polished shoes. The two men also shared an obsession with neatness. Under Lew's presidency, an MCA agent's desktop had to be totally clean by the end of each day.

Galvanized by freedom creative and financial, Hitchcock's work tempo leapt into light speed. Between 1954 and 1960 he would release a new film every year. That pace was reflected in a very good problem he faced in November 1954: Hitch had shot two back-to-back movies, and both were in post-production at the same time.

Movie #1, the silky *To Catch a Thief* starring Cary Grant and Grace Kelly, required months of filming, partly in Monaco. Movie #2, *The Trouble with Harry*, was smaller, quirkier, and more personal, and therefore made with less money and greater speed.

Composer Lyn Murray would be scoring *Thief* until late February, so a second composer was needed for *Harry*. That film's offbeat blend of macabre humor, lyrical imagery, and romance required delicate handling musically.

Hitch was at a loss to name someone up to the task.

Although he played no instrument, Hitchcock considered himself musically sophisticated. His record collection included works by Elgar, Bartók, and Sibelius. In his years of studying silent cinema, he took note of which symphonic pieces worked best as accompaniment. But the street songs of his childhood in London were closer to his heart. Sometimes at his office, he "crooned old music-hall tunes," a secretary recalled.[12]

In film he recognized the need for underscore, but kept it to a minimum. More to his liking was *diegetic music*—the word for music heard by characters within the story, like a singer or a band. In Hitchcock's hands, music that seemed innocuous could create a chilling contrapuntal effect. "You can have . . . a man come in a room and murder a woman," he said, "and have somebody across the road playing the piano, playing pop music—which is even more dramatic, to hear this 'giggly' music playing."[13] That technique was a highlight of 1951's *Strangers on a Train*: as an unfaithful wife is strangled at an amusement park, the only sound we hear is a distant

Example 1.4 During the 1955 filming of *The Man Who Knew Too Much*.

merry-go-round, its calliope chirping the 1895 singalong "The Band Played On." The soundtrack's realism places us *at* the murder scene. It even makes us feel complicit.

Hitchcock used musical metaphors when describing directing. "The size of the image on the screen and its composition is really orchestration. It's no good throwing a close-up on the screen just for the sake of a close-up. It's like music. You have loud brass when you need it."[14] Several of his movies used music as a plot device. The cymbal crash in London's Albert Hall, which conceals an assassin's bullet in *The Man Who Knew Too Much*. The folk tune that is actually a spy's coded message in *The Lady Vanishes*. Hitch's first film, *The Pleasure Garden*, opens inside a music hall, as we see an orchestra accompany dancing chorines. The fact that the women wear blond wigs, as a front row of men grin in voyeuristic delight, shows how early Hitchcock shared his own obsessions.

But working for Selznick, he had little say when it came to music. To be fair, Selznick had played a foundational role in the history of film scoring. While running RKO in 1932, he encouraged Max Steiner to write the first sophisticated scores for talkies in Hollywood. But by the 1940s, Selznick's "desire to actively shape every facet" of a film, including its music, "was insatiable, compulsive, and, in the eyes of his critics, overbearing," observed author Nathan Platte.[15]

On his films away from Selznick, Hitchcock could have more involvement. In 1943 he enjoyed working with Russian-born Dimitri Tiomkin. The classically trained composer scored *Shadow of a Doubt*, Hitchcock's own favorite of all his works, enhanced by Tiomkin's demonic variations on *The Merry Widow Waltz*. (Joseph Cotten's serial killer has been tagged "The Merry Widow Murderer," after his fondness for strangling rich widows.)

Just before moving to Paramount, Hitchcock reteamed with Tiomkin at Warner Bros., on *Strangers on a Train*, *I Confess*, and *Dial M for Murder*. These scores have thrilling sequences, and like Hitch, Tiomkin had an instinct for the commercial. In 1953, Tiomkin won two Oscars for a single film, *High Noon*, for its score and its theme song, "Do Not Forsake Me, Oh My Darlin'."

That success fueled a trend. Hollywood became theme-song crazy, and Hitch agreed that movies could benefit from popular music. For the rest of his career, he looked for the logical placement in his films of songs that could be hits. Tiomkin seemed his ideal accomplice. But by 1954, Hitch had tired of "Dimi" 's penchant for musical bombast, and his inflexibility. "Tiomkin used to say to me, 'Come down, we're going to start to [record the score], I want your opinion.' So I go down, hear the first scene. I say, 'I don't like it.' He says, 'Oh, you can't change it now, it's all been orchestrated.' So there is no way of correcting it."[16] The latter wasn't true: if Hitch had wanted a lighter sound, Tiomkin could have directed some musicians to be silent. If Hitch's quote is accurate, it's likely that the composer did not wish to compromise his role on the soundtrack.

Even the masterful Franz Waxman (*Sunset Boulevard, A Place in the Sun*) struck out with Hitchcock. After two "Selznick" scores the director approved of,[17] *Rebecca* and *The Paradine Case*, Hitchcock hired the two-time Oscar winner for *Rear Window*. The director was "very anxious to get from it a popular song," Hitch confessed. And he had a clever justification within the story: among the apartments being spied on by Jimmy Stewart's hero is that of a composer. As the drama progressed, Hitch wanted audiences to hear the evolution of a hit song, from first experimental notes to lush, unforgettable melody. Waxman's theme, "Lisa," was elegant—but when it failed to stand on its own feet commercially, "I was very unhappy."[18]

By 1954, the director had spent fifteen years making films in America, and he had yet to find a composer with whom he truly connected.

As it turned out, that composer was hiding in plain sight.

As early as 1938, Hitchcock may have heard the music of Bernard Herrmann. The composer's first film score, for *Citizen Kane*, was still three years away. But during pre-production on *Rebecca*, Selznick sent Hitch a radio adaptation of the novel starring and produced by Orson Welles.[19] The broadcast's many virtues included a plaintive Herrmann score. But Hitchcock, who'd already had a bellyful of Selznick advice, may have never listened to the show.

In 1941, Selznick heard in *Citizen Kane* the voice of a major new screen composer. In 1945 he pursued Herrmann for *Spellbound*. Benny admired Selznick's high standards and taste; but he also must have known of his smothering involvement in scoring. Herrmann politely declined. Selznick approached him again for another Hitchcock film, *The Paradine Case*. Again, Herrmann said no.

With each rejection, Selznick's team felt relief—a response that puzzled and frustrated the producer. "I don't understand the resistance to him," he snapped in a memo. "If there is anything against Herrmann that I don't know about, I wish everyone would stop keeping secrets from me."[20]

Indeed, there was.

Like the first screen character he captured in music, Charles Foster Kane, Herrmann was a symphony of contrasting traits. His rigorous intellect. His intuitive creativity. His explosive anger. His need for love.

Example 1.5 Bernard Herrmann, mid-1940s.

The most revealing clues to his nature can be found in his music. So a familiar musical structure may be used to describe them.

First Movement (Allegro, quickly)—Carnegie Hall, 1927

Italian-born Arturo Toscanini is in his first year as co–music director of the New York Philharmonic. Intensely charismatic, the conductor will become the nation's barometer of what symphonic works are worth performing.

Performances and rehearsals take place in Carnegie Hall. And during many afternoons, in the elevated tier of Dress Circle, two small figures hide behind the balustrade. Sixteen-year-old Benny Herrmann has found a broken side door that, after minutes of crawling, leads to a spy post twenty feet above the orchestra. Neither Benny nor Jerome Moross, his fourteen-year-old schoolmate, makes a sound as Toscanini summons the music he desires, through skill, cajoling, and rage.[21]

For Benny, Toscanini's diatribes are spellbinding to watch. "Benny had this great love of the glamour image of the cantankerous conductor," a friend recalls.[22] It is behavior Herrmann will emulate, not through imitation but through shared temperament.

But if Toscanini himself is fiery, his musical taste is conservative: a familiar diet of Beethoven, Mozart, and other canonical greats. The teenaged Herrmann vows that when *he* becomes a conductor, he will play forgotten scores from the past, and the composers of his own generation.

Second Movement (Feroce)—Gramercy Park, New York, 1928

Music fills the home of Benny's parents, Abraham and Ida Herrmann. Abraham's collection of 78-rpm records, including modern works like Mahler symphonies, competes with the din of raised voices, as arguments fly between Benny and sister Rose; between Rose and mother Ida; between Ida and husband Abraham. Adding to the racket is the cat-scratch sound of Benny's violin practice, which is at least "better than his piano playing," according to Jerome Moross.[23]

The Herrmanns live in a spacious brownstone at Second Avenue and Eighteenth Street. Tall, glass-doored bookcases are filled with literature devoured by father and son. There is also a bust of Athena, goddess of war. A servant and car are further reflections of their upper-middle-class comfort.[24]

Abraham, born Avram Dardik, is a successful optometrist. He came to America in 1892, aboard a US whaling ship from his native Ukraine. (Perhaps not coincidentally, his son will write a cantata based on *Moby-Dick*.) He arrived in America with a new name, one fitting a man with social aspirations. He may have borrowed "Herrmann" from an employer or a relative. As for why he added an extra "r" and "n," he probably wished to seem more German than Ukrainian.

Benny, born Maximilian Bernard Herrmann on June 29, 1911, is the eldest of three children. ("Bernard" was reportedly in tribute to a late friend of Abraham and Ida.) Precocious and inquisitive, his maturity is quickened by his father's record collection, by Abraham's library of literature, by his father's company at concerts, and by Abraham's tales of his life and romances. "Benny's father used to buy gloves and scarves for his mistresses," a Herrmann intimate recalls. "He had a lot of mistresses."[25]

By 1910, one of the salesgirls wrapping up gloves for Abraham had become his wife. Ida Herrmann was a Russian immigrant some thirty years his junior, as earthy and uneducated as Abraham was elegant. "His father tended towards the aristocratic in attitude, if not in blood," one of Benny's wives recalls. "His mother was the peasant of peasants. And Benny was exactly half of both."[26]

Fights between Abraham and Ida take many forms. He is agnostic; she is devoutly Jewish. He is articulate; she can barely speak English. But what she lacks in vocabulary she makes up for in decibels. "Ida had the same kind of voice Benny had—very strong," neighbor Sarah Cohn recalls. "Mrs. Herrmann was temperamental. Rose was temperamental. They all wanted their own way."[27] At times, the cacophony drives Abraham out of the

Example 1.6 Ida Herrmann with (from left) her children, Louis, Rose, and Benny.

apartment, presumably to more docile female company. Sometimes, fights are a form of entertainment. According to Benny's daughter Dorothy, "For them, arguing was a wonderful time."²⁸

A lower tension simmers between Benny and his younger brother. Louis Herrmann is handsome and athletic. Benny, already bespectacled, has poor vision, no muscle, bony legs, and a bad complexion. Neighborhood bullies brand the delicate boy a sissy. "Benny was very aware of his lack of physical charisma," a friend recalls. "He was not a pretty-looking fellow."²⁹

But if nature favors Louis, Ida favors Benny. She spoils him from birth, massaging his feet and constantly twisting his hair. He becomes so used to her touch on his scalp that the nervous twiddling of his follicles becomes a lifelong habit. "He liked being coddled," Benny's first wife Lucille will remember. "But he was jealous of the position—*longed* for the position—that Louis had. I think that gave Benny an inferiority complex, to have such a handsome, strapping brother who was very attractive to girls."³⁰

Third Movement (Allegretto, fairly brisk)—New York Public Library, 1927

An indifferent student, Benny comes alive memorizing music scores, which he finds in branches of the New York Public Library. Amid fifteenth-century madrigals and compositions by Henry the Eighth, Benny finds music that will help shape his character, including two composers who become lodestars.

Frenchman Hector Berlioz (1803–1869) may not have fired a cannon while conducting, as depicted in a famous caricature. But his music was a form of detonation. Thirty-five years after the elegant classicism of Mozart, Berlioz composed riotous Romantic fever dreams. None was more outrageous, or more loved by Herrmann, than 1830's *Symphonie fantastique*. Berlioz describes in music an artist tormented by romantic obsession. Overdosing on opium, he dreams that he's murdered his beloved. He watches his own decapitation by guillotine and wakes up in hell, where "ghosts, sorcerers, monsters of every kind" celebrate his death in a "devilish orgy."³¹

Berlioz reveled in using unconventional instruments, many of them detailed in his volume on orchestration. His work opens doors for Herrmann on how to depict psychology in music, often through surprising means.

Another composer who strikes Benny like a thunderbolt is still living. Charles Ives (1874–1954) is a retired native of Danbury, Connecticut. In the first years of the twentieth century, he was a prosperous insurance salesman by day, a musical guerrilla by night. Ives expressed his patriotism, and the Transcendentalism of Emerson and Whitman, by blending folk tunes, church hymns, battle anthems, and other popular melodies into dissonant sonic maelstroms decades ahead of their time. His work included polyrhythms (different rhythms played at the same time), polytonality (music played in two or more keys at the same time), quarter tones (the sounds that live between the notes that make up the traditional Western music scale), and other tools that struck listeners as auditory chaos. What William Blake was to poetry, Ives was to music.

Discovering an Ives score, in the depths of the "Epiphany" branch of the New York Public Library, the teenaged Herrmann experiences just that. He reaches out to the composer, starting a friendship that will last to Ives's death. "He was a great eccentric," Herrmann will recall, "but he was an eccentric with a vision . . . a man who was always to be relied upon to do the unexpected."[32]

> *From now on I have decided that my compositions will be governed by the following idea: Art should be an adventure into the unknown.*
> —Herrmann, age nineteen, 1931 diary entry[33]

Fourth Movement (Scherzo, vigorous and lively)—Manhattan, 1928–1938

Between music classes at New York University and Juilliard, Herrmann builds a social network. His friends run the gamut from symphonic composers to the songwriters of Tin Pan Alley. Always searching for intellectual stimulation, Benny accosts strangers with a reputation for talent. They usually walk away friends. "He was very frenetic in those days, full of energy," composer Morton Gould recalls:

> He wanted very much to be in music, to conduct, to do things. He came up to me in the 58th Street Music Library from between a stack of bookshelves, out of nowhere. He said, "You're Morton Gould, aren't you? I'm also a composer—I'm Benny Herrmann. I heard your concert. I want to get to know you." I said, "Well, fine." He asked me, "Where do you live?" I said, "I live on Long Island." He said, "I'll come out to see you." I had to rush home to get there before he did!

He stood on the piano and made a speech about his music and his conducting. He played violin, not well. He would rant and rave. Benny was very positive about what he was doing. He was a strange mix of great talents and shortcomings, through which he functioned.[34]

Benny introduces himself to George Gershwin, then putting final touches on *An American in Paris*. Gershwin respects the teen's knowledge of modern symphonic music, which exceeds his own. Six years later, Gershwin invites the twenty-four-year-old to a rehearsal of *Porgy and Bess*, his landmark fusion of opera and popular melody. Recalls Benny, "At the end of the crap game fugue, he said, 'Not bad for a songwriter, Herrmann!'"[35]

Gershwin's refusal to limit his genius to Broadway, as well as his car-and-chauffeur lifestyle, leaves a lasting impression.

After the blow of the Great Depression, and Abraham Herrmann's death in 1933—coronary thrombosis, age sixty-one—the family falls into debt. But Benny is convinced he will succeed. He writes concert works that, although heard by few, anticipate his mature style. He visits auto showrooms, where "he tried to convince the staff he was going to buy a Rolls-Royce," recalls a friend. "He never dressed right, and as a young man it must have been even worse. But he used to dream of having a Rolls-Royce when he was young."[36]

In 1932 he joins other fledgling composers, including Aaron Copland, Jerome Moross, and Oscar Levant, to form the Young Composers Group. Its goal is to popularize their progressive music. That aim is mostly unrealized, due to internal rivalries and audience indifference.

Benny decides that if the public will not come to him, he will go to the public. By now he has played violin in a Yiddish theater, and conducted a ballet score he wrote in a Broadway revue. Music, he believes, can be both personal and commercial. "All composers at all times have to do music *of* their time," he tells an interviewer. "After all, Mozart and Haydn were not above writing dinner music while their patrons ate ... Bach certainly thought nothing of writing his weekly cantata for a church service. It's only a question of the time one lives in."[37]

In 1934, he gets his break. The Columbia Broadcasting System, founded in 1928, is among the first radio networks to be heard across the nation. But Depression-era ad dollars are tight. CBS offers several non-sponsored programs that, fueled by the left-wing fervor of the FDR era, lean into the experimental.[38]

Hired by CBS as an all-purpose musician, by 1937 Herrmann is conducting concerts with the CBS Symphony. In contrast to Toscanini's NBC Symphony, Benny programs forgotten and modern music. He writes original scores in days or hours for CBS's finest drama programs. The best come from twenty-two-year-old Orson Welles, the Broadway boy wonder who acts, produces, and directs.

Orson's first dealings with Benny are explosive, a friction partly due to their similar temperaments. But as Welles's coproducer John Houseman observes, "Amid the snapping of batons and the hurling of scripts and scores into the air... the two men came to understand each other perfectly."[39]

On October 30, 1938, a single broadcast, *The War of the Worlds*—America's first and most potent "fake news" drama—makes Welles a global celebrity. Flooded with offers, Orson goes west to make *Citizen Kane*. He's joined by twenty-nine-year-old Herrmann, who Welles insists will write the score.

Example 1.7 Benny and Orson Welles during the filming of *Citizen Kane*, 1940.

Fifth Movement, Finale (Allegro Brillante)—Hollywood, 1940–1942

With *Kane*, Herrmann establishes a template he will use for the rest of his life. He creates a unique orchestration for each film, based on its specific needs. "Since a film score is only written for one performance, I could never see the logic in making a rule of the standard symphony orchestra. A film score can be made up of different fantastic groupings of instruments."[40]

He also displays a talent that will be a hallmark: his gift for making viewers *feel* the psychological states of the characters. "The first step is to get inside the drama," he says. "If you can't, you shouldn't be writing the music."[41]

His score for *Kane* thrills his collaborators. His high-voltage personality exhausts them. "He had a very high regard for himself," says *Kane*'s sound recordist James G. Stewart. "But my God, what a skillful man."[42] "He was bright as hell, irascible as hell," says *Kane*'s editor, Robert Wise. "He could discuss many things, and often did—psychology, philosophy. I was terribly impressed with his quickness and professionalism. I suppose this came from his experiences in radio."[43]

In contrast to his Hollywood contemporaries, his music is "leaner, more sparsely scored, less generic in sound," conductor John Wilson observes.[44] *Kane*'s music is Oscar-nominated. Benny loses . . . to himself. The Academy Award goes to his second film score, for *All That Money Can Buy*. He is thirty years old.

But a heady year of artistic freedom ends in calamity. Welles's second film, *The Magnificent Ambersons*, is a downbeat epic about the death of America's soul, shown through the collapse of a family dynasty. At previews it is jeered and booed; audiences are in no mood for tragedy in the wake of Pearl Harbor. The film is recut and reshot by others, with Herrmann's score eviscerated. The experience confirms Benny's fears that Hollywood is "a racket." For eight years he stays mostly in New York, only working on movies if allowed creative freedom. In an industry typified by obeisance and double-crosses, he gains, as one columnist puts it, "a reputation for telling off the boys in the front office when he feels they have it coming."[45]

Herrmann does consider some filmmakers giants among the hacks. "Saw Hitchcock at the [Brown Derby]," he writes his wife Lucille in December 1942, during a visit to Los Angeles. "He said he was sorry that I didn't do his picture [Hitch's latest was *Saboteur*] as he should have been in closer contact with me from the beginning. Hopes that we do the next one together."[46]

Hitch knows Benny's music through *Citizen Kane*, and from a near-collaboration in radio. In 1940, the director helped develop a CBS anthology series, and suggested its title: *Suspense*. The show didn't launch until 1942, without Hitchcock's involvement. But he heard many of its episodes, which were often enhanced by a malevolent Herrmann score.

Another nexus linking director and composer is Joseph Cotten, star of Hitchcock's *Shadow of a Doubt* and Welles's *Kane* and *Ambersons*. Sensing a possible meeting of minds, Cotten and his wife Lenore arrange a Sunday lunch at their home with Benny and his wife, writer Lucille Fletcher. "The other guests," Lucille recalls, "were Alfred Hitchcock and Alma."

> Benny was a great admirer of Hitchcock's—one of the first pictures he took me to was *The 39 Steps*. We were just about to sit down to a sumptuous meal on the terrace, outside the house overlooking the swimming pool, when who should show up but Orson Welles and his date, Rita Hayworth.
>
> Orson just barged in and said, "Don't let me interrupt your lunch. Rita and I just want to use your pool." They hadn't brought any bathing suits. So Orson took off his trousers and went swimming in his boxer shorts. Rita vanished upstairs to Joe's bedroom, where she selected two Countess Mara ties, each worth about $50 apiece, gorgeous, that Lenore had given Joe for his birthday.
>
> Rita draped one around her neck and bosoms, tying it in the back. She spread the other one out, turned it into a bikini lower part, then languidly vanished into the pool while we ate lunch. It was very distracting, I will say, to eat lunch and watch the two of them.[47]

It was probably best that Hitch and Benny did not connect sooner. Not until the director had full creative control were the circumstances right for collaboration. By 1954, with no Selznick or similar note-giver to send Herrmann stalking off the picture, their partnership could begin without interference.

And it started, surprisingly, with a comedy.

2

Troubles with Harry

"Tell me, Herbie. Who picked this location?"

After three films together, Herbert Coleman didn't need to look at his boss, sitting with him in a rental car, to glean his sarcasm. He knew that Hitchcock was frustrated, contemplating cost overages, and expecting his associate producer to find a Plan B.[1]

The lush colors of East Craftsbury, Vermont, and its environs were crucial for the film they had just begun shooting. Unfortunately, those forest greens, reds, and yellows had been obliterated overnight under snow. It was a bad start for a project that would test Hitchcock's relationship with Paramount. *The Trouble with Harry* was to be an inexpensive lark that would scratch a creative itch for the director. "I've always wanted to do a black comedy," he explained. "This story is perfect for that."[2]

Years earlier, in the highly ordered study in his Bel Air, California, home, Hitch had read *The Trouble with Harry*, a 1949 novel by British author Jack Trevor Story. Its attraction was obvious. A well-dressed corpse lies incongruously in the woods of an English village. He's discovered by several locals—a retired sea captain, a shy spinster, the dead man's wife—who all think they caused Harry's death. A plot that might have served Agatha Christie unfolds instead as a wry satire of social embarrassment.

The farcical saga of Harry Worp's corpse delighted Hitchcock with its blend of the macabre, the amusing, and the romantic. (A handsome painter solves the mystery and falls in love with Harry's widow.) In Hitch's earlier movies, arsenic-laced humor was just one ingredient in a serving of drama. *Harry* would be a comedy of manners, centered on one black joke.

To some in his circle, that joke seemed too slight to carry a feature. Such was the opinion of his most trusted collaborator at Paramount. Forty-six-year-old Herbert Coleman had escaped the rural poverty of his West Virginia childhood to become one of Paramount's most versatile staffers. Starting as a studio truck driver in 1925, Herbie applied his soft-spoken equanimity to problems like the discomforts of location filming, the verbal abuse of

Example 2.1 Jerry Mathers makes a discovery in *The Trouble with Harry* (1955).

temperamental actors, and the exhaustion of all-night shoots. His willingness to tackle hard tasks, and his round-the-clock devotion to each project, made him Hitchcock's ideal associate producer.

For Coleman, *Harry* was "a strange little story with absolutely no suspense."[3] Paramount agreed, although the studio acknowledged that Hitch could make the film if he wished. The director assured them that the budget would stay low: $1 million, two thirds less than that of *To Catch a Thief*.[4] He would not use pricey stars. And since this was an Alfred Hitchcock production, on which his salary was deferred in lieu of later ownership, he was motivated to deliver.

He knew that his partners would need perfect pitch to capture *Harry*'s charm. Fortunately he already had his screenwriter. Thirty-five-year-old John Michael Hayes specialized in writing engaging characters whom audiences could relate to: think James Stewart's L. B. Jefferies in *Rear Window*. Hayes also excelled at sparkling, censor-baiting dialogue. "You want a leg or a breast?" Grace Kelly asks Cary Grant, theoretically about chicken, in *To Catch a Thief*. On *Harry*, Hitchcock told Hayes to stay close to the novel. Their only major change was resetting it in Vermont, where New England propriety replaced British formality whenever a character tripped over Harry's body.

To play painter Sam Marlowe, the sardonic hero, Hitch wanted William Holden. But the rising star had just won a Best Actor Oscar for *Stalag 17* and was fielding bigger offers.[5] Instead, the part went to John Forsythe, a likable TV and B-movie actor, but no box office draw. Despite his promise of no expensive stars, Hitch couldn't resist approaching Grace Kelly, his favorite leading lady, to play Harry's wife-turned-widow Jennifer Rogers. But Kelly was under contract to MGM, and the studio refused to loan her to Hitchcock.[6]

It was Coleman who found a ringer. Watching the Broadway musical *The Pajama Game* featuring Carol Haney, Herbie was enchanted by its lithe, funny, sexy star. Only after the show did he learn he'd been watching Haney's understudy: twenty-year-old newcomer Shirley MacLaine. Intrigued by MacLaine's quirky charm, Hitchcock decided to take a chance on an unknown.[7]

Harry's other major roles—ex-tugboat captain Albert Wiles and tremulous spinster Miss Gravely—went to character actors Hitch loved. Edmund Gwenn, who played Santa Claus in *Miracle on 34th Street*, channeled the rhythms of a Shakespearean clown as the captain who thinks he shot Harry while hunting. As Miss Gravely, Mildred Natwick had Hitch's favorite line: seeing Harry's corpse as Albert drags its leg, she inquires, "What seems to be the trouble, Captain?" On the page that may not seem funny, but Natwick knew how to get the laugh.

Twenty-three days out of a tight thirty were to be shot on location in Vermont. Using Paramount's VistaVision cameras, which yielded lustrous colors, Hitch would start the film by emphasizing green, via hillsides and grassy plains. Green pillows and wallpaper would be an inviting backdrop for the romances between Sam and Jennifer, and the captain and Miss Gravely. But as the town's deputy sheriff begins his search for a rumored body, and Harry's corpse is moved by our heroes from hill to closet to bathtub, Hitch would add a "drop of blood,"[8] as the deep reds of sunset fall over fields of green.

By September 20, 1954, the first day of shooting in Vermont, those plans were in jeopardy. Torrents of rain were followed by snow, which erased the verdant landscapes Herbie found in the summer. Sharing his distress was Robert Burks, Hitch's cinematographer since 1951's *Strangers on a Train*. Burks was "a terrific fellow, hardworking, very intense," recalled C. O. "Doc" Erickson, Hitch's production manager. "He agonized over the look and

Example 2.2 Hitch, John Forsythe, and Shirley MacLaine in Vermont, 1954.

the shots and the camera locations. Bob took his work so seriously, and it showed."[9]

Even working indoors couldn't keep *Harry*'s shoot on track. The sound of pounding rain meant that much of the dialogue would have to be rerecorded. On October 12, an 850-pound VistaVision camera crashed down from the rafters, close to Hitchcock's chair. It pinned a crew member to the floor and grazed Hitch's shoulder. Typically, the director displayed little emotion. But behind his façade of implacability, his stomach no doubt tightened. "He was aware of the innate and uncontrollable terror that can suddenly afflict a human being," observed biographer Peter Ackroyd. "The business of filming itself, for an essentially timid man, was formidable and frightening.... That was why he sought all the time to render himself invulnerable by total control, routine, neatness, quietness."[10]

One day after the accident, it was official: *Harry* would shut down and resume on the Paramount backlot. Crew members scooped thousands of leaves into coffin-shaped boxes and shipped them to Paramount. There, the flora was affixed to artificial trees made of rubber and placed on a set: a copy of the hill where Harry is found and much of Act One takes place.

At least on a soundstage the director felt more in control. "A Hitchcock set was like no one else's," a makeup man recalled. "If anyone—electricians, crews, whoever—had something to say, they'd practically *whisper* it, out of respect."[11] Coat and tie attire was expected. And while the fastidious Robert Burks checked final lighting, Hitch could enjoy the comfort of an on-set trailer, where he discussed the upcoming scene with his actors.

Principal photography wrapped on October 27, 1954. Now began a fresh challenge: overseeing the editing, scoring, and sound mixing of both *Harry* and *To Catch a Thief*. In Paramount's editing rooms, Herbert Coleman got "an editing course in fine tuning a film. I sat for days in the stop-and-go-projection room watching Hitch tell [his editors], 'Add six frames there. Cut two there.'"[12] Two frames are a twelfth of one second.

No matter how finely tuned the edit, Hitchcock saw *Harry*'s potential weaknesses. Much location shooting had been replaced by studio-bound sets. The film had virtually no action. And the cheerful indifference of its characters toward death needed careful underscoring to cue audiences that they were watching a comedy.

When it came to choosing a composer, Hitchcock drew a blank—until Lyn Murray, busy on *To Catch a Thief*, stated the obvious. "I said, 'The perfect guy for that is Herrmann.' He didn't know him, so I had him come in and I introduced them."[13]

Murray was more intermediary than introducer. Hitch and Benny had met at least twice in the 1940s, albeit once distracted by Rita Hayworth, her pin-up body barely covered by two neckties. On September 10, 1950, Herrmann's radio series *Invitation to Music* hosted Hitchcock as a guest. And according to one intimate, Benny and Hitch took a shopping trip together that could have happened no later than 1952, three years before Hitch's face and form were widely known in America.

"Benny always wanted a Bentley Continental, and he and Hitch agreed they both wanted a Bentley. They walked into this showroom in Beverly Hills of Rolls-Royces and Bentleys, and I can imagine what Benny looked like then, because he could make a Savile Row suit look like it came from a thrift store. They asked a salesman about a car. Hitchcock wasn't recognized, and the salesman said, 'Oh ho! Don't you wish you could afford a car like this!' Hitchcock was furious and stormed out. And Benny said to the chap, 'You fool! You've just watched ten thousand dollars walk out of that door.'"[14]

Herrmann later bought a luxurious Alvis—the car he likely drove in November 1954 through the famous double-arched gate of Paramount.

During first meetings, Herrmann often presented a guarded, even hostile front. Herbert Coleman was intimidated by the "short, stocky" man addressing him, "a thick shock of unruly black hair covering most of his brow, his face seemingly frozen in a threatening scowl. I didn't know that Bernie, a highly educated, articulate, sophisticated gentleman, would accept as his equal an uneducated, inarticulate man with a wild, wonderful, Cliff Holler, West Virginia accent. He did, and over the years we became close personal friends."[15]

Herrmann was eager to collaborate with Hitchcock, recognizing in his works a depth beyond their entertainment. "Most people think of Hitchcock as a master of mystery and suspense. Although this is fundamentally true, he is also a great romantic director, his films allowing enormous scope for sensual and lyrical musical treatment."[16] He also admired the consistency of Hitch's output. "Many directors can make one or two good movies. But how many can make fifty great ones like Hitchcock? Somerset Maugham once said, 'Anyone has a good novel in him. It's the second one I'm interested in.'"[17]

Their meeting confirmed that the two men shared what Herrmann called "a great unanimity of ideas."[18] Hitch shared his enthusiasm to collaborate. But why his sudden interest in Herrmann? Perhaps because *Harry* was an American movie with a British sensibility . . . and no composer working in film better embodied that combination.

> *Tonight I was carried back a hundred years. Charlotte [Polonsky, an early girlfriend] read to me A Christmas Carol. We reached Marley's ghost. I was carried away to a fog-ridden London street and the room of old Scrooge. . . . Through the intonation of Charlotte's voice she transported me back into an age which will never return, save through our imagination and Dickens and of course if one is fortunate a gentle one to read to you.*
> —Herrmann, 1930 diary entry

It amused many of Benny's friends that a man usually inelegant in dress, and rough-edged in manner, was a passionate Anglophile. As a youth, he took imaginary trips from New York's Second Avenue "to London through the magic of Dickens's prose and *The Adventures of Sherlock Holmes*."[19] The world's greatest music, he would write, had "the universality of the greatest English literature."[20] And as soon as CBS offered steady employment in the 1930s, he filled his New York apartment with English furniture, first editions, silver, and paintings. "Benny had the most extraordinary knowledge not only of English music but of English literature and art—much more so, I think, than any Englishman," observed his friend Lady Evelyn Barbirolli, wife of conductor Sir John Barbirolli.[21]

During his many periods of stress, Herrmann found calm in the Georgian elegance of Handel; in the Romanticism of Elgar, Delius, and Vaughan Williams; and in the work of British authors of all eras. He "will admit that he can't decide which is really greater, music or literature," a CBS press release stated. "As for books, there are people who have abandoned the idea of ever finding one Bennie hasn't read. Twirling his hair furiously all the while, Bennie can—and does at the slightest provocation—deliver dissertations, complete with quotations, on the works of Trollope, Shaw, Le Fanu, the Sitwells, Virginia Woolf, Shakespeare, Dickens, Graham Greene, or almost any other English author you can think of."[22]

In a tribute to Vaughan Williams's "London Symphony," Herrmann wrote how, from a library cubicle in the 1920s, he first felt "the hush and quietness [that] settled over Bloomsbury of a November twilight, [as] a damp drizzle of rain slowly falls."[23] Further bonding Benny and Hitch was a love of art. Vermeer was a touchstone for the director's lighting and framing. At home, his walls were adorned with Klee, Utrillo, and Braque. Herrmann's favorite painter was Turner, whose canvases evoked the peril of ships at sea, through coloristic swirls emphasizing violent emotion—a tone that Herrmann mastered in music.

Benny had moved to Los Angeles at the start of the 1950s, when for reasons to be explained, his career opportunities were strongest in Hollywood. Now in his forties, he worked steadily, freelancing for two strong supporters: Darryl F. Zanuck, head of Twentieth Century–Fox, and Zanuck's musical director, Alfred Newman. Since 1943 Herrmann's atmospheric scores for Fox literary adaptations like *Jane Eyre* and *Anna and the King of Siam*, his Gothic Romanticism for the thriller *Hangover Square*, and the lyric beauty he brought to *The Ghost and Mrs. Muir* ensured him carte blanche. They also reflected his gift for adding psychological dimension to characters who were emotionally isolated.

Herrmann's stock rose further in 1953, when Zanuck began making a new kind of movie. Facing competition from television, Zanuck unveiled the widescreen process of CinemaScope. Spectacle now trumped quality scriptwriting, making Herrmann's atmospheric soundtracks all the more essential.

> To: Alfred Newman
> From: Darryl F. Zanuck
> Dear Al:
>
> I thought the music score on BENEATH THE 12-MILE REEF was one of the most original scores I have ever heard.... The manner in which Bernard handled the underwater sequence was simply thrilling. The entire picture has been enormously enhanced by this wonderful score. It gives the picture a bigness it did not originally have—yet the music never interferes but adds to the dramatic values.
>
> D. F. Z.[24]

Benny's scores were lucrative: his $15,000-a-film rate would be $175,000 today. And he avoided being stereotyped in a particular genre. But by 1954, the movies he enhanced were increasingly dispensable. The chance to team with Hitchcock promised an exciting new direction.

By December 7, Herrmann was officially on board, and the director raised *Harry*'s music budget. "Mr. Hitchcock now feels that the musical treatment of this picture will be of great importance," wrote Paramount music director Roy Fjastad.[25]

Hitch was confident in his new hire. So much so that, after a screening of *Harry* and a discussion of how music could help the film, the director stated that he would not need to hear any music before recording.[26] At the time, it was difficult to convey a score's content in advance. (Today, a Beethoven symphony can be simulated on your laptop.) Hitch's message was clear: Benny had his trust.

The director did have thoughts about the score. "It is Mr. Hitchcock's desire that the musical treatment should be scored with small combinations such as possibly woodwind octet," Fjastad noted. "However, this may or may not be feasible, depending on what finally is decided in further discussion between Herrmann and Hitchcock."[27]

Benny supported the idea of a chamber-like ensemble. And that December, he started work in his usual method: composing from home.

If Hitch's address near Beverly Hills conveyed status, Herrmann's shouted a desire to be away from the Hollywood establishment: 5119 Bluebell Avenue was a former walnut ranch, in the middle-class suburb of North Hollywood. A faded gray-slat fence circled the front of the property. Towering redwoods were its chief curbside attraction. Only by traveling a long, sloping driveway did visitors see the one-story, dark-brown home, flanked by orange trees "which just rotted," recalled actress Marsha Hunt. Offering a sole cheery burst of color was a rose garden at the front entrance, which Benny tended.[28]

The house was small, its space diminished further by possessions. Music scores and books in the hundreds. Ornate British furniture. Accentuating the Englishness of it all was the light Williamsburg green on the walls.

Upon entering, visitors stepped into a modest living room filled with antiques. It adjoined a small dining room. The kitchen was shaped in the style of a narrow Pullman railway car.

What the house lacked in space was balanced by its backyard. Two brick paths led to a large, shaded swimming pool. Beside it a silver ice bowl offered chilled wine and Beluga caviar. Fittingly, given Benny's love of the macabre, the pool had a ghost. A former resident drowned in it; and at night, Benny's teenage daughters Dorothy and Wendy "swore we heard the sound of someone jumping up and down on the diving board, but never a splash."[29]

At the backyard's far end sat a cozy guest house with kitchen and bedroom. A frequent occupant was Leopold Stokowski, who stayed for weeks when conducting in Los Angeles.

Dorothy, known as "Taffy" to friends, and Wendy were summer visitors. They lived on the east coast with their mother, Lucille Fletcher. Herrmann and Fletcher, a gifted radio dramatist, had married in 1939. They divorced in 1949. That same year Benny was remarried, to Lucille Anderson.

Lucy Anderson, also known to Herrmann friends as "Lucy 2," had given up work as a nurse to serve as full-time attendant to her husband. By his choice, no new children shared their home; instead, Herrmann lavished parental affection on pets. "He was very tender-hearted about animals," Taffy recalled. "I think he felt safer with them."[30]

The home's second bedroom served as Benny's study. It contained a small, upright piano, a desk, and wall-to-wall bookshelves packed with music manuscripts and first editions. He was composing by 5 A.M. and frequently

Example 2.3 Benny at home with mother Ida, Lucy Anderson, and his daughters from his first marriage, Dorothy (Taffy) and Wendy.

Example 2.4 Benny poolside with one of Bluebell Avenue's feline family members.

Example 2.5 Benny works at home, late 1940s.

done by 10. Ideas came quickly, he said, often in his first viewing of the film. He claimed to rarely second-guess himself: "A composer who understands the demands of film can look at a rough cut a couple of times and sense, instinctively, what kind of music will be suitable. It's funny. Rossini had a talk with Wagner. He says, 'I don't have genius like you do, but I have lots of intuition.'"[31]

Joining Benny at the piano was a trio of feline admirers—Boots, Hank, and Inchy. The last was named by Igor Stravinsky, another visitor who came for luncheons by the pool. Even when writing under deadline, Herrmann welcomed interruptions, even a degree of chaos. "At Franz Waxman's house you couldn't make any noise," Taffy recalled. "But Daddy would sometimes compose at the dining room table, and the more noise the better."[32]

Herrmann had a remarkable gift of concentration. He could transport himself to Washington, DC, where a space alien lands on a mission to stop global conflict (*The Day the Earth Stood Still*). He could become a

Hemingway-inspired adventurer trapped on a mountain, recalling past loves as death circles him (*The Snows of Kilimanjaro*).

With *The Trouble with Harry*, Herrmann had a project that tapped into his greatest source of joy: English music and prose. In music, Benny could reveal the bonds he shared with Hitch, and the potential for his music to deepen his storytelling.

Harry required some forty minutes of score. Herrmann had roughly eight weeks to compose them. Using buff-colored manila manuscript paper, he usually wrote in ink—a sign of confidence.[33] He selected every instrument for the notes in his score, a process known as orchestration.

Few composers in Hollywood had that luxury. At Warner Bros., which cranked out more than two dozen features annually, Max Steiner invariably raced the clock, writing forty minutes of score in as little as *two weeks*. For studio staff composers like Steiner, the use of an orchestrator was inescapable. That Austrian composer indicated instrument preferences in shorthand; but other composers were less conscientious. Some used orchestrators essentially as co-writers, leaving their junior partners to flesh out rough sketches.

Herrmann was appalled by such shortcuts. "Color is very important. This whole rubbish of other people orchestrating your music is so wrong. I always tell them, 'Listen, boys, I'll give you the first page of 'Lohengrin Prelude' with all the instruments marked. You write it out. I bet you won't come within 50% of Wagner.' To orchestrate is like a thumbprint. I can't understand having someone else do it. It would be like someone putting color to your paintings."[34] On Herrmann films, two factors were non-negotiable: his $15,000 salary, and having enough time to compose and to orchestrate.

But exactly what instrumentation did *Harry* need? How could the score put viewers inside the story? And what was the central idea that would guide Herrmann's approach?

January 2023. In Glasgow, Scotland, conductor William T. Stromberg sets down his baton and thanks his ninety-three musicians, members of the Royal Scottish National Orchestra. Since 1996, the Los Angeles–based Stromberg, his wife Anna Bonn Stromberg, and score reconstructionist John W. Morgan have collaborated on state-of-the-art re-recordings of Herrmann scores. The BBC ranked their work among the "Essential Recordings" of classic film music.

Relatively little of Herrmann's work was commercially issued in his lifetime. But new recordings by Stromberg, Joel McNeely, and other conductors are embraced by an international audience. That group includes Oscar-winning directors, composers, and editors, who use these new recordings as "temporary track" scores for their movies-in-progress.

Herrmann's scores for radio also have received new recordings, most of them by conductor Michael McGehee. In the pages that follow, these experts and others will offer an insider's point of view on how Herrmann added character dimension and drama with his music.

The Score

Herrmann's approach to *The Trouble with Harry* reflects how astutely he understood its director. The score comprised, as he later wrote, "a musical portrait of Hitchcock. The film is in many ways the most personal and the most humorous of Hitchcock's entire output. It is gay, funny, macabre, tender, and with an abundance of his sardonic wit."[35]

The score consisted of forty separate music cues.[36] Not all will be discussed here. Instead, let us view his approach through a short list of Herrmann trademarks. And, if possible, listen along: all the music discussed here and in later chapters can be heard on the internet, usually by searching "Herrmann" and a film's title.

Trademark #1: Tell the audience what they're about to see.

"The real function of a main title should be to set the pulse of what is going to follow," Herrmann said.[37] In *Harry*, that task takes less than fifteen seconds. It starts with just four musicians, playing four *tutti* (unison) notes.

Like an announcement of Judgment Day, four *fortissimo* (very loud) French horns declaim a powerful E-flat note as the credits begin. Then the horns drop three steps to C-flat. E-flat to C-flat? You've just heard a major third—a happy-sounding two-note chord. Horns then leap up to a questioning A-flat, then plummet down to D-natural, a note that makes the four-note phrase ominous: A-flat to D-natural is a *tritone*, a distance known as "The Devil's Interval" because of the sinister mood it creates. Together, these opening notes pose a question, one that our heroes will wonder throughout the film: What do we do with Harry?

The score has summarized the plot, while introducing a key ingredient in every Herrmann-Hitchcock score: irresolution.

WILLIAM STROMBERG: *I love that motif. This bom-bom-bom-BUM ... we have a death motif for the film right off the bat. It's not the Dies irae [a Gregorian chant of death Herrmann often referenced]. But it's the same idea.*[38]

During this music, a title card appears: "ALFRED HITCHCOCK'S THE TROUBLE WITH HARRY." As text fades, we see what's behind the words: a colorful cartoon of birds and trees, as if drawn by a child. As we register this innocent image, Herrmann's horn call of death gives way ... to a comical, pecking, oompahing pattern for bassoons, clarinets, and bass clarinet. Its clucking rhythm and sharp accents suggest a bird in bouncy motion.

Death, Herrmann tell us, will be funny.

JOHN MORGAN: *It's playful, but very importantly, it's playful in a sardonic way. So it matches Hitchcock's personality perfectly.*

STROMBERG: *And the whole score is based on the chord we're hearing. It's an F-sharp augmented chord, which Carl Stalling used all the time in Warner Bros. cartoons!*

Explaining an augmented chord is easier than it sounds. Play any three-note, major-key chord, including that piano lesson favorite, C–E–G. Now play that G one step higher on the keys, making it C–E–G-sharp. A chord that originally conveyed happy resolution now has tension and mystery, simply by raising its last note a single step. An augmented chord can be frightening. Played lightly and as orchestrated here, the effect is comic.

At story's end, our heroes realize that Harry's death was accidental. They return his body to the hill where he first was spotted by Jennifer's four-year-old son Arnie (Jerry Mathers). At film's end, Arnie again trundles up the hill and, as directed by his mother, rediscovers the body. (Our characters have decided that, with all mysteries solved, Harry can be "found" again by Arnie and reported to the police.) Sure enough, Arnie's return to the corpse is paired with Herrmann's four-note theme that opened the score, bringing everything full circle. Nothing has changed, and everything has changed: the troublesome Harry is gone, Arnie has a new dad, two couples are in love. From death comes new life.

Trademark #2: Choice of instruments is as important as the notes.

Benny agreed with Hitch's concept of using a small ensemble: seven woodwind players, four French horns, a traditional string section, and harp. About forty players for a handful of music cues, but only half as many players for most. The orchestration proved ideal to evoke a bucolic, autumnal tone. Also, horns and woodwinds playing in their low register could convey menace.

Herrmann's main color palette in *Harry* is woodwinds and strings. We hear it in the post-credits montage, of a church tucked amid green rolling hills and trees bursting with red and yellow foliage. A solo English horn (which sounds similar to an oboe) plays a wistful, songlike phrase, supported by a delicate bed of strings. Music invites us to embrace nature's beauty, in the style of Herrmann's favorite British composers.

STROMBERG: *This is Vaughan Williams, Delius type of music, and so beautiful. Herrmann never rips off another composer, but it has that style.*

LUCILLE FLETCHER: *He was fascinated by New England. I think Ives had a lot to do with that. The snowy houses, the small, quiet villages, the church spires. Many writers of his day felt that there lay the real America.*[39]

STROMBERG: *When Herrmann visited Ives he'd see this kind of countryside and come up with music in his mind. I think it may have come back to him for this.*

Beyond his choice of instruments, Herrmann made decisions about how they would be played that also defined his style. Unlike Alfred Newman, who loved "a high intensity, a lot of vibrato [emotional vibration] among string players," Herrmann "wanted a cool sound, almost no vibrato," observed Don Christlieb,[40] Benny's favorite bassoonist. Herrmann used mutes on every instrument whose vibrato could be suppressed. But those muted notes were often to be played *fortissimo*. That mix of suppression and sonic force is a thumbprint unmistakably Herrmann's.

"What people refer to as 'The Hollywood Sound' is the sound of MGM, of Fox musicals," observes conductor John Wilson. "It's essentially theatrical, and the roots of that sound come from the orchestra pit of Broadway theaters. Herrmann's musical language is different. It's symphonic. There's a dark, burnished quality to the way he handles an orchestra. That is his and his alone."

In *Harry*, instruments define character. Take the fragile Miss Gravely, a woman longing for connection. Music is essential to her humanization; when we meet her, Herrmann conveys her delicacy with a solo oboe played in a high register.

MORGAN: *And the oboe is played with character, because it's imitating Natwick's voice, her personality, with a sighing quality.*

"There's very little music in a good film score," Herrmann told a friend. "It is knowing when to bring in the trombones that counts. The *sound* is the main thing, not the music."[41]

A concert piece can take its ideas anywhere, forging a path of its own through the development (changing or restating) of themes and rhythms. But film music, Herrmann pointed out, was collaborative. "The writer, the director, the cameraman and the cutter, all had a hand somehow in its creation. Its form, length, and musical style were dictated by the demands of the dramatic action."[42] Benny had a healthy ego, but he appreciated the importance of his collaborators.

Trademark #3: Short themes are memorable and malleable.

Few composers could get more mileage out of a simple phrase. Throughout *Harry*, that F-sharp augmented chord introduced in the main title, with its pecking, herky-jerky rhythm, is used for long stretches of underscoring. Herrmann ricochets that phrase around the orchestra, altering the choice of instruments, the dynamics (volume), and the phrasing (whether a note is played smoothly or sharply) to keep things interesting.

STROMBERG: *When John Forsythe finds the body and starts sketching it, notice how Herrmann just keeps going back and forth between the two ideas from the opening of the main credits. His orchestration is what makes it so miraculous. He alternates bass pizzicatos [plucking of strings] with low clarinets. That's what makes Herrmann Herrmann.*
MORGAN: *He could take two bars and make them last forever!*
STROMBERG: *It's such a simple idea, but he turns it into magic.*

Early in the film Herrmann takes separate musical ideas and attaches them to characters who, minutes apart, encounter Harry's body on the hill. Watch this seven-and-a-half-minute series of "discovery" vignettes with the volume down. It will feel twice as long. Music adds not only variety but pace.

MICHAEL MCGEHEE: *The sequence is amazing because of the different characterizations he creates. He's always inside the characters' heads. Everything is psychological.*

When Albert sees the corpse he thinks he accidentally shot, his contrition ("Mother always said I'd come to a bad end") is accompanied with a whispering, non-comic "mystery" pattern for low winds, brass, and sepulchral harp pedal glissandos. Did Herrmann already know how central the idea of guilt was in Hitchcock's stories? By playing Albert's soliloquizing straight, Herrmann can gradually escalate to comedy. He progresses from Miss Gravely's oboe sighs ("Embarrassing," she says of the corpse) to a brisk, flighty tune for high strings to describe the town's absent-minded doctor, so immersed in the book he's reading that he trips over Harry and moves on without noticing. Musically it's a rare time that Benny harks back in a Hitchcock score to the light-hearted tunefulness of *Citizen Kane*, with its giddy montages accompanying Kane's youth.

By the time a tramp appears, and trades his shoes for Harry's sporty, two-toned pair, Herrmann has built up to his wittiest theme for the sequence. A waddling, queasy figure in thirds, it is an homage to a favorite composer.

MORGAN: *Ralph Vaughan Williams wrote this phrase for the British film* Scott of the Antarctic, *for a scene with penguins. It's a scene with levity similar to the one in* Harry. *And the way this character moves is like a penguin!*

When Herrmann incorporates music written by another, the reason is referential, not theft. Using the "penguins" theme here is a nod to his friend Vaughan Williams, and to the underlying Englishness of *Harry*'s story.

In his approach to this opening sequence, Herrmann has helped us settle in to the movie's comic rhythms. He has also made a stop-and-start series of actions appear as flowing as the opening of a ballet. "Music is the veneer that bonds these montages together," he explained. "It links the audience in some mysterious way with what is taking place onscreen."[43]

Trademark #4: Rhythm can be content.

Throughout *Harry* Herrmann provides a deliberately dance-like counterpoint to the film's black comedy.

MORGAN: *The movie is rather static. Herrmann comes in and puts everything together, so you feel like you're moving, you're traveling with the characters.*

When Albert is forced to walk past a police car while holding his long rifle, he hides the gun by gripping it to his opposite leg, limping past an officer like a stiff-legged soldier. Gwenn's gait is amusing, but what makes it funny is a demented little waltz for woodwinds—one that incorporates a fluttering "cuckoo" like Delius on helium. A "Waltz Macabre" accompanies Harry's burials and un-burials. But the 3/4 time of a waltz isn't always used as a joke. When Albert brings Miss Gravely into his home, which includes a ship's female figurehead on whose breast Albert casually leans, Herrmann writes one of his loveliest waltzes, expressing the benevolence and reminiscent spirit of two people who, late in life, find connection.

Trademark #5: Be concise.

All but one of *Harry*'s cues last under two minutes. More than half last a minute or less. Scoring radio dramas in the 1930s, Herrmann discovered the power of a short sound bridge between scenes. From *Citizen Kane* onward, he used this less-is-more approach in film—one reason his scores feel modern. Among *Harry*'s loveliest cues is "The Phantom Coach," in which a slow, Debussy-like ascending figure for harp is answered by solo flute and *pianissimo* (very soft) clarinets. The music resembles a poetry setting, as Miss Gravely describes "the call of the phantom stagecoach, that used to pass by here each night two hundred years ago." This cue is all of fifty-five seconds, but it deliberately slows down the film for a last lyrical moment—the sun setting, our characters in silhouette—before the final plot machinations bring *Harry* to a close.

NICHOLAS MEYER, FILMMAKER: *There's a streak of melancholy that characterizes a lot of Herrmann's music. And I think that appealed to Hitchcock.* The Trouble with Harry *has that along with the black humor. And I think that melancholy, that autumnal flavor, was very much part and parcel of Herrmann's inmost self.*

It was a chilly 50 degrees in Hollywood on Tuesday, January 25, 1955, the first of two days on which *Harry*'s score would be recorded at Paramount.[44] In the week leading up to that 9:30 A.M. call, Herrmann's handwritten score had been copied into orchestral parts for each of Paramount's contract musicians. Such was the talent of studio players that after one or two run-throughs of a piece, they were ready to record it, accurately playing the notes, dynamics, and articulations—that is, what notes were accented, whether mutes were needed, and hundreds of other markings.

Paramount music head Roy Fjastad wisely included some extra time each day to deal with any problems. It was no secret that a Herrmann session was often charged with tension. On *Citizen Kane*, "when he stepped on the podium, he was already a basket case even before he gave the downbeat," recalled bassoonist Don Christlieb. "The sticks for the timpani were wrong, the mutes for the horns were wrong, the wooden piccolo mixed with the metal flute was wrong. It took an hour to straighten it out before we began to record the first cue."[45]

Example 2.6 Herrmann conducts at CBS, 1940s.

Adding to Herrmann's anxieties was the fact that *Harry* was his first experience with Paramount's orchestra. Lyn Murray, who had connected Benny with Hitch, visited the musicians before Herrmann's arrival. "I told them he was an old friend of mine and that they'd have a good time together."[46]

As the images of *Harry* silently unspooled on a screen behind the players, so that music could be synced to picture, Benny began recording his largest cues first. This way, the orchestra's size could be reduced as the day progressed.

Almost immediately, Herrmann was unhappy.

The success of his music depended on the subtle difference between soft and very soft . . . between a *sforzando* (sudden, strong) attack on a chord and a *staccato* one (a less forceful accent). A calmer conductor like Alfred Newman could draw that distinction with ease. For Herrmann, the gap between the sound in his head and what he heard from the podium could lead to explosive shouts of anger.

The oboist was struggling to play in the high register Herrmann wanted. Mutes were the wrong kind. And why weren't microphones closer to the French horns?

Invariably "he was suspicious that he'd be working with somebody who didn't know what he was doing," radio director Elliott Lewis recalled.[47] In the opinion of composer Elmer Bernstein, "He was driven by this desire for perfection. He was very intolerant of what he would consider slow-wittedness. He'd be death on a musician, for example, that he thought was second-rate and was trying to pose as a first-rate player."[48]

When Lyn Murray checked with *Harry*'s music editor to see how the day had gone, the reply he got was a glower. "He may be a friend of yours," the editor said, "but he's still a prick."[49]

Herrmann left the session physically ill. But as he processed the experience over the next forty-eight hours (recording was finished two days later), his anxiety lessened. As well it should have: the orchestra's performance was excellent.

By the time Hitchcock and Herbert Coleman appeared on the scoring stage that Thursday, Benny had calmed considerably. No doubt he was also on his best behavior, during the first performance of his music for Hitch. "There were smiles on the faces of the musicians," Coleman observed. "One could anticipate the beauty of the Vermont landscapes by the lilt of the music, punctuated by an occasional hint of danger." Hitchcock's verdict was quick in coming. Said Coleman, "I even heard a muffled chuckle from Hitch when he heard the phrase Bernie had composed for the scene of the sea captain sneaking past the deputy sheriff."[50]

Hitchcock realized that he had, at last, found his musical alter ego.

"*The Trouble with Harry* shows a side of Herrmann you don't get very often in his film scores," notes Michael McGehee. "His output of purely joyful, romantic music for film is rather limited. It's unfortunate because he's so good at it. And because it's for Hitchcock, it's totally unexpected here." Adds Hitchcock historian and filmmaker Laurent Bouzereau, "Herrmann recognized that the movie is all *about* Hitchcock. He knew that Hitchcock always had a cameo presence in his films, but in *The Trouble with Harry,* Hitch is in the film as a character, in the music. I think from that point on, Herrmann gave Hitchcock a musical identity in all of the films they made together."

The fact that Benny's score so perfectly fits the characters, the setting, and the movie's tonal shifts is all the more remarkable given a secret Hitchcock was unaware of: Herrmann had borrowed several key passages from a past project.

From June 1953 to June 1954, the CBS Radio series *Crime Classics* presented true crime stories laced with jet-black wit. Each episode, from Emperor Nero committing matricide, to the Scottish grave robbing of Burke and Hare, relied on Herrmann's music to establish time period and tension.

Radio was the most ephemeral of media: miss a broadcast and it was gone forever. When Benny first watched *The Trouble with Harry*, he realized how many of his *Crime Classics* scores seemed tailor-made for Hitchcock's film. Thus, the four-note horn theme from "The Terrible Deed of John White Webster" became *Harry*'s opening music. A pastorale for harp, oboe, and flute from "James Evans, Fireman: How He Extinguished a Human Torch" became one of *Harry*'s loveliest evocations of nature.

But these and other self-borrowings should not minimize Herrmann's accomplishment on *Harry*. On the most basic level, he eliminated unevenness in sound recording, especially the post-recorded dialogue. He distracted viewers from the imperfect mix of location and soundstage shooting. And he made thousands of separate images, shot over many weeks, seem like a single, inevitable flow. By adding changes of tempo to the film, he gave it pace, and blended its tonal shifts into a unified piece of storytelling.

TROUBLES WITH HARRY 53

Example 2.7 Hitch and Benny in 1955—the first official photo of the pair.

The Trouble with Harry also allowed Benny and Hitch to channel into art one of their deepest fears. "Daddy hated discussing the subject of death," Taffy recalled. "By nature, he was not what one would call a morbid person. He didn't brood about death. He just completely avoided thinking about it."[51] Except, of course, in his music.

As Paramount expected, *The Trouble with Harry* was only a modest box office earner. But it was a creative bullseye in capturing a style that can only be described as Hitchcockian. It also inspired what would be Hitch's favorite Herrmann score—because, he said, "it was comic."[52] Before *Harry*, "Music is music in Hitchcock films," observes Laurent Bouzereau. "It can play a great role. But with Herrmann, Hitchcock becomes the identity of the film in music."

With a single score, Herrmann had joined Alfred Hitchcock's most trusted inner circle. It was a trust reflected not only in the music of their next teaming, but in a surprising way onscreen as well.

3
The Team That Knew So Much

The Trouble with Harry's release, on October 3, 1955, was met with shrugs from critics and moviegoers. But Hitchcock still had much to celebrate. Twenty-four hours earlier, at 9:30 P.M. on Sunday, October 2, he had taken his first bow in a new medium: television. It would mark an epochal shift in the director's life, and impact every creative decision in his future.

"We ought to put Hitch on the air."[1] MCA president Lew Wasserman spoke those words to staff in early 1955, as he brainstormed ways to expand his client's image from bankable director to household name. By 1955, MCA repped most Hollywood celebrities: Brando, Monroe, Mitchum, Newman—even Liberace. Humphrey Bogart, Gary Cooper, and Spencer Tracy were getting percentage deals like the ones Lew orchestrated for Jimmy Stewart. Studios had ended most of their seven-year contracts with stars—too expensive in the age of independent production. Now they looked to MCA, for deals that offered a package team of MCA actors, writers, and director for a film.

Millions of dollars poured into the agency. But Wasserman eyed bigger goals. By 1955, MCA had expanded into an arena once impossible for a talent agency: TV show production.

That scenario had long been viewed as a conflict of interest by the Screen Actors Guild. If an agent's job was to get his client top dollar, how could that agent also be the client's producer? But Wasserman's tenacity led to a precedent. In 1952, SAG president Ronald Reagan—an MCA client—granted the talent agency a waiver, and Revue Productions was born.

Television had little appeal for Hitchcock; he was too busy making movies. But "if Lew said something, my father listened to him," Pat Hitchcock recalled.[2] Wasserman's pitch blended creative opportunity and irresistible profit participation. *Alfred Hitchcock Presents* would be a half-hour series telling standalone stories. Hitch's duties would be limited. He would executive produce, broadly overseeing a team of his choosing. He would approve story selection. He would host each episode, requiring just a few days of filming per season. And, to satisfy sponsor Bristol Myers, he would direct a few episodes each season that he would choose. For this, he would receive $129,000 per program—and all show rights would revert to him after just one broadcast.[3]

Hitch chose trusted colleagues to run the show. He encouraged them to adapt published, already proven suspense stories. The quality showed. From its debut episode, the Hitch-directed "Revenge," *Alfred Hitchcock Presents* was a critical smash, and by Season 2 a commercial one. Movie stars clamored for guest roles. And to Hitch's delight, his macabrely comic host wraps made him a pop culture icon around the world. (Herrmann was not involved in the series until its final two seasons, but he deserves some credit for its style: to convey the tone he wanted for his host wraps, Hitch showed writer James Allardice *The Trouble with Harry*.)[4]

Alfred Hitchcock's Mystery Magazine followed, as did record albums, book collections, and other Hitch-branded products. All of them added to his bank account, and few needed anything from him but his name.

Ironically, one of the world's most famous figures lived an insular daily routine. After a breakfast consisting of black coffee—a multi-course dinner was his end-of-day reward—Hitch was driven by limo twenty-five miles to Paramount. There he led writer conferences, directed his latest film, or both. Ensuring his happiness was a close team that grew in January by one: Bernard Herrmann, for whom Hitch's inner court became a second family.

Easiest to spot was forty-five-year-old editor George Tomasini—tall, movie-star handsome, and quick to laugh, even at jokes made at his expense. "Just his appearance on the set would relieve any tension building up," recalled Herbert Coleman.[5] The husband of actress Mary Brian, Tomasini had a sunny attitude of collaboration. His mastery of editorial rhythm won Herrmann's admiration.

Serving as Hitch's budget monitor, schedule supervisor, and on-set problem solver was unit production manager Clarence Oscar Erickson, known as "Doc" Erickson. Doc was tall and good-looking, with a gentlemanly demeanor and calming voice. To quote Coleman, his "applied expertise, and quiet charm, made him the most sought-after UPM in Hollywood for over three decades."[6]

Joan Harrison began as Hitchcock's London secretary in 1933. After two Oscar nominations as a writer on his films, the elegant blonde now produced *Alfred Hitchcock Presents*. In 1957 Hitch acquired another indispensable

Example 3.1 Hitch during production of *The Man Who Knew Too Much* with (from left) art director Henry Bumstead, unit production manager C. O. "Doc" Erickson, and associate producer Herbert Coleman.

factotum: Peggy Robertson, who had been his assistant on 1949's *Under Capricorn*. Fiercely protective of her boss, Peggy, another Brit, had a "sensitivity to Hitchcock's distress signals," author Stephen Rebello noted, that "bordered on the telepathic."[7]

Secretary Sue Gauthier joined the team in 1960. A former child actress who traded roles in *Our Gang* comedies for a spot in Paramount's secretarial pool, she was the front guard of Hitch's fortress. Her first meeting with Herrmann was typical. "He called on the phone, he demanded to know who I was and why I was there, and what was my name. I thought, oh my goodness, I'm scared to death of this man. He really intimidated me. And when he came into the office, I got a bear hug from him!

"We always had in the office refrigerator things we brought from home— snacks and whatnot. He'd come in, sit in front of the refrigerator, and say, 'What have you got to eat?' Benny had a sweet old heart. I loved him."[8]

Herrmann gained Hitchcock's trust so fully with *The Trouble with Harry* that a friendship began. "Benny admired very, very few people," Herrmann's third wife Norma observed. "But he really admired Hitchcock. Before he knew him intimately he admired his work. And with Hitchcock he behaved a little like a schoolboy. He would seek approval."[9] As Benny returned to Fox and other studios, he "loved to quote things Hitchcock said, his dry sense of humor," a collaborator recalled. "Benny would tell us, 'Now Hitch said this, and it was very funny' or 'As Hitch would say . . .'"[10] At Fox, if sound mixer Len Engel set the music too low, Herrmann had a new comeback: "Hitch wouldn't do it that way!"[11] Not even Orson Welles—twenty-two years old when he first teamed with Herrmann, and more of a peer—inspired such veneration.

The ultimate signs of friendship from Hitchcock, a legendary gourmand, were the dinner invitations he extended to Benny and his wife Lucy. Some took place at his immaculate residence at 10957 Bellagio Road. Others were at his home in Santa Cruz, two hours south of Hitch's beloved San Francisco. Alma was the main host, and Benny watched approvingly as she juggled her dual roles as Hitch's creative collaborator and domestic goddess. "She was extremely bright," recalled *Marnie* writer Jay Presson Allen. "Small. Quick. Very quick. Not a spark of glamour, very plain. But you liked to look at her, because she was so receptive, and so open. You know she read you immediately. Alma was warm. Hitch was warm, but only when he wanted to be. She was real. . . . And Hitch depended on her because he was more fantastical. He needed her to ground him."[12]

As a tribute to Alma's culinary labors, Hitch insisted that he and his dinner guests wash the dishes. Benny loved the tradition, savoring chats with Hitch over rolled-up shirtsleeves and the rinsing of plates. One night Benny mentioned that he dreamed of running a London-style pub. He asked Hitch what profession he'd have chosen other than filmmaking. Hitchcock removed his cleaning apron, folded it over his head, and intoned solemnly, "A hanging judge."[13]

Hitch also gave Benny tours of his private sanctuary. Behind a thick wooden door was a built-in wine cave, filled with hundreds of expensive bottles. Herrmann considered having one built in Bluebell, but the cost was astronomical.[14] Also, Benny drank far less than Hitchcock, who lubricated daytime meetings with liquor, and polished off bottles of fine wine at dinner.

Evenings with the Hitchcocks left Benny invigorated. But they were stressful for his sensitive wife. Minnesota-born Lucy Anderson shared many of Alma's virtues. She was intelligent, a fine cook, and devoted to her husband's demands. She was also attractive—a real-life Hitchcock blonde, minus the danger. But unlike Alma, Lucy had no artistic abilities, or above-average knowledge of Herrmann's favorite topics.

"Lucy was a wonderful, patient, very attractive lady," recalled composer Fred Steiner, "but out of Benny's league intellectually. She was in her own way sophisticated. She was an avid reader. It's just that she didn't know enough about music and art. But compared to Herrmann, who the heck did?"[15]

Once, when Taffy Herrmann was visiting, she found her stepmother in a panic: Hitch and Alma were coming over for dinner. "Lucy was a good cook," Taffy recalled, "but she was a plain cook."[16] That night, Lucy's fears seemed to be realized: the blender making a daiquiri for Hitch shattered. The next morning, she was amazed by the sight of a limousine pulling up outside her door. Out of it stepped Alfred Hitchcock, who presented her with a new blender.[17]

At Hitch's other home, Paramount, *The Trouble with Harry* was just one of many disappointments in 1955. Three producer-directors who had long been based at the studio—Billy Wilder, George Stevens, and William Wyler—had left for more lucrative deals. In Egypt, Cecil B. DeMille was taking drug injections to finish what would be his final epic, *The Ten Commandments*. Directorially speaking, Hitchcock was Paramount's biggest draw. And after the slim profitability of *Harry*, he knew that his next production had to be a home run.

His choice of project was not only commercial; it satisfied a long-held ambition. *The Man Who Knew Too Much* would be a lavish remake of his 1934 thriller of the same name, a film made in Britain and far more modest in scope. The original never satisfied its maker, who dismissed it—unfairly, to many—as the work of a "talented amateur."[18]

In the original, Bob and Jill Lawrence, a British couple vacationing in St. Moritz with daughter Betty, learn of an impending assassination plot. A politician will be shot during a concert at London's Albert Hall, the bullet to be fired as cymbals clash at the climax of a concert piece. To ensure Bob and Jill's silence, the assassins kidnap Betty. But their plans fail when Jill arrives at the concert and screams, just before the gunman pulls the trigger. A third-act shoot-out between police and villains ends in Betty's rescue.

With its focus on the threat to a family—a couple and their daughter—one wonders if Hitch's passion for the story came partly from his own domestic life. The remake retained key story points, but changed nationalities and settings. Hitch's protagonists were now American: Dr. Ben McKenna (James

Stewart, in his third Hitchcock role), wife Jo, a famous, retired singer (Doris Day), and son Hank (Christopher Olsen). Their fateful vacation was shifted from St. Moritz to French Morocco, but the rest of the story, like the 1934 original, took place in London.

This time, Hitchcock would film on location—first in Marrakesh, then in London, before completing the shoot at Paramount. He knew the movie would be among his most expensive. Stewart, with his usual gross percentage deal, and Day, a top recording and film star, didn't come cheap. Shooting in North Africa and Britain required complex travel plans for dozens of cast and crew members. But Paramount executives shared Hitchcock's enthusiasm. And in January 1955, the director began story conferences with writer Angus McPhail, a frequent collaborator.[19]

Equally important was musical planning for the movie's centerpiece: the foiled assassination at Albert Hall. As early as January 25, Hitchcock was researching who owned the faux concert piece written for the 1934 film.[20] No wonder: the cantata "Storm Clouds," with music by Arthur Benjamin and text by screenwriter D. B. Wyndham-Lewis, had served the original movie magnificently.[21] Composed for large orchestra, soprano soloist, and chorus, "Storm Clouds" was calibrated like a time bomb to build from a quietly tense opening to an urgent allegro. It culminates in a loud, penultimate chord, which halts for a beat of silence. In both films, an instant before the piece's

Example 3.2 The assassin (Reggie Nalder) prepares.

climactic cymbal crash, the heroine screams, causing the gunman to miss his shot.

Herrmann would write the new movie's score, and few composers would have passed on the chance to write fresh music for the Albert Hall climax. But Herrmann wasn't most composers. "I could have written a new piece instead of keeping Arthur Benjamin's," he said, "but I didn't think that anybody could better what he'd done in the original version."[22] For Herrmann, the needs of a film took precedence over self-aggrandizement.

Benny also embraced Hitch's notion that, with Doris Day as costar, audiences would expect a song. Day had been cast as part of an MCA package deal with James Stewart. And in what proved an ideal marriage of creativity and commerce, Hitchcock hired Paramount's top songwriters, Jay Livingston and Ray Evans ("Mona Lisa," "Silver Bells"), to write a tune for Day. He told the pair frankly that he didn't know what he wanted. But a description of the plot proved sufficient. Composer Livingston recalled three words from a scene in the Ava Gardner drama *The Barefoot Contesssa*: "Che sarà sarà." When they played Hitchcock the result—"Que Será, Será (Whatever Will Be, Will Be)"—the director's face showed no emotion. Finally, as Livingston remembered, the oracle spoke. "'Gentlemen, I told you I didn't know what kind of song I wanted.' He hesitated, then pointed a finger at us, and said, '*That's* the kind of song I want.' Then he got up and walked out."[23]

Usually, Herrmann railed against the inclusion of a song in a drama. "Benny would go up in the air if you mentioned Tiomkin or 'High Noon,' which he considered dreck," recalled Lionel Newman, brother of Alfred.[24] But on *Man*, Herrmann understood the dramatic purpose of the song. In the movie's finale, Jo sings it to locate her missing son. Benny so enjoyed working with Doris Day, he socialized for a time with the singer and her husband-manager, Martin Melcher.[25]

Herrmann was involved with the movie from the start of pre-production, a system that continued for a decade. He loved Hitch's focus on the script—they shared a passion for the written word—and he appreciated his translation of key sequences into shot-by-shot storyboards. "Talent is the smallest thing about being an artist in anything," the composer later said. "You need many years of apprenticeship to develop the craft that goes with being creative—the discipline, the experience."[26] For Benny, Hitchcock was the ultimate example.

Example 3.3 Sheet music for *Man*'s Oscar-winning song, 1956.

Herrmann understood Hitch's plans so fully that sequences could be shaped editorially to accommodate the score. The director minimized dialogue, telling his story visually in a style he'd mastered in the silent era. While the script was being written, he and Herrmann determined the role of music. "He'd tell just a few words to me, maybe a half-hour discussion, and leave it to me—whatever I felt. It was wonderful to work with Hitch because of this freedom."[27]

The 1934 Albert Hall sequence lasts a mere four minutes and twelve seconds. For the remake, Hitchcock created a set piece grander in scope— one he hoped would be a high point in his career. Benny persuaded Hitch to pay Arthur Benjamin £100 ($3,000 today) to write ninety seconds of new music for "Storm Clouds."[28] The cantata would be played mostly at a slower tempo and orchestrated for a larger orchestra. Hitchcock also authorized Herrmann to oversee revisions in the cantata's text. As a result, on-the-nose phrases like the chorus's "All save the child" were eliminated.

Filming was set to begin in Marrakesh on May 12. There was just one problem: by mid-April, final screenwriter John Michael Hayes had yet to turn in a script. Those pages were urgently needed for overseas casting and location finding.

Hitchcock could not delay his start date: Marrakesh officials had told Herbert Coleman that filming could take place only until the day before Ramadan. After that, any work would be illegal and unsafe. Shooting in Morocco already came with risk. French-controlled since 1912, it was the site of violent protests by North African nationalists. (The French finally left in 1956.) On April 29, Hitchcock left L.A. for London, to finish casting for UK scenes. He then flew to Marrakesh, where on May 13 he had no choice but to start filming with Stewart, Day, and other principals, even though the script was not locked.

In Marrakesh, Hitchcock found the exoticism he wanted. But shooting in a city whose streets were crammed with 225,000 residents pushed filming behind schedule. A script finally arrived from Hayes; but on the cover page, Hayes listed only himself, with no credit for his predecessor, Angus McPhail. "I saw an angry look cross [Hitch's] face," said Coleman. "'How could he have left Angus' name off the title page?' he almost shouted." When Herbie confirmed that the script was solid, "Hitchcock replied, 'Then call the boys. Tell them we're finished with Hayes. And I mean today. I don't want to see him or talk to him again. Ever!'"[29]

The director never used, or spoke with, Hayes again.[30]

As Ramadan neared, Hitchcock flew to London as planned, leaving the last days of shooting in Marrakesh to Coleman. The crew was still filming on the morning of Ramadan. With crowds "becoming hostile"[31] and armed soldiers poised on rooftops, Coleman and his team made a fast exit to London.

During those tense weeks, at least one member of the team was ecstatic. The reason can be found on page 131 of Hayes's screenplay:[32]

```
EXT. ALBERT HALL - (DAY) - LONG SHOT
   The screen is filled with a large poster. It
announces for that evening the commemorative
concert. Further details on the poster indicate
that a Cantata will be sung featuring the London
Symphony Orchestra, The Royal Choral Society, and
a woman as featured mezzo soprano, and Conductor
Bernard Herrmann.
```

Barely three months had passed between Hitchcock's first hearing of *The Trouble with Harry*'s score and his decision to put Herrmann onscreen, in the most crucial sequence of his biggest-budgeted film.

Hitch was rewarding the man he considered a partner. He also knew that for Benny, the role would be no stretch. From the mid-1930s to 1951, Herrmann had conducted the CBS Symphony, in radio concerts that remain milestones in bold programming. Appointed the Symphony's director in 1940, Herrmann conducted modern works by Ives, Bartók, Stravinsky, Barber, Vaughan Williams, and Milhaud, many of whom attended the broadcasts. "Concert programs on radio should not be run from the box-office standpoint," Herrmann told an interviewer. "Radio's artistic function, as I see it, is to expose to listeners the literature of music."[33] No American conductor in the twentieth century played more contemporary or rare scores. And as surviving broadcasts attest, his orchestra invariably delivered excellent performances.

For Herrmann, conducting a symphony concert was the ultimate source of joy. During a trip to Britain in 1946, he was galvanized by the response to his conducting of the world-famous Hallé Orchestra. Noted *Variety*, "Nearly 6,000 turned out to hear one of Herrmann's concerts in Manchester on a rainy night during a bus strike."[34] That success stoked his chief ambition: to become an internationally recognized concert conductor, with writing music as his secondary profession. "He lived and breathed classical music," Taffy recalled. "Daddy enjoyed conducting as he walked down the street. And if he took you to a concert, there were two people conducting: the man on the podium and daddy."[35]

America's most renowned orchestra, the New York Philharmonic, played several Herrmann works in the 1940s, although rarely with their composer conducting. His epic cantata *Moby Dick*, his war elegy *For the Fallen* . . . each had been given well-received performances, at a time when critics often dismissed the unfamiliar, especially from a composer who also worked in film.

In 1947, at age thirty-six, Herrmann was elated to be asked to conduct the New York Philharmonic in a series of summer concerts. They would take place at Lewisohn Stadium, an outdoor venue seating 22,000. If he succeeded, international opportunities awaited, as they had for twenty-five-year-old Leonard Bernstein after his debut with the Philharmonic in 1943.

But Herrmann was never at his best when conducting an unfamiliar orchestra. During rehearsals with the Philharmonic his temper flared. The hostility was mutual, from musicians who'd earned the nickname "Murder Incorporated." And on the night of July 28, with nearly 7,000 people in attendance, the verdict from critics was swift: Herrmann had failed spectacularly.

During Rachmaninoff's Second Piano Concerto, "Benny gave a conducting indication," recalled radio director Oliver Daniel. "Instead of 4/4, he [accidentally] did it in 2/4. So the orchestra did it twice as fast, which created absolute chaos when the pianist came in. The whole thing nearly broke down. I can see Benny wildly gesticulating and trying to get the men back together. That need not have happened, because the piece was sufficiently known to all the men. I consider that a piece of sabotage by the orchestra."[36]

For the first time in his career, Herrmann experienced national humiliation. "Mr. Herrmann is a calisthenic conductor," wrote the critic for the *New York Times*. "His rarely restrained use of large gestures precluded any considered building of climaxes, indicated a lack of understanding of the larger aspects of the music he performed." Vaughan Williams's *London Symphony*, which Herrmann knew better than any American conductor, "became pompous . . . maudlin . . . due to his failure to define its outlines clearly and because he allowed the orchestra to turn in a slovenly performance."[37]

The experience, his wife Lucille Fletcher recalled, "broke his heart. The critics gave him awful reviews, the weather was beastly hot, and night after night the audiences dwindled, until sometimes there were only two thousand people in an amphitheater seating 22,000."[38]

ALEX ROSS, AUTHOR/MUSICOLOGIST: *I'm ashamed on behalf of my fellow critics. Obviously there were technical problems, but the orchestra was misbehaving, the way the New York Philharmonic has done generation after generation. In a case like that, a critic should think, all right, there are some issues here, but what is this man capable of? What else can he bring? There are a lot of conductors like that. Koussevitzky is not someone whom you could have taken away from the Boston Symphony and put in front of the New York Philharmonic. But there's a richness of perspective, and you should make allowances for that.*[39]

Herrmann likely was destined to fail. In 1943, the orchestra similarly torpedoed another film composer, Max Steiner. But the concerts exposed a truth that Benny would never recognize: his conducting, outside of CBS and Hollywood, was seldom first-rate.

Consider these remarks, not from his critics but his supporters:

FRED STEINER, COMPOSER: *He did terrible things with his arms. He didn't have anything even resembling the conventional conducting technique.*[40]

CHARLES GERHARDT, CONDUCTOR: *He wasn't that helpful to the musicians. It was easier for him to be a critic and tell them what he didn't like.*[41]

DAVID RAKSIN, COMPOSER: *It was partly a lack of charisma. He just didn't have the gift of inspiring an orchestra.*[42]

EILEEN FARRELL, SOPRANO: *And he would pick his nose while he was conducting! This is the god's honest truth.*[43]

So why are Herrmann-led recordings of his film scores their best performances? And why were reviews of his CBS broadcasts usually raves?

Two factors rescued him in a studio. The CBS and Hollywood orchestras knew and compensated for Benny's limitations. And his comfort level with those musicians liberated his expressiveness. Conducting a 1956 concert with the Glendale Symphony, an ensemble made up of Hollywood players, "he was so wrapped up in the music, he was dancing on the podium," one musician recalled.[44] Attendee Fred Steiner felt that "he did a wonderful job. And I thought, this guy *is* a good conductor. Sure, he looks funny up there, but he understands the music, and that's the important thing."[45]

Benny's brother Louis put it succinctly: "He never developed a great technique, but he had enormous musical insights."[46]

In 1951, Herrmann's bitterness over his fading reputation as a conductor was dealt its harshest blow, when CBS disbanded its symphony orchestra. The network was putting all its chips on a new medium: television.

With *The Man Who Knew Too Much*, Alfred Hitchcock was giving his friend a chance to reintroduce himself to the world as a conductor.

On May 9, 1955, Benny and Lucy arrived in London for filming of the Albert Hall sequence. Thanks to Hitch, their accommodations were deluxe: a suite at the Savoy Hotel, with all expenses paid.

Herrmann had two responsibilities during his month-long stay:

(1) He would pre-record the "Storm Clouds" cantata with the London Symphony Orchestra. That recording would be played in Albert Hall during filming, so that orchestra and vocalists could perform in time with it. The pre-recording would then be used for the final soundtrack.

(2) He would appear on camera as himself, conducting "Storm Clouds" during three or four of the five days allotted to film in the Hall.

Herrmann arrived so prepared that he needed only two days, not the scheduled three, to record "Storm Clouds," a saving Hitch appreciated.[47] "Benny was clearly enjoying himself during the recording," recalled LSO violinist and friend Henry Greenwood. "He was so on top of the music he was playing. That's how he got the orchestra's respect."[48] Equally happy were the five days of filming inside the glass-and-iron Victorian dome of Albert Hall, a four-tier auditorium that seated up to 8,000. Hitchcock mostly shot medium and wide shots of the LSO, performing under Herrmann's baton. Most of the close-ups—of the gunman, of Doris Day's anguished Jo—would be filmed more thriftily at Paramount.

Hitchcock delighted in having control of one of Britain's most famous buildings, and the performers within it. "These are my puppets," he told Henry Greenwood. "I manipulate them as I see fit."[49] Maintaining control was not merely an ego boost. For Hitchcock, it ensured that life's chaos and disorder—the things he feared most—were held at bay.

On June 6, filming at the Hall was completed. Herrmann was professional throughout, and on the last day, he was touched to receive a gift from the orchestra. It was a book that bore the inscription:

To Bernard Herrmann
"The Man Who Knows So Much"
from The London Symphony Orchestra, June 1955

That week, Herrmann conveyed his own gratitude to Hitchcock, giving him a painting. On June 4, the director responded with unusual emotion.

My dearest Lucy and Benny,
I am so overwhelmed that I'm reduced to writing this note, just because
I would not be able to be in the least bit articulate.
I just don't know how to thank you.
Love, Hitch[50]

The rest of filming, at Paramount in Los Angeles, went just as smoothly. The only note of discord came from Doris Day. After weeks of silence from her director, Day—whose film career grew out of her success as a singer, and

Example 3.4 Hitch directs Benny at the Albert Hall, May 1955. © Academy of Motion Picture Arts & Sciences.

Example 3.5 *Storm Clouds* composer Arthur Benjamin sits between Hitch and Benny. © Academy of Motion Picture Arts & Sciences.

who had no acting training—became stressed. Finally she asked Hitchcock what she was doing wrong. He was puzzled, and explained that he had given her no direction because she needed none. Her performance was exactly what he wanted. The exchange that followed, as recalled by Day, reveals much about the private Hitchcock.

DAY: *I wish you had told me that. You see, I'm frightened of you in a way, and insecure.*
HITCH: *Everyone's frightened.*
DAY: *Don't tell me you are.*
HITCH: *Oh, yes. I am. I'm always frightened. When I walk into the dining room at Paramount, I'm as insecure as everybody else. . . . Everybody's frightened and insecure, and the ones who appear not to be are just appearing not to be. Deep down, they're as frightened as the next fellow. Maybe even more so.*[51]

Behind his mask, "he was afraid of everything," wrote biographer Peter Ackroyd. "He always imagined the worst, and prepared for it. He still did not like to cross the studio floor in case a stranger came up to him. François Truffaut said of him . . . that he was a 'neurotic' and 'a fearful person'; he was 'deeply vulnerable' but as a result became 'an artist of anxiety.'"[52]

It was another bond with Herrmann, whose own anxieties, far more publicly displayed, also fueled his gift for capturing tension in his art.

The Score

Director and composer agreed that *The Man Who Knew Too Much* needed little underscore. Keeping music to a minimum would make the climactic "Storm Clouds" all the more impactful. But Herrmann makes each second of original music count, especially in the opening "Prelude." This music for the main title lasts just two minutes and ten seconds, but it contains the seeds of every key idea developed in the underscore.

The movie opens with Paramount's VistaVision logo—the 1950s equivalent of an IMAX card, promising larger-than-life adventure. We then see a group of tuxedoed musicians who perform Herrmann's main title, written in the style of a grand concert overture. Visually, Hitchcock tricks us. The gilded wall behind the players evokes the Albert Hall, but it's actually a set at Paramount. And there are only thirteen musicians onscreen, but the mammoth orchestra on the soundtrack convinces us we're seeing a larger ensemble.

As the title card appears, eleven percussionists create an explosion of sound: xylophone, glock, two tenor drums, two snare drums, timpani, and the cymbal that will later conceal a gunshot. Muted brass proclaims a *fortissimo* (very, very loud) six-note fanfare, answered by solo timpani pounding a thunderous reply.

WILLIAM STROMBERG, COMPOSER: *This is Herrmann obviously inspired by the Storm Clouds cantata. He starts the film with the same kind of vibrance.*[53]

JOHN MORGAN, COMPOSER: *The timpani part is so important: "Ba BUM, ba BUM...." Herrmann would say to the orchestra, "If ya break the sticks, I'll buy ya new ones."*

Next we hear a shivering figure for strings, winds, and percussion. Play an A-flat major chord, then the D above it, and you'll hear its essence, an unmistakably Herrmann sound of disorientation. In the Prelude, this "Danger" motif (theme) lasts just two measures. Later it's expanded into the score's eeriest cue, "The Warning," as Ben gets a phone call from his son

Hank's abductors. As Hitchcock's camera circles around Ben, the "Danger" theme is played by high, muted strings (*tremolo*, trembling), harp, and two vibraphones. The theme drifts downward in hypnotic triplets (*one-two-three, one-two-three*). It's an intensely psychological effect: we're hearing the whirling gears of Ben's mind trying to process the unthinkable. Herrmann's short themes are malleable: the "Danger" motif will return as a comic scherzo, when Ben goes by mistake to a taxidermist's shop, and the men brawl amid stuffed lions, tigers, and swordfish.

The opening Prelude contains another preview of things to come: a pattern of three rising-falling swells. It's simple on the page. But Herrmann's brutish orchestration and his shifting dynamics from *forte* (loud) to *sforzando* (sudden emphasis) give the pattern the force of a crashing wave in a storm.

STROMBERG: *He uses these minor chords later when Jimmy Stewart is walking through an empty alley, where the music is very slow and menacing. They're also in the fight scene, when Stewart is about to get punched in the church. There it's heard at a much faster tempo as it gets more and more frantic.*

MORGAN: *That's the magic of music. Even if the audience isn't aware that it's based on earlier music, it feels right. It belongs in this sound world he's created.*

Most of the cues are under two minutes long. But inside their brevity is power. Take the back-to-back cues "The Chase" and "The Knife." *Man*'s plot switches into thriller mode when French agent Louis Bernard (Daniel Gélin) runs through a Marrakesh market, trying to escape the man who will kill him. Herrmann scores the chase for just nine instruments. They include a fast *tat-tat-tat-tat-tat* rhythm for snare and tenor drums, rising-falling notes for snarling tubas and bass clarinets, and a fast piano ostinato (repeat figure), playing the "dum-dum-dum-dum" that will become *Jaws*' shark motif nineteen years later.

ALEX ROSS, AUTHOR/MUSICOLOGIST: *Elmer Bernstein said Herrmann was the greatest ostinato writer who ever lived. I think there's something to that. The way he works out ways in which the repetition doesn't turn stale. It doesn't even turn familiar, because there's always these subtle shifts, these ways he finds so that the ostinato takes on a different color.*

When Louis's pursuer thrusts a knife in his back, Herrmann doesn't musically "catch" the moment, as most composers would. The stab happens swiftly, so Herrmann waits until Hitchcock cuts to the big reveal: a shot of Louis's back, knife protruding from his white robe, now blotched with the red of blood.

MORGAN: *It's then that we hear the musical "stinger."*
STROMBERG: *And these chords are fantastic: it's two different minor chords stacked on top of each other . . . A-flat minor and G-minor chords, spread apart, with a weird bass note. We're thrown into something new, a feeling of turmoil.*

With these polychords, Herrmann gives us a preview of what will become his trademark Hitchcock sound. He also achieves it with only nine players: two bass clarinets, four cellos, three basses.

STROMBERG: *Herrmann could do more with less than any other composer in the world. You don't need a full orchestra playing that. All you need is what he did.*

Herrmann also uses simple means to add suspense to shots of Ben and Jo, as they walk through London side streets searching for their son. Against quarter notes for harp, ticking evenly like a clock, Herrmann adds a rising-falling figure—sometimes for ominous low clarinets, sometimes for high violins. What makes this music tense is his detailed articulation. Strings are muted, creating a cold, arid sound. Herrmann asks for down-bows, meaning that players start their bow high on the instrument's strings, and move their bow downward. This can achieve a more accented, agitated sound than an up-bow. Dynamics also add variety: Herrmann's rising-falling pattern starts as a whispery *pianissimo* (very soft), then rises in volume and fades as the notes climb up and down.

JOHN WILSON, CONDUCTOR: *Those shifting blocks of unresolved harmony . . . it's completely ambiguous. It's harmony that can never go anywhere.*
MORGAN: *Herrmann knew that you don't have to have an ending to a cue. He leaves it hanging, unresolved, because the story is continuing.*

Effective as these miniature pieces are, they are side attractions to the main event. The 1956 version of the Albert Hall sequences runs nine minutes and seven seconds, more than double the length of the 1934 original. Since every onscreen image and the tempo of editing are determined by the music, Herrmann effectively became the sequence's codirector.

It begins with wide shots of the hall, as Herrmann takes the conductor's podium. His downbeat initiates Benjamin's dark, minor-key fanfare for trumpets and trombones; their echoing notes suggest the hall's cavernous dimensions. Then Herrmann gets a movie-star close-up. He looks commanding in tails, and displays a clean baton technique.

For a full minute Hitchcock keeps his visuals on Herrmann, the orchestra, and concertgoers, charting the space's geography. Finally we see Jo, listening from the back of the hall. In the music, a flowing passage leads to a lyrical pastorale that reflects Jo's maternal instincts, and her conflict: if she prevents the shooting, her son dies. Music connects us emotionally with Jo's point of view, as she looks up and sees the gunman in a private box. Jo follows the killer's gaze and sees his intended victim: a portly man, his tuxedo covered by a red sash. A tiara on the head of the woman behind him confirms without words that we are seeing a foreign dignitary.

Herrmann takes the cantata at a slower tempo than the 1934 version without losing any of its propulsive movement. This also helps make the cantata's second half, with its brisk allegros and grand finale, more exciting. Lyrical passages of the cantata are reprised, by mezzo-soprano soloist Barbara Howitt and the Covent Garden chorus, as the edit cross-cuts

Example 3.6 Herrmann onscreen in *The Man Who Knew Too Much*.

between the matronly soprano and Jo, who sobs as she sinks helplessly against a wall.

Then, a startling cut: we see timpani, close-up. The player creates a thunderous roll, kicking the sequence into its fast final gear. With only Benjamin's music on the soundtrack (*Allegro agitato*—fast, agitated), we leave the auditorium for the first time as Ben runs into the lobby, silently confers with Jo, then races upstairs to stop the killer. Years later, James Stewart claimed that he had a long section of dialogue here: "I was just talking my head off. At the end of the scene, Hitch said, 'Cut,' and he said, 'Let's do that again. You were talking so loud I couldn't hear the London Symphony. As a matter of fact, let's just cut the whole speech.'"[54] In fact, there is no dialogue in Hayes's script.

During the film's editing in August 1955, Hitchcock realized he wanted to make the sequence even longer. To extend Ben's search for the killer, and to show more footage of Jo, the killer, and his target, Hitchcock and Herrmann re-edited the music, repeating nearly a minute of the *Allegro agitato* section. Close your eyes and the edit is obvious. Now open your eyes and watch: Hitchcock's images make the loop near-seamless. As Herrmann was fond of quoting, "Jean Cocteau once said that a film score should create the sensation that one does not know whether the music is propelling the film, or the film is propelling the music."[55]

The cantata nears its end. The assassin takes aim. Benjamin's music is both symphonic work and movie scoring. A relentless, militaristic ostinato for snare drum, and climbing cadences for orchestra and chorus are matched by faster editing. We see Herrmann conducting furiously . . . a horizontal pan across his music score, the shadow of his hand adding vertical energy . . . a tighter pan across the score . . . the cymbalist, raising his instrument for the clash that will mean a man's death. The hall's magisterial organ signals the cantata's approaching conclusion. Herrmann faces us, symmetrically framed between the two raised cymbals.

A gun barrel emerges from behind the concert box curtain. Cut to "gun in foreground, [the camera] shooting into [its] nozzle with squinted eye of Assassin beyond." Cut to the gunman's POV: the prime minister, passively listening. The camera tilts down to his heart. Chorus and orchestra reach their booming, penultimate chord. Then the long second of silence. Cut to Jo. She screams. The gun barrel wobbles. The cymbals crash, and the prime minister leaps up, grabbing his arm in pain. Ben breaks into the shooter's box. Then five notes, in a triumphant major key, mirror Ben's triumph as the fleeing gunman falls to his death.

Compared to "Storm Clouds," the recording of Herrmann's underscore, at Paramount on November 3 and 4, was a modest affair. But the sessions did expose Hitchcock to Benny's least attractive side, as the director and Coleman "watched him criticize, dominate and sometimes rave at the Paramount orchestra, until the last chord was recorded," Herbie recalled. "The moment the last musical note faded away, Benny's attitude changed completely. Smiling broadly, he thanked the players for their attention."[56]

Throughout his life, Hitchcock loathed and avoided scenes of conflict. With Herrmann, he decided that temperament was an acceptable price to pay for music that greatly elevated his films. Playwright Andrew McCaldon ("Benny & Hitch") has also wondered "whether there was some sense in which Hitchcock tolerated Herrmann's temperament because he admired that candidness. He admired that bravery and that sense of principle. Because although Hitchcock had that in private, it seems that he found that very hard to actually front up to in public."[57]

After an April 29 premiere at the Cannes Film Festival, *The Man Who Knew Too Much* opened across the United States on June 1, 1956. Reviews were generally warm, and box office spectacular. The fact that shooting went over schedule was forgotten, after a box office take of $4.4 million. Best of all for Hitch, rights to the film reverted to him eight years after its initial release. Over the next three decades, reissues and TV sales raised its earnings to $11.3 million.

Its success extended to the Oscars. On March 27, 1957, "Que Será, Será" won the Academy Award for Best Original Song, finally giving Hitch the hit tune he'd wanted. A different musical reward came Herrmann's way. As the movie was being completed, he was thrilled to receive an invitation from the London Symphony, to conduct four concerts in May 1956. Benny couldn't have asked for a better showcase to relaunch his stalled conducting career.

But despite their shared success, Hitchcock and Herrmann could not escape a feeling of frustration that spring. Each man felt acutely a lack of respect within his industry. And in the year ahead, both would tackle new projects they hoped would redress those feelings of rejection.

4

Wronged Men

"The only thing I ever did that was foolhardy was to write an opera," Bernard Herrmann remarked in 1970. "Franz Liszt said that you have to have the soul of a hero to write an opera, and the mentality of a lackey to have it produced."[1]

The most frustrating creation of Benny's life had its roots in both film and his Anglophilia. Hired to score Fox's *Jane Eyre* in 1943, his feeling for the Brontë sisters' writing evolved from admiration to obsession. He decided to compose an opera based on Emily Brontë's *Wuthering Heights*. His first wife, writer Lucille Fletcher, would craft the libretto. And for the next eight years, despite a dense schedule of CBS drama scores, radio concerts, and movie scores, Herrmann invested his deepest emotion in the opera.

He identified with Brontë's anti-hero Heathcliff, an orphaned reject of society the author describes as "slovenly . . . and rather morose." Rejected by his love, Catherine Earnshaw, Heathcliff fixates on revenge. He marries another woman, whom he abuses emotionally.

In Heathcliff Herrmann saw himself, a misunderstood outsider abused by enemies and longing for love denied him. But given Herrmann's success by the mid-1940s—conducting the CBS Symphony, winning an Academy Award, having his pick of films, and enjoying the devotion of Lucille and two daughters—his identification with Brontë's "imp of satan" was more self-fulfilling prophecy than reality. "He was a terribly insecure man," recalled friend Shirley Steiner. "Something led him to be always striving, so that even when he was successful, it wasn't enough. There was some kind of approval he didn't get, some kind of love he didn't get. Nobody ever does. But some people take it harder than others."[2]

During the opera's years of writing, Herrmann grew more resentful. His youthful outbursts of enthusiasm and passing anger hardened into a mood of distrust, punctuated by uncontrollable rages. By the time he finished his opera in 1951, Herrmann and Fletcher were divorced.

But the misery accompanying *Wuthering Heights* had only begun. Benny believed it was his finest creation, but no opera company would touch it. If its over three-hour length weren't deterrent enough, Herrmann's response to any criticism of it sent potential producers running.

He attributed the rebuffs to money-driven music directors and symphony board members he refused to flatter. The truth was more painful. "It's just not good enough, is it?" said Norman Lloyd, a close friend. "It's a derivative piece. He didn't bring any of the suspense or excitement that he did to his film score for *Jane Eyre*."[3] And "for all of Benny's great knowledge of poetry, he had absolutely no feeling for words when it came to their setting," observed musicologist Christopher Palmer. "He invariably accented the wrong word; the musical accent is totally at variance with the verbal accent."[4]

In 1955 Leopold Stokowski, then leading the Houston Symphony, arranged to have his friend conduct several concerts with his orchestra. Not only could Benny make a connection to advance his conducting career; if he made a good impression, the Houston Grand Opera might stage *Wuthering Heights*.

But in January 1956, Herrmann again committed self-sabotage. "He ended up insulting all the trustees," John Houseman recalled. "He had a persecution mania."[5] The board was anti-Semitic, Herrmann told his daughter. Perhaps. But that May, when at last he conducted the London Symphony in four concerts, history repeated itself. Gone was the loquacious Anglophile who charmed the orchestra while making Hitchcock's film. In his place was an anxious, insulting pedant.

"During rehearsals he could be very sarcastic," recalled violinist Henry Greenwood. "Our oboe player was a gentlemanly sort of person and asked, 'Mr. Herrmann, this part is penciled in mezzo-forte, but it's only penciled in. Do you wish me to observe it?' Benny said, 'SURE I do. Whaddya want it in, NEON?' He did so many things like that that the orchestra got tired of him. And when he'd do things wrong, they let him wallow in his mistakes. They just let him sink into the enormity of his own egotry."[6]

Example 4.1 Herrmann rehearsing the Glendale Symphony, 1957.

Many reviews of the concerts were enthusiastic. Vaughan Williams rose from the audience to shake Benny's hand, after a moving performance of his *London Symphony*. But Herrmann would not be asked back.

If spring 1956 was a time of frustration for Benny, Hitchcock's stock had never been higher. Season 1 of *Alfred Hitchcock Presents* wasn't just an Emmy-nominated hit; it had begun to permeate the culture. A second season was in production. "Before TV I'd get about a dozen letters per week," Hitch told a reporter. "Now it's several hundred.... Just the other day I overheard a lady say, 'There's Alfred Hitchcock of television.'"[7]

The director "was accosted with imitations of his booming 'Good evening,'" noted biographer Peter Ackroyd. "He had the most famous silhouette in America. And he now became engaged in what must have seemed like an everlasting process of self-promotion, in which his screen 'character' became in many respects the character that he projected onto the world. He loved it."[8]

But despite that acclaim, Hitch felt dissatisfaction. Nominated only four times to date for an Oscar, he was "ever the bridesmaid," a remark he'd make with a comic sigh, but which masked genuine resentment. Every award lost, each film role rejected by an A-list actor, echoed what he believed the industry said behind his back. *Of course his movies are entertaining. But it's not serious filmmaking, is it? And what real director would appear each week making jokes on television?*

"He really wanted the Oscar," screenwriter Joseph Stefano observed. "He wanted that vote of confidence from the industry. In the midst of so much, he was unhappy."[9]

Hitch's sense of being spurned extended to his homeland. The man born in working-class London confided to Herrmann that he had never been invited into the royal enclosure at Ascot. "Are you interested in horse racing?" Benny asked. "No," Hitch replied, "but I should be invited."[10]

Fittingly, the concept of injustice was at the heart of the next Herrmann-Hitchcock project.

The director had been sent a powerful story from *Life* magazine. It chronicled the wrongful arrest in 1953 of Manny Balestrero, a jazz bassist at New York's Stork Club, who was misidentified as the hold-up man in a string of robberies. Balestrero was exonerated after a mistrial and the real criminal's arrest, but the ordeal broke the musician's fragile wife, Rose. She suffered a breakdown and was institutionalized for two years. She never fully recovered.

Hitchcock often used the ephemeral currency of commercial success to make a more personal or experimental film. In *The Wrong Man*, he did both. Its depiction of Balestrero's story, showing how a life can be wrecked by a flawed, impersonal justice system, echoed a deep Hitchcock fear. It was one that, according to his most oft-told anecdote, had roots in his childhood. "When I was no more than six years of age, I did something my father considered worthy of reprimand.... [He] sent me to the local police station with a note. The officer on duty read it and locked me in a jail cell for five minutes, saying, 'This is what we do to naughty boys.' I have, ever since, gone to any lengths to avoid arrest and confinement."[11]

True or concocted, the story accurately reflected his terror of police. Secretary Sue Gauthier once accompanied him on a drive to his pets' veterinarian (like Herrmann, he loved dogs). "We were driving over when Hitchcock suddenly became very upset. He got absolutely panicky, saying,

'Oh no, I haven't got my driver's license. What if the police stop me?' He was truly petrified that something terrible would happen to him.'"¹²

He also shared Manny Balestrero's Catholic faith. The director who was obsessed with murder tales, in which killers are not always punished, went with his daughter to church, and was obsessed with the causes of guilt.*

Hitchcock also monitored the latest filmmaking trends. Among the most important was the postwar shift to more naturalistic acting, as practiced by trailblazers like Brando and Clift. He also took note of the "kitchen sink" realism of dramas like Elia Kazan's *On the Waterfront*. In 1955, the year Hitchcock lost the Oscar for *Rear Window*, *Waterfront* claimed eight Academy Awards, including Best Director and Best Picture.

Excited by a challenge, the fifty-six-year-old Hitch decided to make *The Wrong Man* in a style he'd never attempted—one that would avoid directorial flair in favor of realism. The decision was made probably not only to challenge himself but also his detractors, who dismissed him as a one-trick entertainer. It would lead to one of his most underappreciated features, and much creative frustration.

The Balestrero home in Jacksonville Heights, the 110th precinct where Manny was arrested, his subway route on the E train from Manhattan's plush Stork Club to suburban Queens—all were meticulously researched by writers Angus McPhail and Pulitzer winner Maxwell Anderson. But even with the casting of Henry Fonda as Manny—Fonda loved projects with social justice themes—Hitchcock worried. He knew that by limiting himself to a docudrama approach, he must give up trademarks that viewers expected from him: tour-de-force action scenes in exotic locales, tension-leavening comedy, glamorous romance, and color itself. *The Wrong Man* was shot in stark black-and-white.

While Hitch had qualms, Herbert Coleman had certainties—none of them positive. He told his boss that the story lacked suspense, and centered on a hero too passive to be sympathetic. But Hitchcock felt that he'd found a vessel to dramatize something personal. He would show an innocent man's arrest and trial from a subjective viewpoint—scenes rarely depart from

---

* Although his films were subject to censorship, which required punishment of the guilty, TV was more flexible. The villain escapes in many episodes of *Alfred Hitchcock Presents*. Hitchcock the host closed these shows with absurdist tales of how the criminal was later captured; once, he tells us, the arresting detective was disguised as a dog. Most viewers recognized these epilogues as mocking jabs at censors' prim morality.

Manny's point of view. Hitch also pointed out that *The Wrong Man* would be made for Warner Bros. He owed that studio one last film, and Warners owned the rights to Balestrero's story.

Manhattan was a source of inspiration for Hitchcock since childhood. In *The Wrong Man*, he hoped to make New York as vivid a character as Manny and Rose. "It would be wonderful to do a story entirely about New York," he said years earlier. "Not the New York as it exists to the tourist, or the casual observer, but *inside* New York."[13] In *The Wrong Man*, Hitchcock believed he'd found the story to achieve that.

Shortly before filming, Herbie and his wife Mary Belle invited Herrmann and Lucy for dinner, at the Colemans' cliffside home in Newport Beach. After two years of collaboration, the couples had become good friends. "As usual, Benny kicked off his shoes the moment he walked into the living room," Herbie recalled. "After dinner we sat on the balcony and watched the sun sink into the Pacific over the west end of Catalina Island. I told Benny the *Wrong Man* story and asked if he'd compose the music for the film. 'For Warners?' Benny exploded. 'They'll never let me on the lot!'"[14]

Jack Warner's studio was infamous for working its staff at the cheapest possible rate. Meanwhile, Herrmann's price per film had just climbed, from $15,000 to $17,500 ($200,000 in modern dollars). As Coleman told his friend that he and Hitch would insist on Herrmann's salary, "Benny couldn't keep from laughing. 'I'd like to see Jack Warner's face when you tell him you've signed such a contract.'"[15]

Herbie kept his word. With Hitch's approval, he sent a contract for Herrmann's services, at his new rate, to Warner Bros.

The rest was silence.

In March 1956, crew members and camera gear arrived in Manhattan. Locations included the Stork Club (a near-continuous thirty-six hours of shooting, necessitated by the club's hours); the Roosevelt Avenue police station where Manny was booked; the courtroom at Queens Felony Court, where his trial was held; liquor stores where the robberies took place; and, most poignantly, the Greenmont Sanitarium in Ossining, where Rose had two years of treatment.

Hitchcock felt on surest ground shooting the lengthy sequence of Manny's arrest. It was played with minimal dialogue, from the accused man's stunned point of view, as he's fingerprinted, photographed, and placed alone in a cell. Its bars are locked with clanging force, a sound Hitchcock may have recalled from his own childhood nightmares.

Example 4.2 Hitch and Robert Burks capture Henry Fonda on a New York subway, 1956.

Through it all, cinematographer Robert Burks was quiet and intense, as he "agonized over the look," Doc Erickson recalled.[16] Days before shooting began, at the 28th Academy Awards, Burks won his only Oscar, for the Technicolor banquet that was *To Catch a Thief*. Burks accepted the award from New York, before returning to the task of how to film Henry Fonda reading a newspaper, as the actor sat in the confines of a real subway E train.

Burks embraced the challenge of using small, documentary-unit cameras for tight locations like the subway. But Hitchcock was losing heart in the project. Despite his expressive use of canted angles and shadows—a style that Fonda biographer Scott Eyman called "neorealist noir"[17]—Hitch worried that his footage belonged in a police procedural, not an Alfred Hitchcock movie. "He knew he'd made a mistake," Norman Lloyd recalled. "The actual shooting of it in New York was very difficult for him, and it got him down. It got him angry."[18]

Anderson and McPhail's script caught the rhythms and feel of a real, non-Hitchcockian world. Fonda disappeared into the role of Manny, and

Vera Miles was painfully believable depicting Rose's breakdown. But was it entertainment?

Meanwhile, one member of the team refused to set foot in what he considered the enemy camp of Warner Bros. Herrmann was incensed when he learned that the studio was only willing to pay him $15,000. Still, he was eager to begin what was now an annual ritual: scoring Hitch's latest movie.

With Hitchcock and Warner in opposite corners, Herbie took a deep breath and wrote a letter to Benny, who was then in Houston conducting. "Warners will only honor a commitment for $15,000. . . . I'm afraid it's a lost cause now. I have discussed this with Hitch, and Hitch doesn't feel that since this is a Warner Bros. Production, not a Hitchcock Production, he can do anything personally to help out. Now don't get upset from the above news and do anything drastic. Just lay the letter down for two or three days and then call me collect. It goes without saying that Hitch wants and expects you to carry on with this project, and we will do what we can on the next one."[19]

Benny would never allow anyone to take his place on a Hitchcock picture. At the same time, he was adamant over money. "Whenever I negotiate for a new project, I'm reminded of the time Stravinsky was asked by David Selznick to do a film. 'I'd love to do the score for $100,000,' said Stravinsky. 'We don't spend that kind of money on film music,' said Selznick, turning pale. "'Oh,' said Stravinsky, 'You don't understand.'" My music is cheap. It's my name that's expensive.'"[20]

Herrmann's possessions may have fit in a small home, but those items cost real money: first editions, English antiques, rare music manuscripts, an Alvis, and a Packard. "He enjoyed the use of money," brother Louis recalled. "My son-in-law was his economic advisor in his last years. He felt that Benny had the greatest control of his financial affairs of any person he ever met—and this is a man involved with people on the highest level of economic matters."[21]

Hitchcock sighed in frustration over the Herrmann dispute. But he also understood. "He hated weak people," assistant Peggy Robertson observed. "He admired people who stood up for themselves."[22]

Four days after his previous letter, Herbie wrote again. "Just talked to Hitch. We're fighting for your top figure. Don't contact Warners. Let us handle."[23]

Five days later, the studio blinked. "Dear Bernie: We have won the battle. Warners agreed Friday to 17,500."[24]

But it was a single win in a larger campaign. By the time *The Wrong Man* was in rough cut form in August 1956, Hitch couldn't wait to hear what Herrmann could do, with a drama whose commercial prospects he increasingly questioned.

The Wrong Man had strong resonance for Herrmann. Since childhood he had been fascinated by the theme of injustice. It was central to the work of his favorite author, Dickens, and to the novel he often quoted: Dostoevsky's *The Brothers Karamazov*, in which the volatile Dmitri Karamazov is convicted for a murder he didn't commit. Also, Herrmann's study of great composers, as well as his own experiences, left him convinced that the lives of artists were filled with injustices.

Watching the film must have triggered a flood of memories. The Stork Club, at 3 East 53rd Street, was just steps from his creative home of the 1930s and 1940s, CBS Radio, at 485 Madison Avenue. Manny picked up the subway home at 53rd Street and Fifth. Benny took a stop ten blocks west. There, from 1934 to 1939, he escorted home to Brooklyn the woman who became his first wife.

Years before the thriller *Sorry, Wrong Number* made her one of radio's most famous dramatists, Lucille Fletcher, age twenty-two, was earning $23.50 a week as a CBS music librarian. When Herrmann, twenty-three, began courting the attractive brunette, "it was like Minerva, the goddess of wisdom, had walked out of my forehead," she recalled. "I was so struck by the knowledge and the talent and the excitement of the man, I was really exhausted. For six years he rode me home. On the subway we would talk about writing and music, all the works we wanted to create. I didn't want to miss any of his conversation. He was brilliant. I had studied at Vassar. In many ways he was far ahead of much that I had learned—not only in music, but in English and history. The Benny I knew was a young man full of idealism. That was what was charming and mesmerizing about him."[25]

But Herrmann's charm ended at the door of Lucille's home. Her parents were middle-class Presbyterians, and Benny's instincts were right this time: Jews were not welcome. "My father and Benny met formally only once, and the evening was a disaster. After that, I saw Benny only outside our home. He had a formidable foe in Matthew Emerson Fletcher." Herrmann also was frustrated by the knowledge that Lucille had another suitor. Her years of resistance to his marriage proposals planted enduring seeds of resentment.

In 1939, Lucille finally acquiesced, and on October 2 the pair wed. Their union lasted a decade.

As Herrmann sat watching his New York haunts reappear in *The Wrong Man*, did he reflect on the parallels between himself and Manny Balestrero? Both were musicians. Both enjoyed successful careers at nearby spots in Manhattan. Both had married and had two children. And both would find their lives violently thrown off course by events beyond their control.

The Score

> *Benny: It's four in the morning, but I'm already up, walking the rooms of the house. . . . I'm not looking for a theme or a melody, that's all too rigid. . . . What I'm searching for is a musical mosaic . . . a small pattern of sound that I can repeat, refract, change. . . . Would I have found more contentment if I stopped this search? Stopped my music? Perhaps. But when the moment comes, when the creating happens—to give up that sensation, that force, is impossible. The sun is just creeping through the windows. And then I have it in front of me. An idea. The pen dashes at the paper. The dreaming begins.*
> —Andrew McCaldon, "Benny & Hitch" (BBC Radio 3)

The Wrong Man would mark a departure in Herrmann's approach to film. In the 1940s, as he concurrently wrote concert music and worked in Hollywood, his film scores featured enough melodic themes and development to turn that music into concert suites. *Citizen Kane* and *The Magnificent Ambersons* became the boisterous "Welles Raises Kane." The suite based on his Oscar winner, *All That Money Can Buy*, was programmed by Stokowski. *Hangover Square*'s "Concerto Macabre" was played on radio, and was a favorite work of a young Stephen Sondheim.[26]

With *The Wrong Man*, Herrmann took a technique he used intermittently in earlier scores—the hypnotic repetition of short, often two-bar patterns—and used it for nearly all of Hitchcock's new film. Subtlety was essential to reinforce the drama's methodical tone. To match it, Herrmann kept his score simple, even repetitious. But maintaining tension was still vital. To do so, he varied his repeated patterns in ways that became synonymous with his style. Orchestration. Rhythm. Dynamics. Accents.

He also used chord inversions—variations of the same chord—played in succession. For example, the ominous C minor chord of C, E-flat, and G sounds like a musical change when the same notes are played in a different order, as E-flat, G, and the higher C.

But try listening to the *Wrong Man* score by itself and your mind is bound to wander. Herrmann would agree. "Film music is a mosaic art," he once remarked. "The music itself must have a great simplicity so that the first time through, the ear and the mind grasp it. There's no point writing a film score that when you see it three times you'll understand it."[27] For Herrmann, dialogue and screen action were the soloists. Music existed to support them. When his score for *The Wrong Man* was blended with the spoken word, his music, almost subliminal, proved that 2 + 2 can sometimes equal 5.

"He's like some of the minimalists today, like Philip Glass," Elmer Bernstein said in 1984. "His music is there to be integrated into a film, not to be the star. It wasn't just a question of being lazy and saying, 'I'm going to repeat this figure twenty more times.' Obviously he was capable of development. People say 'that's very slight material.' And if you attribute that kind of criticism to Bernard Herrmann, then you want to re-evaluate how you feel about the first movement of Beethoven's Fifth Symphony."[28]

Herrmann unveils his approach in the movie's first seconds. Before the credits, we see a high angle shot of a small, silhouetted figure, his features hidden in darkness. His shadow stretches out, huge in front of him, like a sinister alter ego. Trumpets with cup mutes—a cold, brittle sound—play a falling two-note phrase. It's answered like an echo by descending notes for solo bass . . . Manny's instrument. Played pizzicato (plucked), the bass notes have the feel of footsteps. Of a figure creeping up behind you. In five seconds, director and composer encapsulate the story of Manny Balestrero and his criminal doppelganger.

The silhouetted figure onscreen is Hitchcock, who tells us: "This is a true story, [with] elements stranger than all the fiction that has gone into many of the thrillers that I've made before." Dip to black; fade up on the portico of the Stork Club entrance. Inside, beautiful people dine and dance, as Herrmann gives us the last thing we'd expect from him: a bright, catchy rhumba tune.

But as credits appear, listen closely. Conga drums and maracas keep a lively beat. But the major-key tune switches every eight bars to a subtly ominous phrase.

JOHN MORGAN: *The main title is wonderful. It's the only cue where he uses a big, samba-style percussion group, with two pianos and two harps.*[29]

WILLIAM STROMBERG: *And it's one of those great times where a composer creates source music [music heard by the characters] for the opening credits, but Herrmann adds these dark interjections.*

MORGAN: *Anyone could have written the tune and its arrangement, but in those moments you hear Herrmann. Something is not quite right.*

The Wrong Man is mostly a quiet film. Herrmann could have chosen to provide the emotional intensity the movie suppresses. Tunesmiths like Dimitri Tiomkin might have introduced a commercial melody during the Stork Club main titles; suitable for pop recording, the tune could resurface throughout the film, reinforcing the devotion between Manny and Rose.

Instead, Herrmann did something more illuminating. Nearly all of his score is soft, terse, and guarded. *Herrmann becomes Manny.* He becomes Manny's mind, careful and precise. He becomes Manny's heart, increasingly anxious as his world collapses.

Take the film's first piece of underscoring, "The Hallway," as Manny arrives home at 5 A.M. Only eight bars in length, the cue pairs the hushed whispers of one flute, one clarinet, and one bass clarinet against the lonely three-note rhythm of the solo bass. While the woodwinds rise and fall in smooth, close steps, the bass line is pizzicato. This "walking" bass again suggests footsteps, as Manny checks on his two sleeping sons. The pensive woodwinds, combined with solo bass, share with us the gentleness of Manny's character. This also conveys a poetic feel for a time between night and morning, as a man moves silently through a world still asleep.

MORGAN: *If you just heard the bass alone, it would be nothing. It's the flute and clarinets going with it that give it an uneasiness. It's setting us up for what's going to come.*

ALEX ROSS: *The radio work was so important, I think, in evolving this method of working with cells. It was this kind of needlepoint, threading these little corkscrewing intervals and having them appear and disappear. He developed this kind of Herrmann minimalism.*

When two officers stop Manny at his doorstep, Herrmann carefully ratchets up the "Hallway" cue. He uses the same notes but adds four French horns, with metal mutes, against the solo bass . . . the force of the law versus one man. The horn notes are sustained but quietly snarl. The tempo is *Largo* (slowly), as Herrmann uses music to alter our sense of time. "The ear deludes the eye as to what it is seeing," he later said. "It changes time values. What you think is long may be only four seconds, and what you thought was very short may be quite long."[30]

The officers, initially friendly, ask Manny to walk through one of the liquor stores for possible identification. As Balestrero is studied by employees robbed by the gunman, his anxiety can't help making him appear guilty. Herrmann again knows how little to do. Against a three-note string bass ostinato, two bass clarinets and four clarinets moan in their lowest register. The cue repeats when Manny is pressured to do his walk-through in another store. Repetition is key to the score's effect; rather than seem tedious, it reinforces the idea that terrible events will keep happening to Manny.

When Balestrero is arrested, Hitchcock delivers a personally revealing moment as the accused man is fingerprinted. Manny (close-up) looks down at his hand (close-up). The ink stains on each digit look like fingers dipped in blood. His face registers shock, mixed with shame. Musically the softness of woodwinds is gone: we hear the steely force of four trumpets—two played with cup mutes (a hollow sound) and two with metal mutes (a brighter sound). Their blend creates a new instrumental color of chilly stridency.

There is nothing documentary-like about Hitchcock's depiction of Manny's incarceration. We see what he sees in his small cell: a sink, the lock, the shadows of bars on the floor. Herrmann intensifies his sense of entrapment by repeating a two-note pattern incessantly. Music is as imprisoned as Manny is.

STROMBERG: *Notice how he has the trumpet players with mutes playing very loud. You'd think in a scene like this, the trumpets would be trying to play soft. But no, he has it marked Forte. It makes you nervous. And there's no direction to the music. It's almost annoying! But it puts you on edge.*

The sequence ends with a visual flourish that attempts to give viewers a "Hitchcock" moment. Alas, the shot is more showy than effective. The camera faces Manny as he sits in his cell and closes his eyes in despair. Then, the image starts spinning around him in circles, like an accelerating Ferris wheel, for thirty long seconds. Perhaps Hitch would have tamped down his pyrotechnics had he heard the music Herrmann wrote for the scene. He creates a vortex of his own, as his two-note patterns for solo bass and muted brass speed into a whirling blur of triplet rhythms, their chaos heightened by adding two harps and tuba.

MORGAN: *I think that this is a ridiculous cue!*
STROMBERG: *But it adds to the paranoia. The harps are doing glissandos in contrary motion [with one harpist rapidly sliding upward from the lowest notes, while the second harpist slides downward from the highest notes]. And the solo bass is playing very high—that's unique in this score.*

As Manny is transported to a witness line-up, a spitting, staccato rhythm for stopped French horns (i.e., players put their hand into the bell, creating a "buzz") is answered in kind by muted trumpets. Brisk and militaristic, it foreshadows Herrmann's music for the storm troopers in Truffaut's *Fahrenheit 451* (1966).

Paired with the spitting horns is an arresting new theme. A triplet pattern spirals gracefully down from the clarinets' highest range, like flakes of falling snow. Indeed it *becomes* the sound of snow, when Rose and Manny visit the

Example 4.3 *The Wrong Man* publicity still.

ice-blanketed grounds of Edelweiss Farm in search of an alibi. Crystalline harps play the dreamy, floating-down theme, as Herrmann takes note of the beauty of nature (until now, our world has been a harsh urban one). The "drifting" pattern, still for harp, then becomes a "passage of time" idea, as Manny and Rose visit a series of locations, failing each time to find an alibi.

For most of *The Wrong Man*'s runtime, Herrmann's score is like a piece of Manny, making us feel each humiliation he suffers. But two thirds into the drama, Herrmann shifts his point of view to the story's other victim: Rose. Manny and his wife are meeting with their lawyer, Frank D. O'Connor (Anthony Quayle). The dialogue scene is played without music. But gradually we realize that Rose is disengaged. Her eyes drift downward. Asked a question by O'Connor, she replies unemotionally, "Yes. I suppose so."

O'Connor stops to study her. Cut to Rose in profile, an angle that emphasizes the dipped, defeated angle of her head. A subway train's rumble helps Herrmann introduce the score's eeriest effect: a sustained high pitch, played *ppp* (very, very quiet) and *senza vibrato* (without vibration). The pitch is suggestive of the ringing-ear affliction of tinnitus. It steadily crescendos, joined by soft, bitonal notes that add queasy dissonance. Bitonality refers to notes played together but in different musical keys—a perfect metaphor for Rose's disintegrating mind. Two harps articulate, slowly and precisely, four bitonal notes: E, D, B-flat, E-flat. The feeling of a mind frozen by depression is reinforced by the image of Rose's gloved hand, clutching and unclutching her shoulder.

STROMBERG: *"The Glove" is so ahead of its time. Composers in the '60s and '70s picked up on this style, where a simple idea can be very dark, and the composer stays on it for a long time.*

MORGAN: *Believe it or not, he uses a Hammond organ for that first high note. Then flute and piccolo and clarinets join in on the same note periodically. The organ holds the note for a minute and 46 seconds, with harp adding punctuation.*

STROMBERG: *Then Manny's solo bass plays one pluck. "Bom." Then a long space. Then "Bom." You sense this piece more than you hear it.*

WILLIAM V. MALPEDE, COMPOSER: *I remember when my father watched the scene, he said, "What's going on with her?" That's what a great movie score can do.*

This bitonality explodes in the film's one burst of violence. Rose, at her breaking point, strikes Manny with a hairbrush. Blood drips on his forehead as the swing of her arm breaks a mirror, splitting Manny's reflection in two. Bitonal chords... dual images of Manny... Rose's psychic divide—Hitchcock and Herrmann's theme of doubles has reached its apotheosis.

Manny is ultimately proven innocent, not thanks to justice but by chance: the "right" man is arrested during an attempted robbery. Again Hitchcock breaks from documentary style, using a slow dissolve to merge the face of Balestrero, his lips moving in prayer, with the face of the actual criminal about to lose his freedom.

Stop for a moment to imagine the musical road that could be taken here. Many composers would have written a cue of exultant religiosity, seizing the chance for uplift in a film that is mostly bleak. But Herrmann does the opposite. He plays the "prayer" moment for suspense, with a tense ostinato similar to ones we'll hear in *Psycho*. The choice of a dark, repeated pattern, varied by shifts in muted color, helps mitigate the feeling that Hitchcock has gone soft.

The Wrong Man's finale may be the saddest in the director's canon. Manny has taken Rose to Greenmont Sanitarium. A chorale of woodwinds play a melancholy Adagio ("The Parting"), as Balestrero speaks gently to his wife. Her roaming eyes make contact with no one. Later, after Manny is declared innocent, he returns to Greenmont, and Hitchcock has his chance to reverse the story's darkness. A joyous reconciliation between husband and wife ... the Balestrero children celebrating their father's return ... nearly every director in Hollywood would have insisted on such a coda.

Instead, Hitchcock stayed painfully close to the truth. Manny joins Rose at the window of her room, her arm still clutching her shoulder, her eyes projecting suspicion and fear. Herrmann confirms the worst by reprising "The Parting." The same sighing phrase is played by solo oboe, belying Manny's words. "Rose, it's all over ... they caught the man who did it ... we can start our lives all over again." Dialogue continues, but there is no closure.

> *Rose, honey, I love you. This awful nightmare we've been through, it's all over now.*
> *That's fine. For you.*
> *...Don't you want to come with me?*
> *Doesn't matter. Doesn't matter where I am. Where anybody is.... You can go now.*

. . . Rose?

NURSE: *She's not listening now.*

Solo oboist Liliane Lhoest received a standing ovation from the orchestra after playing this piece, which required considerable breath control and expressiveness.

The farewell scene is strong enough to override a final card of text, whose positive message defies belief. "Two years later, Rose Balestrero walked out of the sanitarium—completely cured. Today she lives happily in Florida with Manny and the two boys . . . and what happened seems like a nightmare to them—but it did happen. . . ." It's true that Rose left Greenmont after two years; but she never fully recovered, and Manny spent years struggling to pay for her care. Herrmann's scoring of the onscreen text also lacks conviction: his soaring music is lifted from his 1952 score for *The Snows of Kilimanjaro*.

But Herrmann has a last surprise. From the first piece of underscoring, all trumpets and horns have been played with mutes. In the film's last seconds, those mutes are removed, and brass instruments resound with unrestrained clarity. Like Manny, they are free.

Of all the Hitchcock films he scored, none better displays Herrmann's belief in the "mosaic" role of film music. "There are times when the composer must be content with being very subservient to the screen. Without the music, it's quite a different story. The ear may not hear everything. But yet it's working there all the time."[31]

ATTICUS ROSS, COMPOSER: *I think in many ways, he probably educated an audience far more than he could have ever done conducting orchestras. The music that he was experimenting with, that kind of modular, cell-based collage, incredibly precise. . . . I'm not sure you can get more effective than he achieved. Also I feel it's universal in a sense. Anyone can understand it.*

On October 18, 19, and 22, Herrmann grudgingly set foot on Warner Bros.' recording stage, where he conducted the studio's first-rate ensemble. He was pleased with the result. Jack Warner was not. Soured by his battle with Herrmann, the studio head was also irked that Hitchcock failed to give him another *Strangers on a Train*. His contempt was shown in the scheduling of *The Wrong Man*'s preview. It unspooled after a showing of *The Mole Men*, a sci-fi cheapie aimed at the teenage drive-in crowd.[32]

Released in January 1957, *The Wrong Man* puzzled most critics with its seesawing visual style and lack of suspense. It barely recouped its $1.2 million budget. Today its champions are many, led by Martin Scorsese. "*The Wrong Man* has more to do with the camera movements in *Taxi Driver* than any other picture I can think of. It's such a heavy influence because of the sense of guilt and paranoia ... isolation and helplessness."[33]

By the time of its release, Hitchcock was deep into his next project and eager to move on. But Herrmann still smarted from Warner Bros.' cheapness. Months after the film left US movie screens, he sent Hitchcock a review from an overseas paper. It praised the "classical demonstration of the uses of extreme quietness in developing suspense. The gaunt soundtrack music is a series of plucked low notes from the musician's own double-bass, always in a rhythm to suggest footfalls of a ghost. This gives a weird feeling that ghastly intangibles are stalking the hero in a world of eerie bewilderment and horror."[34]

Benny couldn't resist reminding Hitch of the worth of his contribution.

Months after depositing his final payment, Herrmann received a new job offer. The historical site of Colonial Williamsburg, Virginia, was creating a thirty-seven-minute film for its visitors center. Directed by George Seaton (*Miracle on 34th Street*), the VistaVision, stereo presentation would dramatize Williamsburg's role in the American Revolution.

Music of the Georgian Era? Nothing was more to Herrmann's liking. The score he created for *Williamsburg: The Story of a Patriot* is among his sunniest, as it gracefully incorporates court songs and folk tunes of the period. Nearly seven decades later, the movie was still being shown eleven times daily, making it the longest-running theatrical film in US history.

Asked what his fee would be to compose, orchestrate, and conduct, Herrmann as always knew what he wanted. He informed his client that one of his eighteenth-century cabinets was missing a pane of glass. For his services, he requested a replacement piece.

The producers were quick to agree.

5

I Want You So to Love Me

Vertigo, Part 1

The wailing scream of the ambulance could be heard beyond Bellagio Road in the pre-dawn darkness at 4 A.M. In less than twenty minutes it reached Cedars of Lebanon Hospital.

The patient inside the ambulance, Alfred Hitchcock, was struggling to breathe.

Suffering from a diseased gallbladder and obstructing gallstones, the fifty-seven-year-old underwent surgery two days later, on March 11, 1957.[1] The operation was a success. But he emerged from it "terrified," daughter Pat recalled.[2] Its reminder of death—his crisis had been that serious—would haunt the director through more than a year of obstacles, as he battled to make his most personal film.

The seeds of *Vertigo* were planted long before in London. In 1920, Hitch was mesmerized by the latest play from J. M. Barrie (*Peter Pan*). The poetic fantasy *Mary Rose* centered on a girl who disappears while visiting a Scottish island. Three weeks later she is found; but she insists she was away for only minutes. Years later, Mary—now married, and a mother—returns to the island and vanishes again. She reappears decades later, a young beauty unchanged by time. After her death, she returns a final time years later as a lost, youthful spirit, briefly reuniting with the middle-aged man who is her son.

Barrie's otherworldly "meditation on death and loss"[3] embedded itself in Hitchcock. Mary Rose—a lovely, untouchable ghost—would be echoed in the fantasy women he created onscreen. Privately, Hitchcock agonized over his own looks. "I have all the feelings of everyone encased in an armor of fat," he told art director Robert Boyle.[4] But cinema gave him proximity to the world's most desirable women. And on projects like *Notorious* and *Rear Window*, he made love with his camera to the actresses he adored most, Ingrid Bergman and Grace Kelly. "I always thought of him as the prince locked in the frog," said costume designer Rita Riggs. "He truly loved beauty so much and set out to create it."[5]

From the 1940s onward he hoped to film *Mary Rose*. But its actionless plot, its delicate tone, and the discouragement of studio heads thwarted him.

Instead, he made *Vertigo*.

A 1954 French novel allowed the director to transmute *Mary Rose*'s ingredients of romance, death, and the supernatural into a true Hitchcock film. *D'entre les morts* (*From among the Dead*) was the work of Pierre Boileau and Thomas Narcejac. Their novel *Les diaboliques* had inspired one of the few European films to rival those of the Master of Suspense in popularity.

Hitch sparked to the book after reading a Paramount reader's summary. He retained its foundations while altering its setting and time period. Surprisingly, the novel is set in German-occupied France during World War II. Roger, a French lawyer, is asked by ex-schoolmate Gevigne, a successful shipbuilder, to follow his wife Madeleine. Roger is told that Madeleine, who goes in and out of trances, is obsessed with her great-grandmother, who died young and tragically. A suicide attempt—Madeleine jumps in the Seine—brings the two together. Roger falls in love with her, but vertigo prevents him from stopping her when she jumps to her death from a church tower.

After the war, Roger remains obsessed with Madeleine. One day he is stunned to see her, or her double, in a newsreel. He tracks down the lookalike, Renée Sourange, and forces her to admit the truth: Renée impersonated Madeleine for her lover, Gevigne. Gevigne murdered his wife and hurled her body from the church tower, knowing that Roger could not reach its height. After Renée's confession, Roger, a broken man, strangles her to death.

"Romantic obsession has always interested me," Hitchcock said. "Obsessions of all kinds are interesting. But for me, romantic obsession is the most interesting."[6]

It was a fascination Herrmann shared, and one they discussed during *Vertigo*. As usual, Benny was involved before the script was written. He intuited the story's appeal to his partner, and the voyeuristic link that Hitchcock shared with its protagonist. "He is essentially a puritan," Herrmann told an interviewer. "Yet it's the puritanical artist that achieves real sexual expression, because he conveys his ideas poetically through atmosphere."[7] (What other film composer could have articulated such a thought?)

Herrmann himself was no looker. And while not as overweight as Hitchcock, his once-trim form of the 1940s had expanded into middle-aged obesity. Cigarette butts fluttered down his shabbily treated suits. By 10:30

A.M., according to production designer Henry Bumstead, "his clothes looked like he'd just been shot out of a cannon."[8]

Nevertheless, Herrmann had charisma; and throughout his life he attracted discerning women. "I just recall the electricity of the man," said Alfred Newman's wife Martha. "He and Al weren't beauty prize winners, but their brains were so outstanding that they were extremely attractive. Women were very attracted to him. He was very much a man."[9]

"Bernie had a totally different personality with women," recalled Elmer Bernstein. Once, when the younger composer and his wife saw Herrmann approach them in a restaurant, "Eve really got scared. She had this vision that this maniac was going to come to the table and start shouting at us. Well, Bernie sat down. And he was so charming to Eve, he was a different person."[10] Barbara Ruick Williams, wife of composer John, adored Herrmann. In a town stuffed with self-important players, Barbara said of Benny, "he was a *real* movie star."[11]

He was also no stranger to romantic obsession. In fact, it had cost him a marriage.

Example 5.1 Benny with first wife Lucille Fletcher, Wendy (left), and Dorothy, 1946.

During the summer of 1947, as his conducting career incinerated on the podium of Lewisohn Stadium, Benny and his wife Lucille Fletcher played host to a family member. Twenty-six-year-old Lucy Anderson was pretty, wistful, and nine years younger than her cousin—Benny's wife. She was also emotionally lost after years of unhappiness. Fletcher suggested that she spend the summer with her and Benny.

"Soon, unbeknownst to me, they were having lunch together," Fletcher recalled.[12]

> She told him about her tragic life. She was a lonely child in a lonely brownstone. Her father was a brilliant surgeon who died when he was 41 of lung cancer. Her mother was very negligent, and by the time of his death he'd thrown the mother out, and the mother had dragged my cousin away somewhere. That tore at Benny's heart. It was like something out of Dickens.
>
> For her to meet someone as charismatic as Benny, as famous and brilliant as Benny.... In my primitive analysis it was like getting back Papa. That sense of loss and sadness that shattered her life drew these two people together—Benny who had felt failure, and she who had lost her father and her mother. I suppose in every man there's the desire to be a knight in armor. He didn't have to rescue me from anything; I was pretty solid. But she was like a waif blown in from the night. All his romantic self—and he was very romantic until the day he died—came to the fore. Benny lost all sense of reality.

> *To be opened Friday at Sunset.*
> *My dearest dearest beloved heart.... Have heart and courage. For before us lies the future—the future of rebirth and new life.... Remain tranquil and serene.... For the Lord is watching over you—you are very dear and precious to him.... He has given you my love. My love that now envelops and cradles you—and whispers to you—songs of sleep and tenderness. My love for you is eternal and all encompassing. I love you for the precious fragile and beautiful spirit that is your soul.*
> —Bernard Herrmann to Lucy Anderson[13]

"He was in a tormented, turbulent state of mind," Lucille Fletcher recalled. The life of doing a movie a year in Hollywood, and conducting all summer for CBS, was wearing him out.

The Lewisohn Stadium fiasco helped to break the camel's back.

What he wanted in a wife was not an artist, and certainly not a woman out of his control. He was always harping on the fact that we didn't have any powerful passion in our lives. And that was probably true for me. He was a young man who I don't think had had many love affairs. I don't think he'd ever had any great big sexual experience. He felt deprived. And I hadn't either when I married him; we were two naïve types just feeling our way. He was shy, sensitive. He'd read a lot, but he hadn't done very much.

Even if we weren't totally lovers as in D. H. Lawrence or Joyce—they were thrown at me—we did get along wonderfully. We were happy, we had lots of friends, we traveled about. We had a rapport and fondness for each other. Maybe we didn't have this soaring end of *Tristan und Isolde*. And he didn't seem to miss it, until all of a sudden this bug struck.

> *Come my child. . . . Allow my love to cover thee and sing to thee. Your limbs are relaxing . . . your body is soft and relaxing. . . . Sleep on in the forest of our love—sleep in peace—for the birds and creatures that live there love thee and protect thee. Sleep on beloved—for you have told the bears to keep away from me—and so they now lie at thy feet to guard thee and to tell thee of my peaceful slumber.*

Herrmann decided that Lucy Anderson would bring the peace of mind that increasingly eluded him, along with the constant attention he needed. "He was looking for a nurturing mother type," said friend Shirley Steiner. "But husbands and wives are poor substitutes for those 'beginning' people in our lives."[14]

When Fletcher discovered the affair, Herrmann moved out of their New York apartment, leaving his wife and two young daughters. He spent much of 1948 wandering the country alone, writing emotional letters to both Lucille and Lucy. He eventually decided on divorce.

During their separation, Fletcher was being courted by author Douglas Wallop. (His novel *The Year the Yankees Lost the Pennant* inspired the hit musical *Damn Yankees*.) Fletcher and Wallop married after Herrmann's divorce was complete. "And then," Lucille Fletcher recalled, "he seemed to regret getting it."

Lucy Anderson, accustomed to a life of stress, did her best to make her husband happy. "She was a perfectly nice girl," observed John Houseman.

"But he drove all his women mad. He was apparently sexually inexhaustible. He was sort of famous for that, rushing them off to bed three or four times a day. That I knew from first-hand reports; the second Lucy was a great complainer about that."[15] (Make of this what you will: Herrmann's library included an eleven-volume set of Casanova's memoirs.)

On the heels of personal turmoil came professional catastrophe. In 1951, CBS disbanded Herrmann's CBS Symphony. Benny recognized, bitterly, that his future lay in film work. Leaving New York after forty years, he and Lucy Anderson resettled in North Hollywood. And while screen offers were plentiful, financial need forced Benny to be less selective when choosing films.

With frustration came regret. Recalled Taffy, "He told my mother shortly after he married Lucy that it was like being married to one of his daughters. He meant that in terms of intelligence, she was immature."[16]

By the mid-1950s Herrmann was well prepared to write music for a man obsessed with finding love and carnal satisfaction from a woman of his imagination. *Vertigo*'s story of desire and female doubling may be why Herrmann asked Lucille Fletcher if she was interested in writing the script.[17] (He probably hadn't checked with Hitch first, but the director was open to meeting Benny's literary friends.)

Lucille wasn't interested. But it gave Herrmann an excuse to visit his ex-wife and her husband in their Maryland home. Rifling through their fridge while debating an author's prose style with Lucille, Benny seldom seemed more relaxed.

In Herrmann, Hitchcock knew he had the ideal composer to help him conceal plot implausibility with musical emotion. He was less fortunate in finding a screenwriter.

Ever since John Michael Hayes was cast out of paradise on *The Man Who Knew Too Much*, Hitch had searched for a writer with Hayes's wit, his incisive character touches, and his skill at incorporating the suspense sequences Hitch envisioned.

Creating a script was a multi-month process. Once a writer was hired, the daily work of "breaking" a story usually began after hours of unrelated chit-chat. Hitch delighted in recounting how he'd shot his most famous sequences. Like Benny, he needed company. He also loved playing the teacher. Inevitably, Hitchcock the storyteller took hold, and the day commenced in earnest with a ritual: reciting the script-in-progress from its opening scene.

But even Hayes would have struggled with the logic-defying plot of *From among the Dead*, which was the film's ungainly title until the end of production. (Here, it will be called *Vertigo* for clarity.)

The easiest task was re-setting the story in America. San Francisco would provide the dreamlike backdrop essential to a film that, for most of its runtime, is equal parts romance, mystery, and ghost tale. James Stewart would return for his fourth teaming with Hitch, playing ex-cop John "Scottie" Ferguson, sidelined from the force by vertigo. To play Madeleine and her impersonator Judy, Hitchcock chose twenty-six-year-old Vera Miles. Under contract to the director since 1955, Miles had shown her range portraying Rose Balestrero in *The Wrong Man* and a traumatized rape victim in "Revenge," the premiere episode of *Alfred Hitchcock Presents*. Miles conveyed intelligence that could mask fragility. But she was not a movie star, or a head-turning "Hitchcock blonde." Lew Wasserman advised the director to consider Kim Novak, a rising star at Columbia Pictures. Hitchcock resisted. For a year he had given Miles the attentive—some would say controlling—star buildup he'd bestowed on Grace Kelly. (Grace, to the director's deep regret, was now Princess of Monaco.)

Next came the hard part: finding a writer who could turn a schematic mystery plot into an emotional tragedy—one in which the hero's obsession is both relatable and ultimately repellent. Hitchcock hired Maxwell Anderson, who on *The Wrong Man* had captured an ordinary man's loss of control. But Anderson flattened *Vertigo*'s story into a dull police procedural. When Herbert Coleman asked his boss what to do with Anderson's script, Hitch replied, "Burn it."[18]

Filming had been slated to begin by this time, in fall 1956. But Jimmy Stewart's request for a family vacation bought Hitchcock much-needed time.

A second writer, MCA client Alec Coppel, fared better and put most of the story in place. In it, Scottie Ferguson is hired by shipbuilder/school friend Gavin Elster to shadow Elster's wife, Madeleine. Her obsession with a long-dead relative, Carlotta Valdez, culminates in her leaping into San Francisco Bay. Scottie rescues her and falls in love. But vertigo prevents him from following her to the bell tower at the Mission San Juan Bautista, where she seemingly falls to her death. Scottie is left in a catatonic state—until he sees Judy Barton, Madeleine's double with some differences: brown hair and a street-smart manner.

Scottie pursues her romantically, and convinces Judy to change her hair and clothes to match Madeleine's. Only then is he able to consummate his passion. But when Judy puts on Madeleine's necklace, Scottie deduces the murder plot. Now dangerously obsessed, he drags Judy to the Mission. His vertigo cured, he makes it to the bell tower and forces Judy to confess. A nun in the shadows startles Judy, and she falls to her death, leaving Scottie shattered.

Until the story's last minutes, Hitch instructed, the film "should be a strange mood love story with perhaps the same feeling of Daphne du Maurier's REBECCA . . . MARY ROSE had some of the elements of the first part of this story."[19]

But Hitchcock knew that Coppel's script fell short. Scottie was too gullible, and Judy's behavior too puzzling. Her love for Scottie needed to be emphasized, to justify her staying with him and risking her freedom. Most seriously, the story was unmoored from any recognizable reality.

But *Vertigo*'s shortcomings paled next to a health crisis for Hitchcock. In January 1957, during lunch with Herbie, "he suddenly dropped his fork and hugged his stomach."[20] Doctors at Cedars of Lebanon diagnosed hernia and colitis. Hitchcock underwent surgery, and was told to rest for several weeks.

Vertigo's filming had been rescheduled once. Now it was pushed out further—a blessing in disguise. The same month as Hitch's surgery, MCA talent agent Kay Brown found him the perfect writing partner.

A successful playwright and a longtime San Franciscan, Samuel Taylor was blunt in assessing Alec Coppel's work: the script was unshootable. "The whole story is so unreal and so fantasized," he told Hitch. The director replied, "That's what Jimmy Stewart said."[21] But Taylor had a suggestion. Create a character "who is completely in the real world"[22]—one who could represent the audience, and whose rationality put Scottie's obsession in context. Thus was born Midge (Barbara Bel Geddes), Scottie's ex-flame and friend, who also gave the script humor and pathos (she still loves Scottie).

Vertigo was finally coming to life—but on March 9, Hitchcock's body failed again. His emergency surgery on March 11 for diseased gallbladder and obstructing gallstones was life-threatening. It also led to another filming delay. "For one who has always boasted of never having been sick, I really hit the jackpot this time," Hitch wrote a friend. "Hernia, Jaundice, Gall Bladder removed—and two internal hemorrhages—all in 12 weeks."[23]

He stayed in hospital for a month. And during that time, more bad news arrived: Vera Miles was pregnant. A new leading lady would have to be found.

The director was incensed. For the rest of his life he blamed Miles for *Vertigo*'s delay, conveniently forgetting his own health crises and the Stewarts' unscheduled vacation. But Hitch may have been alone in his disappointment. Paramount and Lew Wasserman were thrilled to see the part(s) go to Kim Novak, who loved *Vertigo*'s script. The actress had been controlled by men ever since her arrival in Hollywood. When she read Judy Barton's plea to Scottie—"I want you so to love me...as I am for myself"—she felt the pain of recognition. "I related to the resentment of being made over," she said, "and to the need for approval and the desire to be loved."[24]

She would find neither love nor approval from her director. Novak's casting meant that shooting, now set for August 1957, was pushed back again: the actress and her boss, Columbia head Harry Cohn, were at war over a salary raise. In truth, Hitch and Samuel Taylor needed every minute of delay. The script wasn't locked until eighteen days before shooting began, on September 30.

By then, each line of dialogue and each visual composition were clear in Hitchcock's mind. Recalled Herrmann, who visited the shoot, "I'll never forget, he said to his cameraman, 'Burk, I want you to light this like a Vermeer.' And he sent him all the color photographs he could find of Vermeer's paintings, till the cameraman had the feeling of Vermeer's lighting."[25]

His direction of Novak was atypically specific, from facial expression—for Madeleine, he wanted none—to the tempo of her walk and voice. Samuel Taylor watched as Hitchcock "succeeded in making her feel like a helpless child, ignorant and untutored. And that's just what he wanted—to break down her resistance."[26] "It was almost as if Hitchcock was Elster," Novak said, "the man who was telling me to play a role . . . here's what I had to do and wear."[27] To Hitchcock, Novak was a flaw in the film that came from his soul. For the actress, shooting *Vertigo* was often an ordeal of demoralization.

Shooting in San Francisco for sixteen days without a break was intense. The large crew was constantly in motion, as Hitchcock directed as many as eighteen separate camera setups a day.

Filming continued at Paramount just hours after the team's return from San Francisco. Back in an environment he could fully control, Hitchcock's desire for perfection grew. So did his frustration, whenever actors flubbed takes, camera timings were missed, and scenes that played well on the page felt flat during shooting.

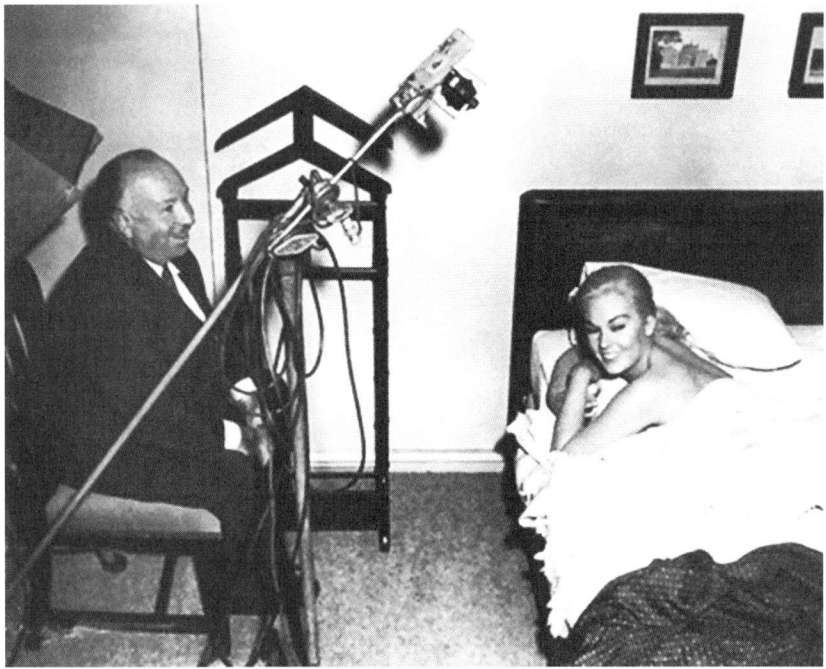

Example 5.2 Hitchcock's smile belies the challenge of filming *Vertigo* (1958).

Example 5.3 James Stewart and Kim Novak, *Vertigo* (1958).

The rhythm of filming slowed, and costs began to climb.

No shot mattered more to Hitchcock than the climactic kiss between Scottie and Judy, who has allowed herself to be physically transformed into Madeleine. Robert Burks's VistaVision camera moves 360 degrees around the lovers for a minute and sixteen seconds. But the actual movement was done by Stewart and Novak. The pair stood on a turntable; the room's changing background (Scottie imagines himself back at the mission, where he last saw Madeleine) was added with rear-screen projection. Lyrical and thrilling, the shot would be one of Hitchcock's most famous. But shooting it wasn't easy. During take two, Stewart slipped and fell, injuring himself. After five attempts, Hitchcock got the shot.

Hitch's editing notes were especially precise. "Trim a frame or two off the first vertigo shot—static too long" (1/24th or 1/12th of a second). "Trim two frames off the beginning of Madeleine sitting up in bed."[28]

Although involved from the start, Herrmann officially joined the payroll on January 6, 1958.[29] He would have ten weeks to write the score; ultimately he needed about seven. A composer of concert music might have required a year or longer. On February 3, 1958, Benny came to Hitch's office for an official discussion. They reviewed the film in Paramount's Theater 3, with Hitch sharing his thoughts about where music should start and stop.

The director had allotted long stretches of the film to play without dialogue—proof of his faith in what Herrmann would contribute. Hitch stressed the importance of a mood of fantasy. He had his staff track down a rare recording as a reference: the music for the 1920 stage production of *Mary Rose*. Hitch was open to Benny's suggestions of edit changes in the film, since Herrmann could always explain his reasons. It's likely that Hitch expressed his disappointment in Kim Novak. Above all, the pair agreed that music must put viewers inside Scottie's head. The key thing, Herrmann said, "was the drive of the emotions."[30]

The brevity of their talks reflected a deepening of their relationship, on a project that would prove a creative zenith. Their first three teamings established Herrmann's ability to express in music Hitch's traumas and pleasures. *Vertigo* went further, transcending commercial imperatives to become a kind of confessional, into which each man could pour his obsessions.

By now, Hitchcock not only "spotted" his movies with Herrmann (that is, discussed the score's placement). He also prepared a list of "Musical Suggestions," usually after meeting with Benny. These comments supplemented Hitch's "Sound Notes," in which he described what effects would be heard in a scene. But after one long passage of direction, Hitchcock writes, "All of this will naturally depend upon what music Mr. Herrmann puts over this sequence."

NICHOLAS MEYER, FILMMAKER: *There's no question in my mind that* Vertigo *wouldn't work at all without that music. If you went through the exercise of turning off the sound and watching it, I think it would be remarkably tedious. It's shots of people driving around in a car or watching somebody in a museum. All the emotional heft and emphasis of the story is supplied by the music.*[31]

The Score

Benny loved *Vertigo* but felt it was imperfect. Despite James Stewart's postwar history of playing damaged, sometimes dangerous men, Herrmann considered him miscast. Stewart was a silver-haired forty-nine-year-old; Novak was twenty-four. "I don't believe that he would be that wild about any woman," Herrmann said in 1975. "It should have been an actor like Charles Boyer."[32] Surprisingly, the composer also took issue with the San Francisco setting. "It should have been in New Orleans, or in a hot, sultry climate. When I wrote the picture, I thought of that."[33] The "New Orleans" comment merits context: at the time he said it, Herrmann was scoring *Obsession*, Brian De Palma's reworking of *Vertigo*. Set in New Orleans, it was Benny's penultimate film, and one that triggered floods of emotion from him as his body was failing.

Even if his criticism was influenced by *Obsession*, his comments reflect a seldom-discussed aspect of film composing. Privately, composers may be writing to the story or actor in their mind versus what is on the screen. If Herrmann's 1975 comments are to be trusted, *Vertigo* may be the greatest film score ever written with a slightly different movie in mind.

Its romantic intensity reflected a part of the composer that wives and friends knew well. "The sentimental side was incredible," said conductor Charles Gerhardt. "He cried in films."[34] Added musicologist Christopher Palmer, "He didn't like music that lacked warmth or passion. He'd say, 'It's got no *temperament!*'"[35]

Overpower my senses and release my soul on its ecstatic flight toward the stars, where the music of the spheres resound forever and ever. Where one

shall embrace his desired one and cleanse his soul, in the early fires of spring… to live amid the orchids of desire and kiss the pure white body of his beloved. To kiss her feet, her hips, until you become part of her.
—Herrmann, age nineteen, 1931 diary entry

Vertigo would be Herrmann's lengthiest score for Hitch, nearly eighty minutes. For a composer who placed music only where he felt it was essential, its quantity—75 percent of the film is scored—reflects his belief that score was essential, to create a mood of spectral mystery and emotional obsession.

His music achieves two almost opposite effects. It makes us feel the vortex in which Scottie is swept up, making his disorientation ours. But music also lies to us. In creating the ghostly atmosphere surrounding Madeleine, it is a co-conspirator in Gavin Elster's murder plot. The supernatural aspect of the music is so powerful that, even when we learn the truth about Gavin and Judy's deception, we leave *Vertigo* with the memory of having visited another world.

ALEX ROSS: *It is a realm of fantasy that he creates. It could be just showing us Scottie's interior world. He's slipping into this hypnotic state, fantasizing about this woman's background, this historical phantasmagoria that builds up around this figure. But it also feels somehow exterior to the character. It is emanating from another plane. Despite the deception, despite the scheme that's underway, you can't discount the reality of this other realm which Herrmann has created with the music. It has such a powerful effect on the consciousness. It has an independent reality, even if it's all part of the manipulation. It's this limbo, this amazing limbo.*

HITCH: *What are you doing?*
BENNY: *Circles. See—with my finger.*
HITCH: *On my wine glass.*
BENNY: *A sound.*
HITCH: *The wine glass I was using.*
BENNY: *A sound circling, searching for an end. . . . There are chords, called sevenths, that are always searching for completion, perfection, but stuck in suspense. Restless, circling, hanging in the air like a question. That suspension, that longing for reconciliation—that's where I find my music.*
—Andrew McCaldon, "Benny & Hitch" (BBC Radio 3)

Example 5.4 Herrmann's pencil score for *Vertigo*'s "Prelude." Courtesy of Norma Herrmann.

Herrmann's "Prelude" stands as one of cinema's most intense, arresting main titles. The visuals conceived while Herrmann composed are no less exceptional; Martin Scorsese called this sequence "a mini-film within a film."[36] For once, Paramount's VistaVision logo is not accompanied by Nathan Van Cleave's studio fanfare. Instead, a harshly accented triplet figure for flutes, clarinets, strings, and three vibraphones rises and falls with hypnotic persistence. After two measures, its airy flutters are joined by a hammering force: a two-note descending pattern for horns, brass, and contrabassoons. It ungrounds us. We are falling.

Then, strings, brass, and winds vanish. Only harp and celeste whisper the original triplet figure, joined by the distant pings of a triangle and vibraphone that echo like ripples in water. The film's first image appears: a close-up of a woman's face fills the left side of frame. The tightness of the image reveals only part of the woman's chin, nose, and lips. This will be a story of objectification.

JOHN WILSON, CONDUCTOR: *The opening credits encapsulate what the film is all about. And I think the music comes from a personal place in Herrmann—something nervous, neurotic. It's a key characteristic of his musical make-up, this nervy, repetitive undercurrent. It never sounds stale, it never sounds overused.*

Now the screen is filled with the mystery woman's lips. The first text flies into the screen—James Stewart's name—as muted brass shatters the harp and celeste's quiet with a dissonant, bitonal sting.

The camera continues its uncomfortably close exploration of the face—nose, eyes—as the names of Kim Novak and Alfred Hitchcock are matched by their own dissonant brass stings. Then, as the mystery woman's right eye fills the screen, the image's monochromatic gray dissolves into a startling, deeply saturated red. The eye opens wider, and from inside the pupil the word VERTIGO emerges. Another bitonal sting is made more violent with the addition of a sustained chord on Hammond organ, a color that will be linked with death.

WILLIAM STROMBERG: *The orchestration is masterful. The way Herrmann captures contrary motion [two parts of the music moving in opposite directions, i.e., one going up, one going down] using two harps, celeste, strings, and woodwinds. It gives you the feeling of descending, especially when he brings in the low brass playing chords that keep getting lower.*

JOHN MORGAN: *And although it's a pretty slow tempo, it has the feeling of moving ahead.*
STROMBERG: *Also, the chords are disconcerting. They're bitonal and they move back and forth, never staying the same. It's claustrophobic.*

The word VERTIGO floats upward out of frame. We too feel a sense of levitation, as flutes and violins play trilling notes that climb upward. During this, the pupil of the onscreen eye dissolves into a swirling geometric pattern moving toward us. It is the first in a series of avant-garde images designed by Saul Bass and John Whitney, and the first of four Bass collaborations with Hitchcock.*

As Bass and Whitney's shapes morph into mesmeric spirals of green, blue, and magenta, Herrmann juxtaposes his triplet-figure "whirlpool" against the score's most important four notes: the love theme. This motif will accompany *Vertigo*'s moments of ecstasy, and its shattering finale.

ALEX ROSS: *The basic harmonic fingerprint of language comes, I think, out of Debussy. This is a post-impressionist musical vocabulary. It's a modified extended tonality [i.e., not staying within the traditional do-re-mi of a "tonic" scale], which often lacks a stable root, but it has this mesmerizing self-sufficiency. He also has a totally distinctive way of working with orchestral color. There's a distinct touch in each of those areas. And when you combine them, this is some of the most unmistakably individual music that there is in the 20th century.*

Surprisingly, the "Prelude's" triplet-figure "whirlpool" ostinato will not return in the rest of the score, with one brief exception.

WILLIAM STROMBERG: *Herrmann brings the audience into* Vertigo *by writing a separate overture. It's captivating music, but he's not going to use the main ostinato later, except for one short scene.* The Snows of Kilimanjaro *[1952] is another example of this: you have a rambunctious, wonderful overture, and he never uses that material anywhere again in the film.*

---

* Hitch wanted something unique for his main title, and hired Bass early in December 1957. On February 25, 1958, Herrmann reviewed title boards of the sequence-in-progress, to ensure that music and image would create a single effect.

LAURENT BOUZEREAU, FILMMAKER: *The music is a repetitive motion that signifies yes, vertigo, but it also signifies this in-between state between life and death, the purgatory that Scottie will be in.*

2011. In "Born This Way," one of the year's most talked-about music videos, Lady Gaga appears as an alien queen, in an elaborate sci-fi prologue that precedes her song. For two minutes, thirty seconds, her narration about "the birth of evil" and dramatic camera swoops are timed to Herrmann's Vertigo *"Prelude," heard at full volume. "Hitchcock," writes* The Atlantic, *"is one of the singer's noted inspirations."*[37] *On its website, MTV reports that the Herrmann-scored sequence is viewers' favorite part of the 7.5-minute video.*[38]

As *Vertigo*'s first scene begins, Herrmann doubles down on the "Prelude's" idea of linking triplets with disorientation. A churning ostinato for strings and winds sustains the "Prelude's" tone of anxiety, as we see . . . a steel bar against an out-of-focus background. This abstract visual holds for a full five seconds; this will be no ordinary Hitchcock film. A man's hand bursts into frame and grabs the bar. It is a fugitive, chased by Scottie and a uniformed cop. A location shot orients us: we are on the rooftops of San Francisco at night. (The music's energy and menace help smooth the scene's blend of soundstage and location footage.) Ferocious waves of brass join Herrmann's swirling ostinato. A motif of panic, this music will return during Madeleine's run to the mission bell tower before her apparent suicide.

ALEX ROSS: *"The Rooftop" becomes a kind of postlude [a concluding piece of music] to the main title, very much extending its frenetic, supercharged state.*

During the chase, Scottie fails to make a jump between two buildings. He clings from a rooftop's rain gutter. And as his point of view becomes ours, *Vertigo* delivers its first iconic shot: the street far below seems to move closer and move away at the same time. Hitchcock achieved this visual "stretch" by having the camera simultaneously zoom in as it tracked backward. Herrmann scores the moment with bitonal chords of E-flat minor and D major. Played simultaneously, the notes would become a signature. Search "Herrmann Vertigo chord" online and you'll find over 270,000 references to it, in languages from English to Spanish, Russian to Korean.

ANNA BONN STROMBERG: *It's a great big polychord, with major-minor chords stacked on top of each other, and two harps going in opposite directions.*
JOHN MORGAN: *So the harps are doing what the zoom and dolly back is doing.*

Example 5.5 Visual innovation that finds a musical analogue: *Vertigo* (1958).

The cop lowers his arm to Scottie, but this would-be rescuer slips and plummets to his death. As Scottie looks down at the corpse below, a two-note pattern for brass and low strings snarls against a sustained chord in Hammond organ. In Herrmann's universe, electronic instruments augur danger. This powerful two-note motif will reappear after each death fall in the film.

Director and composer agreed that scenes based in "reality" would either be silent or offer musical contrast. In the scene after "The Rooftop," a radio in Midge's bright apartment softly plays Mozart . . . music of sublime rationality. Dialogue establishes that Scottie has retired from the force, that he and Midge were once engaged, and that Scottie's vertigo retains a paralyzing hold on him. When he tests himself by climbing a stepladder Midge sets by a window, Herrmann brings back chaos, triggered by Scottie's POV of the street far below. Hitch did not plan for music here—another example of his deference to Benny.

WILLIAM STROMBERG: *Those harsh trumpets are muted, and you hear this ringing Hammond organ chord. Again he uses bitonality, a G minor chord against A-flat minor. It's almost the same chord as when we see the knife in*

> *Louis Bernard's back in* The Man Who Knew Too Much—*two chords on top of each other.*
>
> MORGAN: *Herrmann is creating a Hitchcock-Herrmann language that will run throughout their films.*

"Reality" returns as Scottie meets with Gavin Elster, who hires his ex-schoolmate to follow Madeleine. During this, *Vertigo*'s most expositional scene, music has no place.

> ALEX ROSS: *Herrmann is not part of this contemporary world. He just lies in wait until this dialogue is finished. When he comes back, the re-entry is in a very different mode from the "Prelude." The movie has taken a turn toward his world. This really establishes Herrmann's voice as an independent, equal player in the drama.*

Scottie's first sight of Madeleine in Ernie's restaurant inspires a visual transformation. Colors are vivid as she walks closer to Scottie and to us. Her green dress and coiffed blond hair stand in bas-relief against the deep red walls of the dining room. Hitchcock's dubbing notes had suggested "a silence" as Scottie sees Madeleine, while adding, "I don't know what Mr. Herrmann has in mind musically here." When Hitch found out, he conceded to his composer. Score enters quietly as Madeleine appears, *Lento amoroso* (slowly, with love). The velvet color of muted strings and harp matches the lyrical, questioning phrase we hear—Madeleine's theme. Like the character, music invites us closer but will not fully reveal itself.

> WILLIAM STROMBERG: *This music is from Scottie's point of view. It's ambiguous, but the love theme that comes later will develop out of it.*

Herbert Coleman caught a glimpse of Herrmann at work, when Benny "took me to his music room to play what he called 'Madeleine's theme.' Two pianos, keyboards facing each other, with only enough room for a swivel chair between them, dominated the small room.... He sat down before one of them. His whole body seemed to change. His shoulders rounded, and his head bent forward toward the keyboard. His stubby fingers gently caressed the keys, and the soft sound of a haunting melody filled the room."[39]

With the introduction of Madeleine, something new happens in the Hitchcock-Herrmann canon. Thirteen minutes—more than a reel of film—elapse from the end of Scottie's talk with Elster until the next full dialogue scene. Scottie's following of Madeleine, the start of his obsession, is paced with a deliberation that would seem aimless without music. Hitch is working with Herrmann in mind, as Benny would proudly recall. "Hitchcock would call me and say, 'Do you feel you'll need music in this scene? Because if you do, I will shoot it differently, giving you more elbow room.'"[40]

The score stays rooted in Scottie's perspective, as he follows Madeleine in his car to a string of puzzling sites. The "driving" music begins with a soft ostinato of five mysterious rising-falling notes. It's the aural version of Scottie's thoughts: Where is she headed? What is going on?

ALEX ROSS: *In the driving sequence Herrmann casts a spell. He takes the images and transfigures them, transports them into a sort of different world, and almost literally puts a different kind of light on them. It changes the quality of the image in a powerful way.*

MORGAN: *The music is simple, but it makes us want to know more.*

For Madeleine's visit to the flower shop, Hitchcock initially outlined a soundtrack of "the pleasant sounds of the interior." Instead he chose Herrmann's approach: a delicate, ethereally high statement of Madeleine's theme as Scottie studies her from behind a door. Her theme then assumes a graveyard whisper as Madeleine visits Carlotta's grave.

WILLIAM STROMBERG: *What's notable is the register [the "height" or placement of a note]. You have violins in mutes, pianissimo, way up at the top of their range playing the Madeleine theme. Underneath, you have held notes for bass clarinets, way down at the bottom of the register. There's no rhythm, but that combination of high and low instruments is hypnotic.*

With Madeleine's trip to the art museum, film and score transition into a world of the supernatural. As she stares at the nineteenth-century portrait of Carlotta, a solo harp introduces the rhythm of a habanera, a slow Latin dance form.[41] Over the rhythm, two flutes purr a seductive new melody that climbs and falls, mostly in half-steps. It is Carlotta's theme, played *senza vibrato* (without vibrato, creating a cool sound). It will be linked with the idea that Madeleine is possessed by her ancestor.

NORMA HERRMANN: *Benny wasn't religious at all, but he really liked the supernatural. And because there was something supernatural about* Vertigo, *that moved him.*

ALEX ROSS: *Herrmann uses these familiar dance rhythms, like the habanera. What is that exactly? It could almost be a cha cha! But this is not dance music. It's so brilliant what Herrmann does in playing* off *of dance elements. You recognize them, but they're at a distance. They're cool, they're detached, they become pure ostinato. Real dance music is not purely ostinato. This is calmly relentless.*

WILLIAM V. MALPEDE, COMPOSER: *When strings take up the Carlotta theme, Herrmann has them play "sur la touche"—at the fingerboard. It creates a ghostly sound when the bow of the instrument plays at the fingerboard [where a player's fingers move to create different notes]. And the clarinets run air through the instrument, but it's almost not heard. It's just a breathy, ghostly sound.*

The ingenuity of Herrmann's scoring—simple but memorable themes, shifting of orchestral color—allows Hitchcock to delay the first meeting of Scottie and Madeleine until forty-four minutes into the film. After that encounter, music assumes another purpose, as Hitchcock makes one of the boldest choices of his career: Scottie transforms from audience surrogate into antagonist . . . a man whose obsession will prove self-destructive and deadly.

6

We'll Just Have the Camera and You

Vertigo, Part 2

Death came close to Alfred Hitchcock in the year before *Vertigo*'s filming. The threat of it inspires the next major plot point in our journey through the score.

After half an hour of hushed conversations and wordless cat-and-mouse, a riot of cascading horns and high woodwinds accompanies Madeleine's leap into San Francisco Bay, and her rescue by Scottie. Herrmann gives us the sound of panic—Scottie's terror of losing her.

> WILLIAM STROMBERG: *Herrmann could all of a sudden slap you in the face with a big cue like this, because it's important. He wanted to startle the audience along with Scottie. Horns are playing very fast, piccolos are descending.... It's like the contrary motion of musical lines in the "Prelude." It's one of the biggest musical "hits" in the whole score, which is mostly dreamlike.*[1]

The Production Code Administration, Hollywood's censorship division, had loosened its fangs slightly since the retirement of arch-conservative Joseph Breen in 1954. But Hitchcock still had to tread carefully when filming the scene of Madeleine awaking nude in the bed of Scottie's apartment. The sight of Scottie removing her clothes could not be filmed, but we imagine it thanks to a shot of her hanging garments. Herrmann also knew the power of restraint. He evokes mystery, not lust, as a soft, crying two-note pattern for high violins passes downward through the strings, until they whisper under Scottie and Madeleine's first conversation. Herrmann is telling us the truth—Scottie is falling in love—while also lying to us with his music's seductiveness: the "possessed" Madeleine is really Judy Barton, luring Scottie into a murder plot.

Example 6.1 James Stewart, Kim Novak, and Fort Point, San Francisco, in *Vertigo* (1958).

JOHN WILSON: *If you're asking what a film composer can do for a scene—well, a composer can sustain an illusion for half an hour, forty minutes, or more as Herrmann does here.*

    This music serves another purpose. Hitchcock shot more takes than usual of this scene. He may have feared audience laughter at Madeleine's trance-like state, or the hesitant dialogue between an apparently suicidal woman and the stranger who undressed her. Originally he directed Herrmann not to score the scene.[2] Later, he realized the value of adding the quietly restless dialogue for strings, and hints of Madeleine's theme, which imbue the scene with romantic tension.

    Perhaps for contrast, Hitch envisioned a passage of levity, as Scottie follows Madeleine the next day in his car from her apartment—to the door of his own address. Music for the scene, Hitch wrote, should "by degrees get more comic—developing when Scottie starts to throw up his hands" in bafflement at where she's going. But Herrmann ignored the directive. There isn't a sixteenth-note of humor in *Vertigo*'s score. Instead, it stays within the mind of Scottie.

No scene in the film evokes the spirit of *Mary Rose*—its spectral island where people vanish, and human time stops—than Scottie and Madeleine's walk through Big Basin Redwoods State Park. For Madeleine, the sight of a 2,000-year-old tree conjures thoughts of "all the people who have been born and died while the trees went on living. I don't like them ... knowing I have to die." She is speaking the thought that frightened Hitchcock most.

Capturing the scene was stressful. Hitch worried about Novak's performance, and Robert Burks felt the pressure of matching the park location's dimming sunlight with close-ups to be shot at Paramount. Again, Herrmann was the unifying force, providing music as eerily beautiful as any he would write. Three muted trombones set the sepulchral mood. They play bitonal chords in parallel motion—that is, each musician plays a different note in a chord, then moves up or down the same interval from each other, like spirits floating up and down on the same plane.

Another wisp of darkness emanates from low string harmonics. Harmonics are a frequent tool for Herrmann, and not as intimidating as the name suggests. Simply put: when a musician plays a single note (like a key on a piano), sound waves create near-subliminal pitches above the note being played. What better choice for *Vertigo* than an effect that creates ghost sounds?

WILLIAM STROMBERG: *The harmonics in this cue, "The Forest," are low—they're on violas, cellos, and basses—which creates a haunting quality. When you touch the ends of the strings on an instrument, to create a harmonic effect, it makes an airy sound ... a kind of "whoosh" that goes along with the main note. That's what he's doing here. Herrmann also has a Hammond organ pedal chord going through the whole scene. And bass clarinets make a subtone sound—the clarinetist blows air softly to create a kind of airy whistle. Another ghost sound.*

The combined effect captures Hitchcock's description of the scene: "I want Madeleine to feel the world is closing in on her. The density of the trees is a wall around her. There's no escape. Only suicide is left."[3]

With the next cue, "The Beach," Herrmann shifts into a forceful intensity that will continue to the end of the film. After a quote from Carlotta's habanera theme—a summons from the dead—the love theme, heard only fleetingly before, unfolds in a full orchestra statement. And as Scottie and Madeleine share their first kiss by water (with crashing waves behind them—Hitch dares to use a cliché to evoke sexual desire), Herrmann ends the cue with a rare chord of musical resolution. Scottie believes he has won Madeleine.

Another musical tour de force comes with "Farewell/The Tower." During the sequence's seven-minute length, Herrmann carries us from Scottie's excitement at solving Madeleine's mystery, as they arrive at the Mission San Luis Bautista, to Scottie's desolation over Madeleine's suicide leap from the top of its bell tower. The music begins with a phrase that is strangely familiar. Herrmann is reimagining the best-known theme in Wagner's 1859 opera *Tristan und Isolde*—the "Liebestod," or "love death." One source defines "Liebestod" as a "theme of erotic death or 'love death,' meaning the two lovers' consummation of their love in death or after death."[4] Herrmann is linking *Vertigo*'s story, of a man in love with a dead woman, to a mythic opera in which, as a critic wrote, "love is both the ultimate end and a destructive force."[5]

Inside a barn at the mission, Madeleine recalls supposed visions sent to her by Carlotta ("We were forbidden to play here...") as flutes play Carlotta's quietly insistent habanera. Scottie and Madeleine kiss, and as Scottie first speaks the words "I love you," Herrmann boldly restates the love theme—his reworking of Wagner's "Liebestod."

The theme becomes delirious, spiraling upward in strings that anticipate what happens next: Madeleine's race upstairs to the tower, and Scottie's failed attempt to follow due to his vertigo. As George Tomasini's edits accelerate during the chase, Herrmann readies us for tragedy, reprising "The Rooftop"—the churning terror music from *Vertigo*'s opening, which ended in a policeman's death. As Scottie watches Madeleine's body plummet to the ground, Herrmann combines not two but three minor chords, to create the ultimate dissonant scream.

An inquest scene gives us respite from score, before another virtuosic display of terror in music: "The Nightmare." Hitch's visuals are deliberately arty—part animation, part live action, as Scottie dreams of a living Carlotta, her eyes blazing defiantly. Scottie's head, minus body, floats down a corridor of flashing colored light. He falls into Carlotta's open grave. From its blackness we shift to the animated silhouette of a figure floating listlessly down from the mission tower. (This image would be central to *Vertigo*'s advertising art.) Herrmann unifies this surrealist mélange with a grotesque statement of Carlotta's habanera: it is now a pounding declaration of death's triumph. Finally, Scottie leaps up in bed, waking in a pool of sweat. The sledgehammer chord accompanying him includes the notes of the famous "whirlpool" chords from the main titles. No matter where the story goes, Herrmann provides unification.

As Midge tries to comfort a catatonic Scottie, now in a sanitarium, an album of Mozart—refined, orderly—creates the sharpest of contrasts from Herrmann's maelstrom. Midge recognizes the futility of the therapy. As she slowly walks away from camera down a long corridor, mournful low strings signal a farewell. This is the last time we will see her, and with her goes the last champion of rationality. When Scottie goes home he will be a different man.

His chance sighting of Judy Barton launches *Vertigo*'s last act, thirty-four minutes of highwire filmmaking. Hitchcock slowly turns us against Scottie, shifting our identification to Judy as she is forced to become the fantasy woman she impersonated. Herrmann quietly foreshadows disaster to come: as Scottie spots Judy, muted strings play the Scottie-Madeleine love theme. Far from euphoric, it is *Lento e mesto*—sad and pensive.

During *Vertigo*'s writing, Samuel Taylor made a crucial realization. "This is not pure Hitchcock," he told the director, "unless the audience knows what has happened"[6]—that Judy and "Madeleine" are the same woman. Hitchcock agreed. The resulting scene unmoors us again with a surprise revelation. After Judy agrees to a date with Scottie, the camera holds on Judy's face, alone in her apartment, and dissolves into a flashback: Elster hurling the real Madeleine's body from the tower, then shoving his hand over Judy's mouth as she realizes the horror she is part of. The flashback fades, and Judy writes a letter to Scottie confessing all (a letter she then destroys). The music that accompanies it marks the beginning of our shift in sympathies. As we hear Judy's letter in voice-over, low strings plays a sustained chord, over which Herrmann adds chilly, high muted strings *divisi* (divided, playing different notes in a chord).

Again there are harmonics—ghost tones accompanying the notes we hear. As Judy details the murder plot ("He planned it so well, he made no mistakes"), high *divisi* strings slowly climb upward in a simple major-key scale—the musical version of a plan done well, a pattern with no "mistakes" (i.e., surprising notes). But as Judy's words shift to her emotions—"*I* made the mistake, I fell in love.... I'm still in love with you"—violins shift into an exquisite diminished chord that begs for release . . . something Judy will never have.

ALEX ROSS: *There are these momentary glimpses of a stable, tonal world. In "The Letter," there's this rising scale. It's like [happy sigh] Ahhh! Then everything seeps away, which is something Debussy does as well. There are moments in* Pelléas et Mélisande *where you get this fleeting glimpse of tonal harmony, which is not available to people in this world. The withdrawal of it can have a shattering effect.*

WILLIAM V. MALPEDE: *With "The Letter," now it's Judy who is sympathetic. We feel her pain and suffering in these* divisi *chords, so simple, so beautiful.*

Ironically, a scene without scoring—Scottie's description of Judy's new wardrobe, a copy of Madeleine's, as Judy listens, powerless—had an echo in Herrmann's life. "Benny and Lucy made frequent shopping trips to Bullock's on Wilshire, where you can drop a fortune on the simplest of clothing," recalled actress Marsha Hunt. "I might not notice the new clothes because they were so understated. Indeed, it looked so right on Lucy that you didn't comment. I learned to pay attention to what Lucy was wearing, because if a comment was not made, Benny wouldn't be able to stand it. Eventually I got my eyes peeled for something I hadn't seen before and say, 'Isn't that new?' and Benny would just beam."[7]

Like Scottie, Herrmann's behavior toward Lucy had a dark side. Recalled a friend, "He was against sleeping pills, aspirins, anything. When Lucy would be in pain and I would offer some aspirin, Benny would say 'NO! She doesn't take those!' " Said another: "He hated it when she went out and had coffee with girlfriends. He said that all those drunken Los Angeles women poisoned her mind." The real reason for Herrmann's control was different: "Benny never wanted to be left alone. Ever."[8]

Scottie's obsession culminates in the most passionate love scene of Hitchcock and Herrmann's career. Agreeing to become a dead woman—"I indulged in a form of necrophilia," Hitchcock told François Truffaut[9]—Judy changes her hair from brown to blond. The montage of Judy at a beauty parlor was to be unscored. Days before recording, the director changed his mind. Herrmann quickly penned ten bars, reprising the main title's "whirlpool" motif. It is arranged here for two harps—an alluring color Herrmann used to evoke beauty within an uncomfortable setting. (*The Twilight Zone* and *Fahrenheit 451* are two examples.)

WILLIAM STROMBERG: *There's a note in the score here: "In a hard, brittle manner." It's Marcato [forcefully] and fortissimo. It's not supposed to be pretty.*

MALPEDE: *And as we hear the music from the "Prelude," the close-ups of Judy in the beauty parlor remind us of the tight images in the main title of the woman's face.*

For nearly two hours, Hitchcock and Herrmann have slowly constructed a dreamworld. It builds to the sequence at the heart of *Vertigo*, what Herrmann titled "Scene d'amour" and described as "a long crescendo of emotional fulfillment."[10] Herrmann never forgot the trust Hitchcock placed in him. "[Hitch said,] if we're going to have music, we won't have one word of dialogue. We'll just have the camera and you."[11]

As Scottie sits anxiously in Judy's hotel room, waiting for her to appear as Madeleine, Herrmann uses another favorite tool for suspense: suspended chords. This means that a note or chord is held, unchanging, as other notes shift around it, changing the harmony. The result: uncertainty.

ANNA BONN STROMBERG: *Herrmann puts crescendo-diminuendo marks [loud-soft] on every bar. It's like breathing, pulsing. And these shimmering, tremolando [trembling] strings are like Scottie, shaking. Then, five bars before the big moment, Herrmann has them play* sul ponticello *[the musician's bow plays near the string instrument's bridge, creating ghostly harmonics], and the effect becomes eerier. Then, when she appears, he releases it.*

The ecstatic statement of *Vertigo*'s love theme, as Judy/Madeleine steps out of a ghostly green light toward Scottie, unspools into Herrmann's most celebrated expression of passion. The composer called it "eight minutes of cinema without dialogue or sound effects—just music and picture. Whatever music can do in a film is something mystical. The camera can only do so much. The actors can only do so much. The director can only do so much. But the music can tell you what people are thinking and feeling."[12]

JOHN WILSON: *The chord that begins the love theme comes directly from* Tristan and Isolde, *and it reflects the great Wagnerian influence on Herrmann. Let's not underestimate the opening-up of harmony that Wagner gave us. The fact that it could roll on endlessly and never find a resolution was central to Herrmann's harmonic language writing for the movies.*

WILLIAM STROMBERG: *I think people make too much about the Wagner connection, because Herrmann took one chord from the "Liebestod." It's a chord that is poignant and very inspirational. But Herrmann took it and ran with it, basically finishing the melody where Wagner meanders around it. Where Herrmann took the chord is even more poignant, especially when it goes into a quasi-waltz as the camera goes around Scottie and Madeleine 360 degrees.*

ALEX ROSS: *Vertigo is so emotionally rich, especially when Herrmann opens up the Wagnerian dimension. And it's unusual that he makes this choice, because he's not a pastiche composer. The "Scene d'amour" is not a pastiche of Wagner. It's Herrmann all the way through. But the Wagner elements are very recognizable. I feel that the audience is supposed to recognize these Wagnerian devices—that's part of how the movie works. The way that it plays on Scottie's romantic delusions and romantic obsessions. The music is doing the same thing to the consciousness of the audience.*

But harmonically, because he turns toward this Wagner template, the harmonic logic changes, and you hear things that you don't otherwise hear in Herrmann. Like that hyper-romantic fake-out cadence [i.e., the musical buildup] right before we see transformed Madeleine. We're going up by chromatic steps to the tonic [a musical resolution] and at the top Herrmann immediately inserts his own motif [the love theme] and the Wagner atmosphere disappears. There's a playfulness in terms of having manipulated Wagner. It's a fantastic moment. We're about to fall head-first into the Wagner pool, but we veer away at the last moment.

2011. *Director Michel Hazanavicius is unhappy with the music that accompanies the climax of his feature film* The Artist. *He replaces Ludovic Bource's original score with Herrmann's "Scene d'amour."* The Artist *wins the Academy Award for Best Picture; but Kim Novak takes out a full-page ad in* Variety *decrying the use of Herrmann, stating, "I feel as if my body—or at least my body of work—has been violated."*[13]

2023. *With an audience of 15,000 behind him, John Williams raises his baton under the circular shell of the Hollywood Bowl. Violins from the Los Angeles Philharmonic play the soft first notes of "Scene d'amour"—a piece that is a favorite of the orchestra's principal conductor, Gustavo Dudamel. By the 2020s, the piece has entered the repertoire of symphony orchestras around the world.*

The resolution of *Vertigo*'s story unfolds swiftly. After Scottie and Judy's sexual consummation, implied by the music's ecstasy, only ten minutes of film remain. Scottie sees Judy put on Madeleine's necklace, unlocking for him the truth we already know. Stabbing French horns play Carlotta's theme: it's the sound of Scottie's mind connecting the pieces. He drives Judy to the mission. There as he grips her, the love theme returns darkly, Herrmann accenting each downbeat of its waltz rhythm with hammer force. Love is veering into madness.

WILLIAM STROMBERG: *Strings are* tremolando *[trembling] and* ponticello *[strings played close to the bridge to create harmonics]. They're steely and scary. There's a timpani roll, subtle. He creates an intense feeling of dread, as Scottie drags Judy up the staircase to the tower and the orchestra plays the love theme in a big, minor-key unison. The music is sadistic—we're in Scottie's head.*

During their final dialogue in the tower (Judy: "I walked into danger, let you change me, because I loved you"), Herrmann offers a poignant restatement of the love theme. But one last ghost interrupts the pair: a figure in the shadows, made more chilling by Herrmann's chord for Hammond organ.

It is a nun. Off-camera, Judy screams. We do not see her fall, but thunderous low notes for brass, strings, and timpani—the music heard during each fall in the story—confirm the second death of Scottie's love. He stands on the ledge, his vertigo cured, his soul destroyed. A *fortissimo* statement of the love theme ends this monumental score with a surprise: the most common of chords, C major, played in unison. A C major chord offers the fullest resolution possible, but nothing is resolved at the end of *Vertigo*. Herrmann is only telling us that the story ends here. We are left standing on an abyss.

ALEX ROSS: *Was* Vertigo *the peak of his career? It's one of the greatest film scores ever written. But Herrmann can't be reduced to a single piece.* Citizen Kane *is a very different kind of score, but a staggeringly brilliant one, especially for his debut as a film composer. And the romanticism, the wistful atmosphere of* The Ghost and Mrs. Muir, *and later in* Obsession. *So this is an output that has a lot of peaks.*

But if I did have to pick one, it would be Vertigo. *I can listen to it as a purely musical experience and not necessarily be thinking of the film. Of course, you can't not think of the film. But these musical episodes have an internal logic and internal interest, and it's sustained all the way through. Wherever you dive in, it's rich, it's layered. And I think it was very much an opportunity that Hitchcock created for him. He made the film differently, knowing that Herrmann would be writing the music.*

As Herrmann composed his richest score of the 1950s, Hollywood was falling into its own state of chaos. For three decades, the major studios had maintained in-house orchestras, until television's arrival slowed their slate of product. When feature production dipped in the 1950s, producers fought demands to raise musicians' salaries. In February 1958, James Caesar Petrillo, the bull-headed leader of the American Federation of Musicians, declared a strike.

By late February, Herrmann had almost finished the score that he knew was among his best. Sixty-five musicians would perform it under his baton at Paramount, as long as the AFM strike was resolved.

It wasn't.

Example 6.2 A famous Herrmann portrait, c. 1958, here unretouched.

"Faced with the possibility of a very long delay," Herbert Coleman recalled, "I decided to score the picture overseas."[14] Paramount's UK branch assured Hitch and Herbie that London musicians could record the score. But Herrmann was a member of the AFM, which forbade its members from conducting during the strike. "I was happy I wasn't around when Benny got the news," Coleman said. "It was enough when he walked into my office and vented his feelings against . . . England, America, the rest of the world, and most of all, the LIBERALS, meaning me."[15]

Herrmann knew that the score's effectiveness wasn't just in the notes. It was in the careful observation of dynamics (quick changes from loud to soft), the articulation of instruments (like the "ghost" harmonics in the strings), and countless other details that only he fully understood. But Paramount's deadlines left him little time to sulk. The studio hoped to complete *Vertigo* by March 21, for a US release in May. By late February, pressure was on to complete the costly film, as its budget crept toward $2.5 million.

Hitchcock knew that Herrmann's music was essential to *Vertigo*'s success, and he sided with Benny in demanding the best musicians possible. By March 5, Coleman had hired Scottish-born Muir Mathieson, widely considered the best conductor of film music outside Hollywood. Two days later, Herrmann and Mathieson spoke on a transatlantic call, in what must have been for Benny a state of immense frustration.

That same week, Coleman and music editor Leon Birnbaum arrived at London, greeted by sheets of snow and rain. Bad weather portended trouble to come: the scoring session was delayed until Mathieson, the recording studio, and the musicians Herrmann wanted were all available. Nine days passed, each one an extra expense. Hitchcock decided that his presence could accelerate the pace. He flew to London and arrived the night before the first session.

The next day, Hitch and Herbie felt a wave of relief: the score was magnificent. Its most important cues were recorded first, and in stereo, unlike previous Herrmann-Hitchcock scores. At day's end "everyone was on a high," Coleman recalled.[16]

It didn't last long.

During Day 2, after the recording of thirty-eight minutes of music, "a stranger walked in and called Muir aside," Herbie said. The stranger was "the head of the Musicians Union in England. He told us his organization had held an emergency meeting the previous night and had agreed to support the strike. The musicians didn't agree when they heard the news, but had to pack up their instruments and leave the stage."[17]

Hitchcock and Coleman had no choice but to find an orchestra outside Britain. Rome? Paris? Stockholm? Brussels? Despite Herbie's best efforts, all he heard was no. "I'm going home," Hitch finally announced.[18]

Eventually Coleman got a break. Paramount's office in Vienna assured him that studio musicians in their city were at his disposal.

A stormy flight to Austria's capital added to Coleman's stomach pains. But on arrival, the producer found a "wonderful orchestra"[19] that responded strongly to the score. Mathieson assured Herbie that Herrmann would be pleased. Knowing Benny, Coleman was less sure.[20]

On March 17, three weeks after Coleman left Paramount for what was meant to be a four-day trip, the recording of *Vertigo* was finally complete. Herbie came home to find Herrmann "bitter. . . . He grumbled about the quality of the recordings but had to accept what he heard."[21] Indeed, there were errors in the playing—"Mathieson missed notes all over the place," Benny growled.[22]

WILLIAM STROMBERG: *There's a moment in the "Prelude" where one of the two vibraphone players comes in a bar early. And Saul Bass used it for the start of the animation, when the film's title card comes out of the eye toward you. Bass made it worse because he pointed out the mistake. And there's a really sour note in the horns on Muir Mathieson's conducting credit!*
JOHN WILSON: *But the players on the soundtrack sound incredibly engaged. And that communicates an intensity to the audience.*

The un-budgeted overseas travel and recording added $10,000—$108,000 today—to *Vertigo*'s budget. During the tense mixing sessions, as music was combined with dialogue and effects, each mistake in the orchestra triggered an "outburst from Benny that Hitch would squelch by lowering the dry end of his Havana cigar from his lips and softly remarking, 'Now, Benny.' "[23]

Meanwhile, a different struggle over music was playing out at Paramount. Studio executives wanted a song—ideally one that would explain the meaning of *Vertigo*'s damn title. (For months, Hitchcock refused their entreaties to give the film a more accessible name.) Soon Herrmann "was screaming, in his usual fashion, 'I'm not going to give them some goddamn score of pop music,'" recalled CBS producer William Froug. "At that time, the pressure was on every producer, Hitchcock included, and that went against everything Benny believed in."²⁴

Herrmann enlisted colleague Jeff Alexander to arrange *Vertigo*'s love theme as a song. Conveniently, its first four notes could be stretched into "Madeleine," the tune's final title. But Hitch and Paramount wanted something catchier. Recalled *Laura* composer David Raksin, "Benny told me a funny story. When Hitchcock wanted to needle Benny, he'd say, 'Listen, Benny, why don't you write me a theme like *Laura*?' And Benny would say, 'If you want garbage like that, why don't ya get Raksin?' I loved that. Benny liked *Laura*, but he just had to say that."²⁵

Herrmann's love theme was deemed insufficiently commercial; so Jay Livingston and Ray Evans signed on to provide "an exploitation song titled 'Vertigo.'" Paramount hoped that the duo who wrote "Que Será, Será" might add an audience-friendly element to the publicity campaign for Hitch's dark fantasy. But their tune had just one recording. Even jazz great Billy Eckstine couldn't persuasively sing, to a bossa nova beat, "This vertigoooo is driving me insane, my love . . . This vertigoooo that has me spinning like a top . . ." (Mel Brooks must have heard it, before writing his histrionic title song for the 1978 Hitchcock parody *High Anxiety*.)

Despite a successful premiere on May 9—in San Francisco, of course—*Vertigo* had one last creative convulsion. Paramount president Barney Balaban had already ordered the shipping of 500 film prints when Hitch screened the film for Joan Harrison, producer of his TV series. After hearing her review, the director told Herbie that the movie must be recut. Audiences, he decided, should *not* know that Judy had impersonated Madeleine until Scottie makes the discovery in the picture's last minutes. Judy's "letter" scene was to be cut.

Coleman took a deep breath, then told Hollywood's most powerful director that he was wrong.

"He didn't like that, and we began to argue. We were standing face to face. Our voices were rising."²⁶ But the argument was unwinnable. And after Coleman supervised the cutting of the scene and its memorable music, he was tasked with showing the edit to Herrmann, who "blew his top."²⁷

Five hundred new versions of Reel 11 were hastily printed. But just as they were about to ship, Barney Balaban screened the recut for critics. Their reaction was as negative as the premiere audience had been enthusiastic. Hitchcock was literally called on the carpet of the studio chief's office and ordered to restore *Vertigo* to its original edit.²⁸

Example 6.3 Jay Livingston and Ray Evans's title song was recorded only once. Signed by Livingston, courtesy of Paul Farrar.

At least the Paramount chief loved the film. He called it "a masterpiece," which may have emboldened the director's choice of text on its posters. "ALFRED HITCHCOCK'S MASTERPIECE" was a surprising declaration of artistic ambition for someone who liked to insist that he was merely an entertainer.[29]

The saga of *Vertigo* began with a petrifying episode for Hitch—his emergency surgery. It would end with another. In April, as he planned his international publicity tour, Alma told him that a routine medical checkup revealed that she had cervical cancer and needed immediate surgery. At the time, cervical cancer was usually considered a death sentence.

The possible loss of his closest emotional confidante was devastating for Hitchcock. After fulfilling each day's commitments, "he would drive straight to the hospital, weeping and shaking convulsively," biographer John Russell Taylor wrote.[30] During a drive home from Paramount with Norman Lloyd, Hitchcock began sobbing. "What's it all about?" he asked Lloyd. "What would it all mean without Alma?"[31]

Example 6.4 Saul Bass and John Whitney's spiral design for the main title inspired the visuals of *Vertigo*'s ad campaign.

The surgery was a success. But Hitchcock "remained a complete wreck and believed she was going to die," daughter Pat recalled.[32] Pat took Alma's place alongside Hitch at the San Francisco premiere of *Vertigo*. Afterward, in his high-floor hotel room, "he just broke down in tears and said that he couldn't live without her and that he might as well jump out the window. . . . I really do feel that, had anything happened to her, he probably couldn't have gone on."[33]

One month after Alma's health crisis, on May 28, *Vertigo* opened across the United States. Legend has it the picture flopped in 1958, unloved by critics and audiences. The truth is more nuanced.

"Hitchcock tops his own fabulous record," wrote Jack Moffitt for the *Hollywood Reporter*. "It is a picture no filmmaker should miss. . . . Bernard Herrmann's music conducted by Muir Mathieson keeps the audience hovering with expectancy on the threshold of every thrill."[34] Several reviews praised its "artistic" merit. But there were prominent dissenters, with *Time*'s putdown—"a Hitchcock and bull story"—leading the pack.[35]

Moviegoers were initially attracted by the stars and director. But the film's strange rhythms, its increasingly unlikable hero, and its bleak ending took a toll. With a cost of $2.5 million, *Vertigo* grossed $3.2 million—profitable, but below expectations. Audiences that year preferred musicals like *South Pacific* and *Gigi*, comedies like *Auntie Mame*, and sexy dramas with upbeat endings (*Cat on a Hot Tin Roof*). Hitchcock and Herrmann blamed James Stewart's age, and Benny also criticized audiences: "People in America thought [the word *vertigo*] was a backache or something."[36]

A year after its release, writer Joseph Stefano, then working on *Psycho*, asked Hitch if he could see *Vertigo* in the director's private screening room. Up to that time Stefano considered Hitchcock emotionally remote. After the screening, his feelings changed. "Here was this incredibly beautiful movie he had made that nobody went to see or said nice things about it. I told him I thought it was his best film. It brought him to near-tears."[37]

Fortunately, Hitchcock was far from paralyzed creatively. His next movie promised to be a colorful, and commercial, super-production. And financially, 1958 was another boom year for the director. A rival studio, Universal-International, was stumbling financially after making too many second-rate titles. Its biggest stars were Rock Hudson and Francis the Talking Mule. That December, MCA made an offer to buy Universal's 423-acre backlot. The price was $11.25 million.[38] Universal took the cash. Lew Wasserman now had ample turf to produce MCA's hundreds of hours of TV product. And although the agency wasn't running the studio, it now essentially owned it.

As an MCA stockholder, Hitchcock's finances continued a climb that hadn't stopped since 1954. The heft of his bank account and the continuing success of his TV show were just the boost he needed to tackle the most logistically complex film of his career. And to Herrmann's delight, it would showcase a side of Benny's talent like no project before.

7

On the Rocks

> LUCY ANDERSON: *(laughs) You should have seen him, Alma! Parading me around in front of the store girls at Robinson's.*
> ALMA HITCHCOCK: *So you see, animals aren't the only thing that melts Benny's heart, my dear.*
> LUCY: *You're so sweet. And so kind to keep inviting us back. Such a novelty! Benny can be…*
> ALMA: *You mean he's not everyone's cup of tea?*
> LUCY: *Your English sayings are just so—polite!*
> ALMA: *Hitch and I are very fond of you—both of you. I've never seen him put quite so much trust in someone.*
> LUCY: *Mutual respect, Benny says.*
> ALMA: *Mutual pig-headedness, too.*
> LUCY: *You're telling me! But Benny gets along with the difficult people. Says it's the nice ones you've got to watch out for… I—I didn't mean that Hitch was one of those difficult people. You do understand that?*
> ALMA: *Oh, no, no, no. He* is *difficult. But only because he knows what he wants to control. Same newspaper in the morning. Same suit. Same steak and salad for lunch. Same Dover sole for dinner. Same filming hours.… I think he needs life to be like a studio shoot, you see? That's contentment for him—everything perfectly controlled. Sealed off from the incompetence and chances that your Benny loathes too.*
> LUCY: *Loathes? That's an understatement.… He goes into battle with the whole world every day.*
> ALMA: *Hitch simply hides from it.*
> —Andrew McCaldon, "Benny & Hitch" (BBC Radio 3)

The hour was late as George Tomasini sat in his edit bay at Paramount. His focus was interrupted by a call from the front gate.

"There's a gentleman here to see you," the guard explained, "but he doesn't have any identification on him. He says his name is Benny."

"Does he look like a mad bomber?" Tomasini asked.

ON THE ROCKS 133

Example 7.1 Benny poses his with his beloved dog Twi, c. 1960.

Pause. "Well, yes, as a matter of fact, he does."

"Send him up!" George replied.[1]

Over the last four years, Tomasini and Herrmann had formed an easy friendship. George accepted, even enjoyed, Benny's eccentricities, just as he could laugh with no hurt feelings at Hitchcock's barbed critique of an editing choice.

At his best, Herrmann was capable of many warm friendships. "Benny loved to give gifts," recalled horn player Alan Robinson. "In London he had an instrument made for me—a natural horn that plays in about twelve different keys. They had to make it special. He knew I loved natural instruments."[2]

One night, Herbert and Mary Belle Coleman were visiting Bluebell. "We'd just settled down when Benny's beloved cat parade commenced. . . . One in particular always headed straight for Mary Belle. . . . I watched Benny watching Mary Belle and knew he was studying her to decide if she was worthy of mothering one of his children." Weeks later, Herrmann appeared at the Coleman doorstep. "Snuggled in his arms was that same little, long-haired gray kitten. He handed it to Mary Belle. 'His name's Babo.' He pulled some pages from a pocket. 'Here's how you care for him, what you feed him, and when, the name and address of his vet.'"[3]

But a night with the Herrmanns was fraught with variables that gave many friends pause. They knew that one of two scenarios was equally possible. (The following details and quotes are taken from actual events.)[4]

Scenario #1. Arriving at the door of Bluebell Avenue, you straighten your tie and jacket—customary dinner attire of the time. Benny opens the door, smiling and already in conversation with you. Stepping inside, you smell steak and other savories—Lucy is in the kitchen. Benny dashes into the hall and returns with his latest book purchase from Sotheby's: *Fine Eighteenth and Nineteenth Century Drawings and Paintings*. Flipping its pages and stopping on a Turner watercolor, his voice rises with excitement. You try to ignore the compulsive movement of his right-hand thumb and forefinger, as they twist strands of hair together—an action he repeats for minutes.

Dinner is excellent. Benny serves the wine, and has just one glass: alcohol gives him migraines. After the meal he lights a cigarette, kicks off his shoes, and sets his feet on the coffee table. Relaxed, he begins an amusing dissertation on Samuel Johnson's thoughts about human flight. (Johnson was against it: too much risk from falling objects.) Benny emulates Johnson's aphoristic style; an evening with Herrmann is an evening of quotes. Now he's recalling his favorite teacher at Juilliard, the eccentric genius Percy Grainger. By midnight, he is reflecting on the size of the universe, and the distance between stars. Itchy the cat trots into the room. Benny nuzzles it gently, as Lucy wordlessly refills your drink.

Scenario #2: As you approach the doorstep, the ugly sound gets louder. Benny is yelling inside. The door flies open. It's Herrmann, who says nothing as he turns back to Lucy, his scratchy falsetto now a string of profanities. He's on a tear about a meeting today, with a producer who wanted him to score a film. Midway through the screening, Herrmann stormed out of the room. He proudly shares that he told the producer his picture was "garbage." "They're a bunch of empty-heads," he snarls, moving close to you. His voice drops to a conspiratorial whisper. "They pretend to be nice guys. But it's a disguise. They're not nice." His voice jumps two octaves: "They're *vicious, vindictive people who try to make sure that anything good hasn't got a chance!*"

A second couple has arrived. Lucy, trembling, greets the newcomers and hands out drinks. Herrmann lights a cigarette and sulks. One of the new arrivals, the wife of a university professor, breaks the silence with a comment she hopes will impress her host. She praises the latest recording by Leonard Bernstein, the thirty-something wunderkind who moves easily from concert conducting to symphonic writing to film music to TV lectures. Herrmann despises Bernstein, who has everything Benny longs for. He snarls at his guest that he has no time for "vacuous, stupid people." Lucy has left the room, but can be heard crying in the hall.

Within minutes, you and the others are driving home, as your companion expresses sympathy for Lucy. "It's like she's living on top of a volcano."

Among Herrmann's friends was a sub-group with much in common: talent, wit, and emotional neurosis. They included pianist and professional neurotic Oscar Levant and forty-year-old screenwriter Ernest Lehman. Like Benny, Lehman's personality careened between charming (especially around women) and complaining (especially around collaborators). Also like Benny, his work was outstanding. In the last five years, his screenplays included *Executive Suite, Sabrina, Sweet Smell of Success,* and *The King and I. West Side Story, The Sound of Music,* and *Who's Afraid of Virginia Woolf?* would follow.

"Benny was *very* likable, very irritable, loved to ruffle feathers, to speak with anger in his voice, and above all, be provocative," Lehman recalled. "I suspect, however, that he was a highly gifted, somewhat unappreciated pussycat."[5]

Herrmann admired Lehman's talent for story construction and sparkling dialogue. Hitchcock was always looking for writers who could create the tree on which to hang his set pieces of suspense. Benny proposed a meeting. On August 30, 1956, the trio met for lunch, and Herrmann's instincts proved on target: Hitch and Lehman hit it off, and agreed to collaborate.

MGM had been courting the director to leave Paramount long enough to make a picture for them. From the mid-1920s to the late 1940s, Metro dominated the industry by making lavish, star-driven escapism. But by 1958 the studio was in trouble, as it struggled to find new stars and more adult material in a post–Gable and Garland world. Hitchcock said yes to MGM's offer, and Lew Wasserman arranged the deal. Hitch would get $250,000 ($2.7 million today), plus a percentage of the box office. He also would have the team of his choosing, including Herrmann, and total creative control.

Although Hitch's TV series was as popular as ever, his attempts to make more personal films—*The Wrong Man*, *Vertigo*—had been rejected by the masses. He was hungry for a hit, but couldn't find a story that excited him. Working in Metro's elegant Thalberg Building, Hitch and Lehman tried to adapt a story that MGM owned: the courtroom drama *The Wreck of the Mary Deare*. The pair soon agreed that it was a talky bore. But a eureka moment arrived soon after, when Hitch recalled unused story fragments he'd collected. They included the notion of a movie that began with the stabbing of a UN diplomat. Another involved a pursuit across Mount Rushmore—an idea Hitch called "The Man on Lincoln's Nose."[6] Lehman sparked to the challenge of writing the ultimate Hitchcock chase thriller, filled with wit and romance, and a story strong enough to anchor its showpieces.

The result was *North by Northwest*, Hitchcock's silkiest and most seriocomic thriller. Its story—Manhattan ad man is mistaken for a US spy, falls in love with an undercover agent, and traverses the country to prove his innocence—was flexible enough to go wherever Hitchcock wanted. It could shift from terror to farce, thanks to plot twists from a writer who excelled at painting himself into corners, then finding ingenious ways out. "The audience never knows what's coming next," Lehman said, "because I didn't either."[7]

Hitchcock was getting excited. He envisioned Cary Grant and Eva Marie Saint in the leads. MGM pushed for Gregory Peck (cheaper than Cary) and Cyd Charisse (already under contract). The director held firm. Hitchcock and Grant had already made three hits together—*Suspicion*, *Notorious*, *To Catch a Thief*—and the actor embodied Hitch's most successful screen formula: "Beautiful people, beautiful scenery, a love story and suspense."[8]

Unbeknownst to his audience, Grant was also depressive and insecure. His outward persona, like Hitchcock's, was mostly a construct. In Grant's case it concealed a psyche scarred by childhood hurts, which manifested itself in distrust. After signing on to the project, "Suddenly all Cary could think about and talk about was how desperately he wanted out of the movie," Lehman recalled. "The role was all wrong for him. The picture would be a disaster."[9] Grant even groused within Hitch's earshot that the director didn't understand light comedy.[10] For seventy-eight days of shooting, which began in Manhattan on August 27, 1958, Grant's complaining rarely stopped.

Throughout the shoot, Hitchcock was frustrated by a litany of no's. No, he could not film the exterior of the United Nations building. No, more security wasn't possible to control crowds on New York streets. No, he could not film on the faces of Mount Rushmore. But the director ultimately got what he wanted. A hidden camera captured Grant walking into the UN building. As for Mount Rushmore, Hitch always planned to shoot the chase on stages at MGM. He only needed large-scale photography of the presidential heads to use as background, a request finally granted.

The production was Hitch's largest and longest. After New York, the crew moved to Chicago—then South Dakota, for brief shooting near Mount Rushmore. Then back at last to MGM, where the comfort of working on soundstages was mitigated by front office worries over budget. Despite Herbert Coleman's protestations, MGM and Hitchcock had agreed to the fiction that the movie would cost no more than $2.3 million. It ultimately cost $4.3 million, as Coleman predicted.[11]

The footage was a jigsaw of real locations, studio sets, special effect stages, and matte paintings of places that lived only on painted canvas. The risk of the movie lacking visual continuity was high—that is, if the team were less experienced than Hitchcock, cameraman Robert Burks, and production designer Robert Boyle. Boyle's Oscar-nominated work remains one of cinema's greatest examples of elevated realism and attention to detail.

The number of visual effects meant a long post-production schedule. As Hitch and George Tomasini tightened the edit, the director was confident

Example 7.2 Hitch makes the most of limited time at Mount Rushmore, filming *North by Northwest* in 1958.

that he had a hit. He also knew that the movie that would be his lengthiest—136 minutes—needed music to keep up the excitement.

For Hitchcock, even *North by Northwest* had a personal element. Nothing terrified him more than loss of control—the scenario Roger Thornhill faces from start to finish. Herrmann intuited Hitch's emotional connection to the film. And if *The Trouble with Harry* was "a portrait of Hitch," *North by Northwest*'s score would be a portrait of Hitch's anxiety, lurking behind humor.

The director brought him onto the production as soon as location filming was over. On October 2, not long after shooting at MGM began, Hitch made time for lunch with Benny.[12] Then again, on October 31 (imagine lunch with the duo on Halloween); then again, as filming was close to wrapping, on December 15. Herrmann was in good spirits throughout. While Hitchcock had been away filming, the forty-seven-year-old composer had begun a fertile new partnership, with stop-motion animation producer and future Oscar winner Ray Harryhausen.

At the time, the Harryhausen-Herrmann movies were critically dismissed as kids' fare. But *The Seventh Voyage of Sinbad*, *Mysterious Island*, *The Three Worlds of Gulliver*, and *Jason and the Argonauts* would be nearly as influential on a future generation of filmmakers (Spielberg, Lucas, Burton, Elfman) as Benny's Hitchcock titles. Harryhausen's mythic creatures—a skeleton army, a rampaging cyclops, a giant statue brought to life—unleashed Herrmann's passion for dazzling orchestral color and musical grotesquerie. Hollywood took note. And for the next five years, Herrmann lent scope and poignancy to several sci-fi and fantasy projects, most memorably Fox's *Journey to the Center of the Earth* and Rod Serling's TV series *The Twilight Zone*.

North by Northwest brought its own fresh challenge. Pleased that his introducing Hitchcock to Lehman had led to gold—Alma called the script Hitch's best since *The 39 Steps*[13]—Benny loved writing music with as much dry humor as it had menace. The result is a master class in balancing suspense and comedy in music—one often pilfered from, but never equaled.

The Score

Most of *North by Northwest*'s music is rooted in a single concept—one that baffled MGM's old-school music department. Opening credits appear over shots of scurrying commuters on the streets of Manhattan, which made Metro want "to know why I didn't write something that sounded Gershwinesque," Benny recalled. "They thought that anything that had to do with New York had to be pop-sounding. I wasn't interested in New York. I was interested in this kind of crazy dance that was going to happen now between Cary Grant and the world."[14]

Crazy dance. The concept was pure Herrmann: surprising, instinctual, intellectually clever. Taking his cue from Grant's "Astaire-like agility,"[15] the composer decided the best way to unify the film's dizzying geographical leaps was by linking them with a dance theme. He turned to the Fandango. Originating in Spain and Portugal in the 1700s, the Fandango's rhythm was usually a hard-driving triple meter. Imagine *West Side Story*'s "America" for a similar pulse and intensity.

Herrmann injects excitement before credits even begin, by starting his music during MGM's opening logo featuring Leo the Lion. Leo's roars are ingeniously timed with the first murmurs of score: *DOM-da-da-da-da-DOM ... da-da-da-da DOM, DOM, DOM....* Herrmann's 3/8 rhythm starts softly in timpani and other percussion; the final three notes of the phrase are playing as an answering snarl by low strings. Like a building storm, the orchestra expands, its dynamics (volume) rising, as strings and winds introduce *North by Northwest*'s main theme, his earworm Fandango. It is played *Allegro vivace e con Bravura*—fast and lively, brilliantly, boldly.

The MGM logo is tinted a surprising lime green. As the logo fades away, that bright burst of green fills the screen, until diagonal dark lines streak across it. Saul Bass's second title sequence for Hitchcock is simpler than *Vertigo*'s, but a perfect curtain raiser for this faster-paced film. Opening credits appear as slanted text, which flies up from the bottom of the screen before "landing" on one of Bass's diagonal lines. Those lines match-dissolve into footage of a Madison Avenue skyscraper. Each new block of credits is accompanied by Herrmann with a thrilling *whoosh* of cymbals. They intensify the feeling that we're in for something spectacular. They also hint at the multitude of height-based thrills to come: a careening car on a cliff, a crop duster firing bullets from the sky, a climb down Mount Rushmore.

ELLIOTT LEWIS, CBS DIRECTOR: *To this day,* North by Northwest *is a stunning example of what music does for a film. Look at the opening. Benny's overture is so exciting it knocks your brains out.*[16]

Example 7.3 Cary Grant and Eva Marie Saint, publicity still.

LYN MURRAY, COMPOSER: *Stanley Wilson [a musical supervisor at Universal] said, "Benny can really make an orchestra roar."*[17]

Castanets and tambourine add exoticism to the riotous dance, as Herrmann flings his Fandango theme back and forth across the orchestra. But although the theme is in constant movement, we're hearing variations on one idea. Musically speaking, it's going nowhere—just as Roger Thornhill will bounce across America, searching for an exit from the farcical nightmare he's trapped in.

The Fandango returns throughout the movie, most notably during its Mount Rushmore climax—a musical sequence Benny drolly titled "On the Rocks." The Fandango is also heard early in the story, as Roger tries to escape his captors by car. It was for this sequence—"The Wild Ride"—that Herrmann first wrote the Fandango. He later reverse-engineered it for the movie's main titles.

JOHN MORGAN: *The main title is usually the last thing a composer gets, because the studio is still working out who gets credit. Sometimes you take internal material from the film, you combine your different motifs together, and you think, "Ah, I've got my main title." And this is one of Herrmann's best. The sharpness of music. The way it goes nowhere but up and down, like Roger Thornhill, who's mistaken for a spy who doesn't exist. Throughout the score, Herrmann gets away from tonality [an agreed-upon order of notes and harmonies, like a musical scale]. There's no real home base musically. It goes all over, like Thornhill heading to all these different places with no idea what's going on.*[18]

In past scores, Herrmann used bitonality—the clashing combination of two or more chords, played in different keys—to evoke terror. In *North by Northwest*, bitonality is just as likely to evoke a grin. As Cary Grant's name appears in the opening credits, we hear a quirky bitonal phrase within the Fandango. Herrmann will reuse this phrase throughout the score, whenever Roger is stuck in scenes of comic humiliation.

WILLIAM STROMBERG: *To me, that phrase is the heart and soul of* North by Northwest, *because it captures the movie's feeling of whimsy, but it also has a darker overtone. Using bitonality, the top chords are fun and whimsical, but the bass line underneath has a more sinister quality.*

Herrmann mixes levity and danger in another recurring theme. For centuries, composers have incorporated the *Dies irae*—a Gregorian chant of death—to invoke an ominous mood. Herrmann often reworked it as music for figures of power or menace, from Charles Foster Kane to Dracula on radio. In *North by Northwest*, Herrmann has fun for once with the gloomy chant. When Roger is arrested for disturbing the peace (he has made a scene to escape the villains), the policeman snaps like a scolding parent, "You oughtta be ashamed of yourself!" Herrmann buttons the rebuke with the *Dies irae*'s famous opening rhythm—BOM bom BOM bom, BOM bom BOM bom. But here, played as staccato sixteenth notes by four blasting French horns, the *Dies irae* sounds like a child's *nyah-nyah* taunt. Later, as Roger sneaks away from a new set of captors—the CIA—strings recall the theme with a playfully shivering *tremolo*.

Herrmann also shows how a pint of invention can produce quarts of musical drama. Early in the film, Roger waits alone in a room after his abduction ("The Door"). Muted strings play a soft, despairing pattern. Those same twelve measures of tension return two hours later. But now they've become a hammer of brass and winds, as Roger and Eve Kendall find themselves on top of "The Stone Faces"—the presidents of Mount Rushmore. Few viewers will catch the repeated music, but Herrmann is subliminally adding unity to the movie through music.

He also helps make its hairpin turns of pacing and tone feel inevitable. After forty-five minutes of mystery and action, Hitchcock gives audiences a breather by introducing Eve Kendall to Roger, during a Chicago-bound train journey. Eve's blunt romantic proposition in the dining car ("I never discuss love on an empty stomach") is the cue for Herrmann to switch gears: the propulsive rhythm of the train is mirrored in a gentle syncopation for strings. Over it, a solo oboe plays one of the composer's loveliest, most lyrical melodies. Observed writer Frank K. DeWald, "It is a perfect reflection of the characters' relationship—sensual and insinuating without being overtly passionate; exquisitely beautiful yet always reserved."[19]

MORGAN: *Later, when they kiss in her stateroom, high violins in octaves play the love theme. The orchestration is like Sibelius, just gorgeous, with Herrmann keeping motion like the train going underneath with the lower strings.*

ANNA BONN STROMBERG: *He makes you feel that there's real emotion between these two people who've just met. And he was brilliant at ending a*

Example 7.4 A twenty-four-hour seduction is deepened by music in *North by Northwest*.

> *cue. A great example is at the end of their kiss. Eve's eyes shift away from Thornhill, and Herrmann adds this little extra "off" note in the chord, so it's unresolved, a bit dissonant. And you know that she's lying.*

Herrmann also knew when to be silent. While "spotting" the picture—determining where music stops and starts—Hitch and Benny agreed that the crop duster attack on Thornhill would be unscored. "If you're a painter, it doesn't mean that you can't use black," Herrmann later said. "And that is a sound: *black*. Every good artist uses black at times."[20]

LAURENT BOUZEREAU, FILMMAKER: *North by Northwest is an action-adventure story, and at times you feel the limitation of the technology, particularly in the Mount Rushmore climax. The camera hardly moves, because it's all matte paintings, right? The artificial side of it is so heightened, it's impossible to look at it without music. The music becomes the motivator of the action. It does that in the opening credits, it does it throughout*

Example 7.5 "Every good artist uses black at times": Herrmann stays silent during a legendary set piece.

> *the film, and it prepares you for that final sequence that does not work without music.*
>
> MICHAEL MCGEHEE, CONDUCTOR: *To me, this is the pinnacle score for Hitchcock and Herrmann. The music is integrated. It's joyous. There are no throwaway cues that mean nothing. He took an abstract notion—this dance across the country—and turned it into a Fandango. That's brilliant. And from the simplest passage to the most complex, you never lose interest.*

On April 23, Herrmann ascended the podium of MGM's fabled scoring stage, where *The Wizard of Oz* and other classics were recorded.[21] There, he led with unflagging vigor the first of four sessions with an orchestra of fifty players. After the debacle of *Vertigo*'s overseas recording, the composer reveled in his authority. He had assembled an all-star team that included trumpeter Uan Rasey, the bluesy soloist in 1951's *An American in Paris* and later 1974's *Chinatown*; oboist Arnold Koblentz, whose reed work graces Verve's *Ella Fitzgerald Song Book* albums; and violist Virginia Majewski, whose solos in 1951's *On Dangerous Ground* were so exceptional

Herrmann insisted on sharing his screen credit with her. No fewer than eight percussionists ensured that Herrmann's recurring Fandango would explode with demonic rhythm.

Hitchcock was delighted.

Unlike Paramount, MGM recorded its tracks in stereo, and Herrmann's insistence on close miking of instruments resulted in a thrilling, you-are-in-the-orchestra sound. Its clarity is further enhanced in modern editions of the film, which deliver those stereo tracks in 5.1 surround.[22]

Herrmann often approached mixing sessions—the final combining of dialogue, sounds, and music—like a warrior entering enemy camp. At MGM, "the mixers, who worked for the sound department, not the music department, had a lot of power to voice their opinions and change things," engineer Ralph Ives recalled. "One day, the chief mixer said, 'I don't think we need that cue. It's nothing. Let's take it out.'" The movie was previewed, and "the next day, the mixer said very sheepishly, 'You know, there's something about Benny's music. When you see the picture in its entirety, you see the reason for it. It belongs in.' If there's anything Herrmann knew more than any other

Example 7.6 Benny relaxes between takes in 1959 with bassoonist Don Christlieb. Courtesy of Don Christlieb.

composer, it was dramatic import. His knowledge was keener than anyone I've ever known."[23]

Did Hitch weigh in when Benny objected to the initial dropping of the cue? Probably, but not for long. "Hitchcock loathed conflict," Norman Lloyd recalled. "There was never a voice raised on the stage. He would just walk off if there was any conflict at all. If it were even arising, he would just walk off."[24]

The director did say no when MGM executives made a familiar request: they wanted a song. Recalled Ernest Lehman, "One day, Sammy Cahn, the great songwriter, came into my office and sang 'The Man on Lincoln's Nose.' It was just like Broadway in the '30s. It was a love song, but it sounded like something from a Kaufman and Hart farce."[25] The song was not used.

North by Northwest opened at Radio City Music Hall on August 6, 1959. Hitchcock summed up the reaction in a telegram to Lehman: "RECEPTION F--- ENORMOUS."[26] The movie grossed just under $10 million ($109 million today), making it the sixth highest grosser of 1959.[27] After two highly personal films that audiences mostly rejected, the director had made his ultimate entertainment without compromise. He even got a memorable apology from Cary Grant. One day while Hitchcock dined in MGM's commissary, Grant entered, knelt at Hitch's table, raised his arms, and did a silent, bowing salaam to the Master.[28]

Eva Marie Saint, a Herrmann friend, cabled the composer after seeing the film in Spain. "YOUR SCORE TREMENDOUS STOP WISH YOU COULD HAVE HEARD THE STAGGERING APPLAUSE." Benny replied, "I am not surprised they liked the music in Spain since it is based on Fandango music."[29]

Other fans included author Ian Fleming and producers Harry Saltzman and Albert Broccoli, who brought Fleming's 007 to movie screens three years later. Herrmann was accurate in stating that "*North by Northwest* was the forerunner of all the James Bond films."[30] The second Bond title, *From Russia with Love*, featured an aerial attack on its hero that can be considered homage, plagiarism, or both.

Nineteen fifty-nine had been one of Herrmann's most creatively varied years. That August, he conducted the music of his beloved Handel at the Los Angeles County Museum. He also wrote one of his most moving scores for any medium, for the *Twilight Zone* episode "Walking Distance." Its writer, Rod Serling, thanked Herrmann for "one of the most beautiful music scores I've been privileged to hear. Thank you for lending a great talent to our project."[31]

In a reflection of Benny's hope for a conducting career abroad, he and Lucy set up a second home, purchasing a London flat on Cumberland Terrace.

Nineteen fifty-nine would be a year of celebration for Hitchcock as well. That year, MCA offered its stock to the public. Its full name, Music Corporation of America, was changed to reflect reorganization. "MCA Inc." now had twenty separate divisions. Most important for Hitch was Revue Productions, which made MCA's TV shows. By 1960, according to Wasserman biographer Dennis McDougal, "MCA would utterly dominate television, controlling more airtime than any other single entity, including studios, networks, and independent producers. About 45% of prime time alone would belong to MCA."[32] Thanks to his stock shares, Hitchcock was getting a piece of all of it.

Once again, financial security and *North by Northwest*'s success emboldened the director to experiment. And no movie in his fifty-six-year career would be riskier, more controversial, or more impactful on cinema and popular culture than the unlikely shocker he chose to make next.

8

Something Terrible Is Going to Happen

Psycho, Part 1

The thin strands of hair over the skull's hollow eye sockets were the trickiest to attach, since they were arranged like tiny crosshairs. But eleven-year-old Jerry Mathers wasn't complaining. Sitting in the cheerful living room built on Universal Studios' Stage 17—home to Mathers's TV series, *Leave It to Beaver*—America's favorite sitcom kid considered himself lucky. Makeup supervisor Bob Dawn, who worked on *Beaver* and other shows, had said yes when Jerry asked if he could help Bob with his latest task: preparing the mummified skull of Norma Bates for Alfred Hitchcock's next movie.[1]

"I want this to be a *shocker*," Hitch had told Jack Barron, head of *Psycho*'s makeup department. "This woman has been sitting around a long time."[2] Now, Jerry and Bob sat in Mathers's TV home, gluing hair to the skull provided by a medical supply company. The makeup team aged and darkened the bright white head. They created the illusion of leather-like skin pulled tight across bone. They replaced the skull's generic jawbones with rows of large, crooked teeth, twisted in a rictus grin.

Mathers had been directed by Hitch five years earlier, playing Arnie in *The Trouble with Harry*. Now he delighted in helping groom Mrs. Bates. "I was fascinated. As a young boy, I thought, *what could be cooler than this!*"[3]

Hitchcock would have phrased it differently; but on the subject of *Psycho*, he was in total agreement. And it's telling that Jerry, one of the baby boomer generation that made up much of the moviegoing public by 1959, only needed a skull to get excited about the film.

Meanwhile, the sixty-something heads of Paramount Pictures, *Psycho*'s releasing company, had a different opinion. They were convinced that Alfred Hitchcock had lost his mind.

Today, *Psycho* may seem the surest of bets—the movie that launched six decades (and counting) of serial killer tales in every medium. At the time, it was the unlikeliest of screen projects, especially for a director who had just scored big with Cary Grant in a Technicolor romance. For Hitch, making

Psycho was no rash impulse. He had tracked over years a shift in moviegoing.[4] Films made in Europe, free from the strictures of Hollywood censorship, were more sexually explicit and cynical. Directors like Henri-Georges Clouzot used that frankness to out-Hitchcock Hitchcock. Clouzot's 1955 thriller *Les diaboliques* was a global hit, thanks in part to a killing in a bathroom that viewers were urged not to divulge.

In 1958, US movie ticket sales plunged an alarming 12 percent. Big studio titles were getting trounced by cheap exploitation flicks that frontloaded sex, blood, and rock 'n' roll. Hitchcock was especially intrigued by the output of independent producer and distributor American-International. Movies like *Girls in Prison* and *It Conquered the World*—the latter from an upstart named Roger Corman—were grossing up to forty times their bargain-basement costs. What if, Hitch wondered, a *real* director made a movie of quality... but on a shoestring budget, and with enough shock elements to attract the young drive-in crowd? The challenge was especially attractive after *North by Northwest*'s $4.3 million price.

That ambition crystallized in April 1959, after a *New York Times* book review intrigued him. It described a novel inspired by the grisly true story of Wisconsin loner Ed Gein. After the death of his mother, Gein dismembered female victims and used their skin to make furniture and his own "woman suit." Even in author Robert Bloch's less graphic reimagining, the novel *Psycho* was, according to the *Times*, "more icily terrifying than all of the arcane horrors summoned up by a collaboration of Poe and Lovecraft."[5]

It took Herbert Coleman just one hour to finish the book Hitch had dropped on his desk, with the comment "Read it, and we'll talk."[6] For Herbie, each page brought fresh agonies. First there was the main character, Norman—a fat, middle-aged, pornography-loving motel owner who hacked up women and preserved the corpse of the mother he had murdered. Then there was the stabbing death of Mary Crane, the only remotely sympathetic character, who leaves the story early and horribly: "It was the knife that, a moment later, cut off her scream. And her head."

Coleman returned the book to Hitch with a question: why was he asked to read source material—and bad material at that—for one of Hitchcock's TV episodes? When the director replied that *Psycho* would be his next feature, Herbie was speechless. So great was his disappointment that after shepherding the project through script stage and budgeting, Coleman left

Hitchcock's unit. Herbie had aspired for decades to direct a movie of his own; *Psycho* gave him the final push. For both Hitchcock and Herrmann, his departure was painful. Coleman's dedication to a film's smallest details, his gift for untying logistical knots, his loyalty and his honesty—all would prove irreplaceable.

Herbie wasn't alone in hating *Psycho*. In June 1959, Paramount's front office made it clear that, while they couldn't stop the director from making the movie, they agreed with their in-house reader, who deemed Bloch's novel "too repulsive for films."[7] Paramount had just told reporters that it would be focusing on "'blockbuster'-type features." Hitch had given MGM *North by Northwest*, and everyone involved made a fortune. Couldn't he do something similar for the studio that supported him most?

The director refused to back down. So he proposed a risky compromise: Hitchcock would personally pay for *Psycho*'s entire shoot and post-production. He would be reimbursed by Paramount only when the final film was delivered. And he would be paid no salary as director or producer. Instead, he would own 60 percent of the negative, and ultimately have full ownership, after Paramount received a percentage of profits from its initial release.

After the low grosses of *The Wrong Man* and *Vertigo*, Hitchcock had good reason to give up on *Psycho*. Its making was a risky move that could lead either to a financial windfall, or—if Paramount was right—a wasted year, lost income, and professional embarrassment.

To Paramount's relief, blood would be spilled not on the walls of its soundstages but at Universal, where Hitch's TV series was produced. Universal's backlot was now MCA-owned, and Lew Wasserman gave his friend soundstages, cameras, and an inexpensive crew, all without a penny of overhead. His motives weren't altruistic. As Hitchcock's contract with Paramount neared its end, MCA's president had a larger plan in mind. *Psycho* was Phase 1.

With his salary based solely on *Psycho* turning a profit, Hitchcock approved the lowest budget possible. The tally came to $800,000, roughly equal to three one-hour TV episodes. Little went to "below the line" (non-actor, non-director) talent. For the first time since 1950, cinematographer Robert Burks would not be at Hitch's side. Instead, TV veteran John L. Russell would be shooting in stark black-and-white, as he did for *Alfred Hitchcock Presents*. And so it went down the call sheet—with two exceptions. Retained from the feature unit were editor George Tomasini and Bernard

Herrmann. Each, the director believed, would be needed to elevate *Psycho* from a B-grade shocker into ... possibly ... something special.

For a screenwriter, Hitchcock wanted someone young. Enter thirty-seven-year-old Joseph Stefano, an MCA client with more credits as a songwriter than scriptwriter. But agent Kay Brown saw in Stefano's slim output a talent for characterization, something the novel lacked. "They thought it was a very inferior book, a very sleazy kind of property," Stefano recalled.[8] After urgings from Wasserman, Hitchcock met the inexperienced writer, who told the director of forty-six movies how disappointed he was in Hitch's choice of project. A fat, drunken voyeur? A "horrendous murder of a stranger I didn't care about"? Why would anyone want to watch these people?

Hitchcock silenced him with a question. "How would you feel if Norman were played by Anthony Perkins?" At the mention of the handsome twenty-seven-year-old star, a budding teen idol known for romantic roles, Stefano's attitude changed to excitement. He countered with an idea of his own: what if the story began by focusing on Mary (later Marion) Crane? Instead of a cipher we meet on the run, with $40,000 stolen from her employer, the

Example 8.1 Hitch as master of publicity: *Psycho* (1960).

movie could make us care about this woman. We would understand her theft as an irrational act, triggered by love for a man she's afraid to lose. Then Stefano said the words that sealed the deal. "I told him, 'I'd like to see Marion shacking up with Sam on her lunch hour.' Hitchcock, being a very salacious man, adored it."[9]

Soon, another breakthrough. "What if we got a big-name actress to play this girl?" Hitchcock asked. "Nobody will expect her to die!"[10] With that, he made *Psycho* his own. Weeks of often giddy story meetings with Stefano yielded a script with relatable characters, sudden scares, and an overarching sense of dread. "We decided this was going to be a picture of Gothic horror," Stefano recalled, "something he had not really done before."[11] Further buoying Hitch's spirits was his latest deal with MCA. Thanks to its vast TV output (some 1,650 episodes), the company had never been more successful. As Stefano recalled, *Psycho* script meetings paused when one man stopped by: "Lew Wasserman used to come in and they'd talk stocks and money, money, money."[12]

The freewheeling phase of writing was followed by the months Hitchcock dreaded: making the thing. Most of the elaborate camera shots he and Stefano imagined were sacrificed on the altar of budget. And his desire for a fast shoot was heightened by threats of a strike by the Screen Actors Guild. As a result, the filming that began on November 11, 1959, was devoid of location shooting.

At least the cast was close to perfect. Perkins as Norman; Janet Leigh, a star since the late 1940s, as Marion; Vera Miles as Marion's sister Lila; and Martin Balsam as Arbogast, the detective Lila hires to find her sister. Hitch especially loved working with Leigh, who appreciated his hands-off direction and playfulness after a take. Unlike some actresses, she was amused by his penchant for lewd jokes. She showed her own bawdy side by giving him a photo of her diligently studying the script—while sitting on a prop toilet. The inclusion of that bathroom fixture in the film was in defiance of the Production Code. Hitchcock featured and flushed it onscreen for the first time since censorship was enforced in 1934.

The only dud in the ensemble was John Gavin. The Universal contract player and MCA client delivered the beefcake Hitch wanted for the opening scene, showing Marion in a bra and half-slip, and Sam half-dressed, in bed in a dirty motel room. But during that scene's filming, Hitchcock was frustrated. Gavin was giving a TV-grade performance. The sexual tension the director counted on, to startle viewers as soon as credits ended, was nil. The scene "had to establish the passion of the relationship right from the start," Leigh recalled, "so that Marion's tremendous sacrifice and dangerous act makes sense."[13] Gavin never improved, inspiring Hitch to give him a nickname: The Stiff.

On the plus side, much of the shoot moved with impressive speed. Many films captured six or seven setups (new camera angles) a day. The *Psycho* crew was getting up to eighteen. But with speed came error. When Marion arrives at the Bates Motel, John L. Russell left a production light in the shot. Hitchcock simmered but said little—until the day Russell photographed the light bulb swinging over Mrs. Bates's corpse. (A horrified Lila has hit the bulb with her arm, motivating the swing.) Hitch told Russell that he didn't want to see a nimbus—that is, a light ring around the swinging bulb, which can appear if the camera is placed incorrectly. Russell photographed a nimbus. After viewing the shot, "Hitch let him have it," recalled assistant Peggy Robertson.[14]

Inevitably, Hitchcock's fast-and-cheap mantra collided with his instincts as an artist. He envisioned Marion's shower murder as *Psycho*'s showpiece. By slaughtering the main character and audience surrogate forty-seven minutes into the film, moviegoers would be both terrified and unmoored: where are we going now?

The scene was originally scheduled for a single shoot day.[15] But that was pure fantasy: the murder montage contained seventy-eight separate camera shots. Hitch conceived the scene with a musical rhythm in his head: "I'm going to shoot and cut it staccato, so the audience won't know what the hell is going on."[16]

For seven days, Janet Leigh and Marli Renfro, her nude double, screamed and struggled on a tiny bathroom set surrounded by protective screens. The process was tiring and claustrophobic. Hitch, attired in black suit and tie, waited with silent impatience whenever water struck the lens or Leigh's protective moleskin peeled off her private parts. "Mr. Hitchcock sometimes walked away because he became so exasperated," recalled wardrobe supervisor Rita Riggs.[17]

The murder of Arbogast required fewer shots but also proved challenging. It was filmed on Universal's massive Stage 28, which still housed the Paris Opera House set built for 1925's *The Phantom of the Opera*. For *Psycho*, Stage 28 served as the second-floor landing of the Bates mansion. As Arbogast reaches the top of its staircase, a figure in a dress races out and stabs

Example 8.2 Directing the shower scene, 1959.

his face—an act we see from a God's-eye perspective, looking down on the action. Not only is the angle startling; it conceals that the killer is Norman in drag. For over a week, the end of each work day was spent rehearsing the shot, which required the building of a metal bipod "run by pulleys that would lift a cinematographer and a relatively lightweight camera."[18] On the day of the shoot, Hitchcock woke up with the flu and had to direct the shot by telephone. The next day's shooting was canceled until he recovered.

Filming the murders put *Psycho* behind schedule. And so did a brief spell of indecision on the director's part. After one day's shoot, "My God, we had—I've forgotten how much footage," recalled George Tomasini's assistant, Terry Williams. "There was just a lot of coverage.... George comes over and says, 'God, the old man got lost.'... He meant that Hitch got lost and covered everything."[19]

Psycho completed principal photography on February 1, 1960, nine days over schedule. With its director on the hook for cost overages, the customary wrap party was canceled. But Hitchcock wasn't done filming. After watching Tomasini's first edit, he paid for retakes of Arbogast's murder and Lila's discovery of Mrs. Bates (the lighting wasn't sinister enough). Ironically, one of *Psycho*'s most essential players was among the lowest paid.[20] George Tomasini made $433.10 a week for his cutting, which included the tour de force of his career: fifty-two edits during the forty-five-second shower scene.

Joseph Stefano remained close to the project, and his youth and passion for the movie may be why Hitchcock shared with him his early, unscored cut of the film. It ran nearly two and a half hours and shocked Stefano for all the wrong reasons. "I thought it was a truly terrible movie. I came out sick. It was long. It had no tension. It looked careless. When we came out, Hitch saw the look on my face. 'A lot of work to do, it's just the rough cut,' he said."[21]

But privately, the director was worried. The movie cried out for intensity... and an exceptional score. But Hitchcock almost lost the collaborator he needed most. According to Dorothy Herrmann, "Daddy was very insulted that Hitchcock offered him a car instead of his fee."[22] Later, Herrmann told record producer Tony D'Amato that *Psycho* had such a paltry budget he almost turned it down.[23]

As on *The Wrong Man*, Herrmann played financial brinksmanship during the first weeks of December, holding out for his usual $17,500. Eventually Hitch gave in. "HAVE AGREED TO YOUR TERMS," he telegrammed Benny, then in London. "YOURS IN SUNSHINE, HITCH."[24] The deal was announced in *Daily Variety* with a phrase that no doubt amused the composer: *"Bernard Herrmann Will Lilt Hitchcock 'Psycho.'"*

In early January 1960, Hitchcock stepped away from shooting to meet with his composer. Contrary to his telegram, Hitch's mood was anything but sunny. "He *loathed* the picture," Herrmann recalled. "He said it was no good, that it didn't work, that he was ashamed of it."[25] After the pair screened an incomplete cut, "Hitch was nervously pacing back and forth, saying it was awful and that he was going to cut it down for his television show.... He was crazy—he didn't know what he had."[26] Herrmann's account of the meeting was supported implicitly by the director, in the authorized biography *Hitch*.

Never before had the director revealed so much self-doubt and anxiety to Benny. But it wasn't a new experience for the composer. "Many times, directors have lost perspective on their films."[27] On *Psycho*, Herrmann became the dominant force in the room. "'Wait a minute,' I said, 'I have some ideas.'"[28] As usual, Hitchcock told Herrmann to "do what you like" with the score. He had just one stipulation: "Please write nothing for the murder in the shower. That must be without music."[29]

Watching the rough cut, with its scenes of a woman in jeopardy, rainstorms, and a sinister Victorian house filled with secrets, Herrmann was struck by a literary parallel. "Hitch has his own world of film," he said in 1964. "He's created characters, places, and stories for it very much the way Dickens did.... Although many of the stories that he has told are stories of our time, I believe the way of presentation, and the motivating psychology, is essentially of the period of Dickens and the great Victorian writers. *Psycho* is very much like the Wilkie Collins stories. I think this was part of Hitch's great heritage, and one that he's been able to transmute and carry forward in the world of cinema."[30]

The mystery novels of Dickens's friend Wilkie Collins are widely considered the first to be written in that genre. They include *The Woman in White*, about a girl trapped in an isolated Victorian mansion and marked for death. *Psycho*'s tone is mirrored in a statement by one Collins heroine: "I feel the ominous Future coming close; chilling me ... forcing on me the conviction of an unseen Design ... now fastened round us." Or as Norman Bates tells Marion, whom he will soon murder, "I think that we're all in our private traps, clamped in them, and none of us can ever get out. We scratch and claw, but only at the air, only at each other, and for all of it, we never budge an inch."

Benny had reassured Hitch that he had "some ideas." They included the concept that would make *Psycho*'s score a seminal example of how music can transform a film.

The "scratching and clawing" Norman describes ... a phrase that evokes entrapment, the taxidermic birds in Norman's parlor, *and* Marion's killing... that scratching and clawing would become literal in Herrmann's score.

And he would do it using only strings.

"Once Hitchcock made his decision to shoot *Psycho* in black-and-white, I knew that musically I had to ... reinforce his decision. I decided to use only string instruments throughout the entire movie."[31] By eliminating brass, woodwinds, and percussion, "I was able to complement the black-and-white photography of the film with a black-and-white sound."[32] The result, he later said proudly, was "pure ice water."[33]

Many directors would have rejected the concept, but Hitch agreed. "Mr. Hitchcock had a wonderful relationship with Benny," script supervisor Marshall Schlom recalled. "And the way to maintain that was to give Herrmann the latitude to do what he wanted. Mr. Hitchcock only wanted people around him who knew what they were doing."[34]

Example 8.3 Herrmann embraces the darkness, c. 1960.

The Score

If Hitchcock felt deflated that January, Herrmann was on fire. In a little over four weeks, he composed and orchestrated nearly all of *Psycho*'s fifty minutes of music, as chilling as they were visionary. And contrary to the belief that he chose strings due to budget limits, *Psycho*'s score required more musicians than his first three films for Hitchcock.[35] The composer employed fifty string players: fourteen first violinists, twelve second violinists, ten violas, eight cellos, and six basses.[36] As scholar Thomas Yotka observed, "*Psycho* exceeded budget/actual music expenses of almost all their previous films. Herrmann could have reduced the number of strings, which was enormous by Hollywood scoring standards. But he instinctively realized a huge string section would make his music all the more powerful and terrifying."[37]

Herrmann's idea set off warning bells among some. Joseph Stefano, a composer of pop music, discussed it with Benny and "thought it was weird. No drums? No rhythm section?"[38] Herrmann friend Fred Steiner, composer of the jazzy *Perry Mason* TV theme, was "a little wary about his using just strings, although I liked the idea. But I thought to maintain the suspense if he'd just have timpani . . . there was precedent for that. But he said, 'Nope! Nope!'"[39]

Asked once to name his favorite orchestral combination, Herrmann replied, "strings and a harp."[40] A violinist in his youth, with *Psycho* he was allowed to explore the vast range of effects string instruments can produce. And just as a black-and-white image contains an uncountable range of grayscale tones, Herrmann's "black and white" sound offered infinite varieties of orchestral color.

Since *Psycho*'s main title was the last element finalized, Herrmann likely used Marion's flight with the stolen money as his creative starting point. Those cues—"Flight," "The Rainstorm"—were synthesized into the most famous main title cue of Herrmann's career. "After the main title, nothing much happens in this picture apparently for 20 minutes or so," Herrmann later said. "Appearances of course are deceiving, for in fact, the drama starts immediately, with the titles! The climax of *Psycho* is given to you by the music, right at the moment the film begins. . . . That is the function [of the main title]: to set the drama."[41]

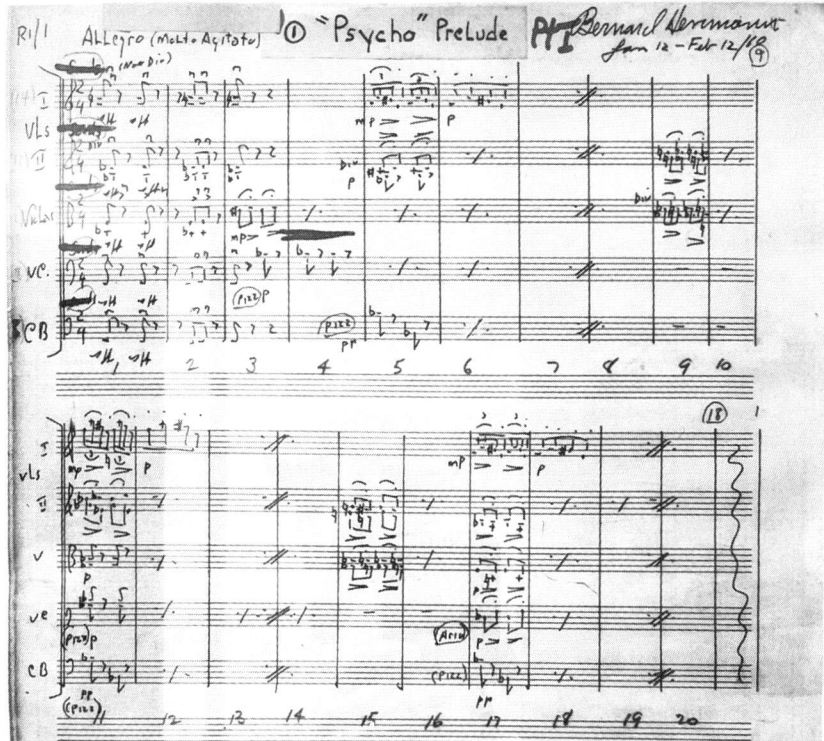

Example 8.4 Original pencil score for *Psycho*'s "Prelude." Courtesy of Norma Herrmann.

LAURENT BOUZEREAU, FILMMAKER: *With* Psycho, *Herrmann is using music as a weapon. It just assaults you in a way that is the weapon Hitchcock cannot show because of censorship.*[42]

BOM BOM. BOM-BOM. The first notes of *Psycho*'s "Prelude"—the same chord, played four times—stab like a knife. This chord is unresolved; and its frenzied, brutal rhythm continues as Herrmann introduces the first *Psycho* theme. This new "tune"—*DA-DA-dum, DA-DA-dum*—sounds like the convulsive leaps of a skipping heartbeat. Played high in the strings, it is juxtaposed against a chugging, clocklike rhythm in contrabasses and cellos. The ferocity of these low strings was a sound Herrmann admired in another conductor's work. "I remember Koussevitsky always used to say to the

Boston Symphony, 'Now, *deep* in the bow, *deep* in the bow.' This was an obsession, the deepness of sound."[43]

Onscreen, Saul Bass's fractured horizontal lines, animated to Herrmann's cue, slide and un-slide, forming the text of the credits. "The music is fast, urgent, nervous," wrote musicologist Christopher Palmer. "The constant hard, forward-driving motion anticipates the key emotion of the first part of *Psycho*: fear bordering on panic."[44]

WILLIAM STROMBERG: *The tempo is crazy. One quarter note equals 156 on a metronome. I can't even imagine the players' fingers moving that fast. And those low contrabasses are just playing evenly on the beat. CHOMP. CHOMP. CHOMP. CHOMP.*

JOHN WILSON, CONDUCTOR: *One of the trademarks of Herrmann's sound world is this nervy energy. He strips the main title back to this two-bar phrase, with the gritty string sound that gives us this incredible tension.*

JOHN MORGAN: *The sound has a brittleness, with very little reverb. The "boxy" recording quality adds to that frightening, black-and-white feel, not warm and beautiful like strings normally are. And you would think that this is the one cue that you would not have the strings muted, because of the violent nature of the music. But typically for Herrmann, he has the strings muted!*

ANNA BONN STROMBERG: *Having the mutes adds an extra edginess. All of the instruments are marked* sforzando *[forcefully] and* fortissimo *[very loud], and they have to try to play loud with mutes on. Then he adds this secondary theme, a quasi-lyrical theme, rising and falling, for high legato [smooth] strings. But it's an incomplete idea, it never resolves.*

Los Angeles, 2000. Rapper Busta Rhymes's latest single "Gimme Some More" earns a Grammy Award nomination for Best Rap Solo Performance. Its driving beat is accompanied by an insistent phrase for violins that rises and falls. Critics and many listeners recognize the source: Herrmann's "Prelude" for Psycho.

As the "Prelude" nears its end, cellos play with violent force a variant of the three-note theme we will come to know as "The Madhouse."

MORGAN: *It's a perfect main title. It sets the mood for the film. It introduces fragments of themes you'll hear later on.*

WILLIAM STROMBERG: *It adds to his vocabulary as a composer. Herrmann never did anything quite like this before or afterwards.*

London, 1966. Inside Studio Three at Abbey Road, the Beatles listen as their producer, George Martin, leads a rehearsal of the four violinists, two violists, and two cellists called for the day.[45] *Paul McCartney has requested strings for "Eleanor Rigby," a song on their next album,* Revolver. *"I wanted a series of E-minor chord stabs," McCartney later says. Martin combines "my idea of the stabs and his own inspiration [from] Bernard Herrmann [and]* Psycho. *George wanted to bring some of that drama into the arrangement. And of course, there's some kind of madcap connection between Eleanor Rigby, an elderly woman left high and dry, and the mummified mother in* Psycho.*"*[46] *Martin directs the string players to hit each downbeat harshly. The influence of* Psycho's *main title is clear. "That's it!" one of the players says. "Deadly."*[47]

Although nearly half of *Psycho* is scored, its content focuses on just a few character-driven themes, brilliantly reworked throughout the film. After the "Prelude's" urgency, Herrmann scores the movie's first images—a slow pan of Phoenix, Arizona—with the most languid music possible, as Hitchcock's camera travels into the window of the hotel where Marion and Sam have made love. Even before we see Marion, Herrmann has told us what she's desperate to escape: the oppressive monotony of her city, a place where the love she finds is measured in minutes.

The director had planned an ambitious aerial shot for this opening, which was scrapped due to cost. No doubt he asked Herrmann to help the awkward transition from the wide shot of Phoenix to the studio-shot window we "enter."

MISCHA DONAT, BBC COMMENTATOR: *Its slow, descending chords seem to suck us down with it, establishing the slow, heavy atmosphere that's to characterize the score throughout the early scenes of the film.*[48]

WILLIAM STROMBERG: *Many composers would score this so differently. Some would have bustling city music, some stupid thing. Herrmann sets it up with this eerie, cold-sounding music for the desert. There's not one passage of this score that sounds happy or hopeful.*

For Hitchcock, Marion was mostly a device to shock the audience with her sudden death. For Joseph Stefano and Herrmann, she was a woman who carries the film's humanity . . . and whose death strands us in an amoral universe. The talents of Stefano, Janet Leigh, and Herrmann make Marion's warmth and her yearning for love palpable.

"Marion and Sam," Herrmann's scoring of the hotel scene, does more than bolster John Gavin's flat performance as Hitchcock had hoped. The cue's first notes rise, suggesting a melody. But after just three notes, the pattern repeats and repeats, moving "continually downwards [through the orchestra] in quiet despair," wrote Christopher Palmer. "This melancholy music exemplifies Herrmann's tuneless approach—no melody . . . only an oppressive atmosphere."[49]

For the wordless scene in which Marion looks at the money she's been entrusted to put in a bank, but which now sits on the bed in her apartment, Hitchcock told Tomasini to add more cross-cuts between Marion and the envelope of bills. "I always want the audience to think what she's thinking."[50] Herrmann's accompanying cue, "Temptation," makes her thoughts as clear as any dialogue could. It also strengthens our identification with Marion, with its quietly sinister, repeating syncopation.

WILLIAM STROMBERG: *It really is like the devil tempting her. It's hypnotic. It sighs back and forth, with high string chords and the low string chords rising and falling, with that little ostinato [repeated pattern] going through the whole thing.*

MICHAEL MCGEHEE, CONDUCTOR: *It's not like a horror movie score of today. It's purely psychological. He's inside your head and carrying you along, and you're not even aware of it, because it is quiet and it is subtle.*

One of many frustrations for Hitchcock during editing was the failure of the images to convey that Marion isn't just driving—she is leaving town with the money. "That scene always gave trouble before it had any music," Herrmann recalled. "What you actually saw was a very good-looking girl driving a car." Benny chuckles. "She could have been just going for a ride before going back to work. Hitch said to me, 'We'll put voices in [of her boss, of Sam] occasionally, from her mind. They're missing the money now.' I said, 'That's all right, but that still doesn't make it terrible.'" Instead, Herrmann jolts the audience with the music we know from the "Prelude," which "gives the audience, who don't know something terrible is going to happen to this girl . . . that it's *got* to."[51] Herrmann's voice, as he says these last words, is impassioned. As he confided to a friend, he often felt that he was "with" the characters while composing, experiencing their joys and, most often with Hitch, their terror.⁵²

The return of the "Prelude," as Mischa Donat observed, makes us "realize why the composer has been careful to maintain such a lethargic feeling in the score before this point. By so doing, the moment of decision—the point of no return—is quite unmistakable when it comes."⁵³

In Hitchcock's sound notes for Marion driving, he details the need for traffic noises, the engine of Marion's car, and the loudness of "passing car noises when headlights show in her eyes." During the rainstorm "there should be a progression of falling rain sound ... windshield wipers should be heard all through." The final soundtrack has almost none of these sounds. All it needed was Herrmann's music—anxious, then hysterical, as the "Prelude's" metronomic quarter notes match the fast-moving windshield wipers. "It's the music," Herrmann said, "that tells you that she has embarked on a dangerous, horrifying experience."⁵⁴

MARTIN SCORSESE: *That driving music is what propels the picture emotionally and psychologically. The music is driving the characters, taking the characters ineluctably to their doom.*

In their early discussions, Hitch suggested to Benny that there be no music from the time Marion arrives at the Bates Motel, until after Marion's murder and the hiding of her body and car. Herrmann disagreed. And the music he wrote for that section of the film would not only make cinema history; it contained a piece that the composer considered the dark center of his score—a cue he later called "the real *Psycho* theme."

9

The Real *Psycho* Theme

Psycho, Part 2

For Herrmann, no scene in *Psycho* was more key to its story and philosophy than Marion's conversation with Norman, which occurs innocuously over sandwiches in his parlor. The two are surrounded by stuffed birds, whose dead eyes add to Norman's monologue—the one about people in traps.

Hitchcock originally wanted no music for the scene. Later, he was grateful for the quietly unnerving cue Herrmann wrote. "The Madhouse" is based on a three-note figure for low strings (cellos and basses): a low F, played at a startling *fortissimo* (very loud); then a leap up nearly an octave, to E-flat; then a final D that is lower than the first note. The three notes sound like a flare of anger that softens into a murmured threat. It begins after Norman challenges Marion about "putting" his mother "someplace": "Do you mean an institution? A madhouse?" Herrmann's three-note theme unites *Psycho*'s trilogy of horrors: Norman; his alter ego, Norma Bates; and madness that links them. For Herrmann, "The Madhouse" was "the real *Psycho* theme."[1]

Remarkably, the theme did not originate with *Psycho*. Benny had written it twenty-five years earlier in 1935, for an obscure concert piece, "Sinfonietta for Strings." He adapted other brief passages from the "Sinfonietta" for *Psycho*. But his reason wasn't to take a shortcut. He knew that the nihilistic passages he wrote as a young man would find their fullest realization in *Psycho*.

Béla Bartók also hovers over *Psycho*, especially his *Music for Strings, Percussion and Celesta*. As in Bartók, "The Madhouse" has no tonal center. Instead, the string orchestra twists the notes through repetition, crawling around them like a spider circling a fly. It's no coincidence that Marion's theme, heard in the first scene, is a variant of "The Madhouse": both she and Norman are in "private traps" and can "never get out."

JOHN MORGAN: *This is the closest that Herrmann comes to twelve-tone music.*[2]
[Created by composer Arnold Schoenberg after World War I, twelve-tone

Example 9.1 Herrmann, c. 1960.

music rejects traditional scales and harmonies, in favor of a math system. The result is a dissonant departure from tonal writing.]
ANNA BONN STROMBERG: *It has that twelve-tone feel, the way the violins and violas play in this canonic style, where the tune starts in one instrument and then it starts in another instrument halfway through the tune. Which creates all these "rubs" between the notes, the dissonances. And that creates tension.*

Denham, England, 1977. From the conductor's podium inside the largest stage at Anvil Studios, John Williams leads a sharp downbeat, as George Lucas listens to the score for his new film, Star Wars. *Low strings dig into their instruments, playing a three-note phrase. It is "The Madhouse." This music will be heard as Luke Skywalker, Han Solo, and Chewbacca emerge from their hiding place in the Millennium Falcon, after landing on the Death Star. The theme's inclusion is homage—to the composer who taught Williams much as a colleague and friend.*[3]

"The Madhouse" ends just before Marion smiles, having decided through her conversation with Norman that she will go back to Phoenix and return the money.

MORGAN: *Herrmann made the decision that if there was a lighter moment or tinge of hopefulness in* Psycho, *he would not have music. Music is in this other world, because he knows the outcome of the film.*

Norman's inner feelings, unlike Marion's, are opaque to a first-time viewer. Until the climax Herrmann walks a fine line, hinting at Norman's dark side without giving the game away. A prime example is Norman spying on Marion through a peephole as she undresses. Herrmann keeps a chilly neutrality, contrasting the warm resonance of muted violas with the coldness of violins, slowly climbing through their highest register.

WILLIAM STROMBERG: *That violin part is very difficult to play, getting that intonation [accurate pitch]. It would be easier if they came up to that high note on a run. But just starting them on that high C—it's really iffy. I'll bet there were a lot of retakes.*

DAVID NEWMAN, COMPOSER: *The effectiveness of* Psycho *isn't just the main title and the shower music—it's the* dread *music.*

Music has stopped by the time Marion steps in the shower. Hitchcock "was very clear about what he wanted," Janet Leigh recalled. "The shower was a baptism. . . . He wanted the audience to feel her peacefulness, her kind of rebirth."[4] Hitchcock made the white tiles around her as bright as possible— "almost blinding," per the script. They create a tone of optimism . . . until through the shower curtain, we see the bathroom door open. A silhouetted figure approaches Marion.

MORGAN: *Some composers might have brought the music in when we see the shadow on the shower curtain. But what makes it so scary is the silence. We just hear the water.*

JOHN WILSON: *When I conduct the score live with the film, when it comes to the murder, everybody in the audience knows what's coming. There's a palpable tension in the air. You feel the hairs on the back of your neck. And it's often greeted by nervous laughter. Of course, that's the audience's way of coping with the horrors about to unfold. The second the music kicks in, I can sense the terror behind me in the audience. The music immediately changes the atmosphere.*

As the shower curtain rips back, we hear screams, stabs... and no music.

At least this was the request of Hitchcock, during his January review of *Psycho* with Herrmann. But Benny felt differently. On most of their films, he had written cues that were not used; it was a standard part of the scoring process. No harm would be done, he reasoned, in writing the piece he titled "The Murder."

We all know the sound. As the shower curtain is whipped back and Marion screams, violins—unmuted for the first time in the score—play *Molto Forzando e Feroce* (very forcefully, ferocious). Three E-flat notes, in the first violins' highest register, are joined by shrieking second violins, playing E-natural. E-flat and E-natural, notes that are next to each other, create dissonance. And so it goes, down the musical scale and down through the instruments, until the first violins' piercing screams have been joined by the same violent rhythm in the low contrabasses. The result, one critic wrote, was a "marrow-scraping intensity."[5]

The notes were played with hard downbow strikes and leaping glissandos (up- or downward slides). Until now, the constant use of mutes on instruments has created a "dry" sound. For "The Murder," Herrmann requested a reverberant echo. Observed composer and friend Laurie Johnson, "It was this ability to see and hear the end product in his mind that made these things work. He knew *exactly* the sound mixture to have that effect."[6]

Example 9.2 "For the first time, movies weren't safe": *Psycho* (1960).

Contrary to many film theorists, there are no added electronic effects. "People laugh when they learn it's just violins," Herrmann said. "It's just the strings doing something every violinist does all day long when he tunes up. The effect is as common as rocks."[7]

But the phrasing of those slashing glissandos . . . the precisely chosen cluster of dissonances—those were anything but common. In one of his last interviews, Herrmann confirmed that the strings were intended to hark back to "Norman Bates' irrational association with humans and stuffed birds."[8] In other words, he tells us in music who the killer is. The cue also invokes the hacking knife and Marion's screams. But its ultimate purpose was more elemental. Asked what he thought of when writing the cue, Herrmann answered: "Terror."[9]

California, 2014. Studying the composer's handwritten score, at UC Santa Barbara's Special Collections, scholar Thomas Yotka makes a surprising discovery. Judging from the order of Herrmann's revisions, it appears that he initially did not score the shower scene. However, that music's origin is heard in a different cue: "The Body." This music, for Norman's discovery of Marion's corpse, was written as Herrmann worked from Hitch's unfinished rough cut. "The Body" started with what later became the shower music's signature opening notes. After Hitchcock tightened Psycho *to its final length, Herrmann reworked his idea for "The Body" into a new cue: "The Murder"—aka the shower scene. In "The Murder," four shrill notes from "The Body" became "The Murder's" opening pattern of three notes. Herrmann also added a slashing glissando effect, and slowed the music to an agonizing length of over a minute. Thus was born the most famous film cue in history.*

Norman's disposal of Marion's corpse initiates *Psycho*'s longest section without dialogue: ten minutes. With Marion suddenly gone, music now accompanies the actions of Norman, while maintaining a cold objectivity. Bitonal chords and ostinatos (repeated patterns) almost take us inside Norman's mind, as he methodically mops the bathroom's blood. But music goes no further than to keep us tense and intensify our disorientation. Marion is dead . . . who is this young man we're left with?

MICHAEL MCGEHEE, CONDUCTOR: *What's interesting to me about* Psycho *is how meticulous it is. It's very subtle. It sounds repetitive, but there's actually* almost no perfect repetition. It's constantly evolving, in note changes, in the articulation. He can stretch one idea out for minutes.

STEPHEN SONDHEIM: *Those unresolved chords . . . keep going on so that nothing ever reaches a cadence [resolution]. And so you're constantly upset, because it's all a kind of—irresolution, is the best I can say. It promises something else: You're not through yet . . . you're not through yet . . . something else is going to happen. . . . Herrmann was the master of that.*[10]

Initially Hitchcock suggested that, like Marion's death, the murder of Arbogast have no music. Benny disagreed. By February 2, a new typed list of directorial "suggestions" includes a change: "Continue [music] through Arbogast's death."

When Arbogast steps cautiously into the Bates mansion to question Norman's mother, Herrmann's score is again transformative.

WILLIAM STROMBERG: *We hear a hushed strumming effect in the strings. The players are strumming their instruments like a guitar, probably holding them sideways. One of Bartók's quartets has the same sound, and it's perfect.*

ANDREW MCCALDON, PLAYWRIGHT: *It's one of those moments where your heart jumps. That sort of shimmering delicacy and fragility in the music. Suddenly it's very, very tentative, microtonal, like Ligeti almost.*

Arbogast slowly ascends the staircase. The strumming players mirror his movement by taking one musical step upward. Then another. Over these *tremolo* (trembling) notes, Herrmann adds high violin harmonics—the "ghost" sound that adds subtle extra tones above the note being played. The high violins oscillate up and down nervously, as Hitchcock cuts from Arbogast walking up the stairs . . . to his hand on the railing . . . to a low shot of a door slowly opening on the second floor. Violins hold a high, *pianissimo* seventh chord—more musical "ice water"—while softly, a dissonant note in low strings rubs against the high violins. The effect is like time frozen. Until . . .

"The Knife—Molto Forzando e feroce (Vivo)." Forceful, ferocious, brisk. The shower music is back, louder, faster, even more terrifying, as Arbogast's face is slashed by his offscreen assailant. Herrmann and Hitchcock's slow buildup

Example 9.3 *Psycho* publicity still (1960).

to the slaughter, followed by an explosion of sound, proves that violence can be just as frightening when the audience knows it is coming.

After Arbogast's disappearance, Lila and Sam begin their own search. It takes them to the Bates Motel. Herrmann is mostly hushed or absent in these scenes, a choice that helps make *Psycho*'s last minutes a nerve-shredding escalation of horror.

Sam distracts Norman in the front office, as Lila climbs the steep ascent to the Bates mansion, alone. Director and composer join forces to tell us: this is the beginning of the end. Hitchcock shows Lila, walking toward "us" (the camera). Then he cuts to her point of view of the house, as it grows larger in the frame. On the soundtrack, Herrmann uses an ingenious corollary to these two camera shots. In his cue "The Hill," first violins start in a high register, then tentatively climb down the musical scale, half-step by half-step. It is the aural equivalent of Hitchcock's high angle framing of Lila, walking toward the camera. While the first violins play these falling notes, the second violins, violas, and cellos play low notes that climb *upward*—the equivalent of the camera angle showing Lila's low-angle perspective of the Bates house coming closer. Herrmann's descending-ascending musical lines finally converge, just as Lila reaches the house.[11]

As Lila walks through the mansion's dark, overstuffed rooms, cellos and basses play a steady pulse that throbs like a heartbeat. Its sense of movement toward something, as Lila walks through rooms that may hide a killer, creates a mood so tense that even jaded twenty-first-century audiences gasp during it. When Lila enters Norman's room and spots a doll and toy rabbit, violins sigh a falling pattern. It is a rare moment of compassion: Herrmann is reminding us of a child's lost innocence. The violins' phrase echoes a score he wrote months earlier, *The Twilight Zone*'s "Walking Distance," about a man who longs for the lost freedom of childhood. Herrmann's universe is filled with subtle interconnections.

As Lila makes the grisly discovery of Mrs. Bates's remains in the cellar, listen closely: there's a sloppy music edit, hidden in live showings of *Psycho* by audience screams. Herrmann did not plan to use the shrieking violins of "The Murder" for the reveal of Mrs. Bates's corpse, or the appearance of her knife-clutching, cross-dressing son. But in the final film those screaming violins return, for reasons to be explained. The soundtrack reconnects to Herrmann's original music for the scene as we see the close-up of Mrs. Bates's skull, her eye sockets animated by the swinging light bulb, matched by frantically spiraling violins.

In *Psycho*'s finale, Simon Oakland's psychiatrist gives a wordy explanation of Norman's mental breakdown. Yet the film ends in the most unresolved way possible. Norman sits in a cell. He is wrapped in a shawl like Whistler's Mother, as we hear a female voice speak the words in his head. "Let them see what kind of person I am. . . . 'She wouldn't even harm a fly. . . .'" Beneath her voice, Herrmann brings back "The Madhouse"—softly dissonant, and surprisingly sad.

JOHN WILSON: *The end of the film is terrifying, with very little happening in the music. It's incredibly measured. It's incredibly quiet. There are very few notes. And yet it penetrates deeply into your psyche.*

Herrmann was among the few who venerated forgotten Russian composer Nikolai Miaskovsky, a despairing "sick soul" whose "morbid emotions" and death-centered pessimism attracted Herrmann at an early age. "In Miaskovsky's music," he wrote in an essay, "there is no love, hope or any intense lyrical utterance."[12]

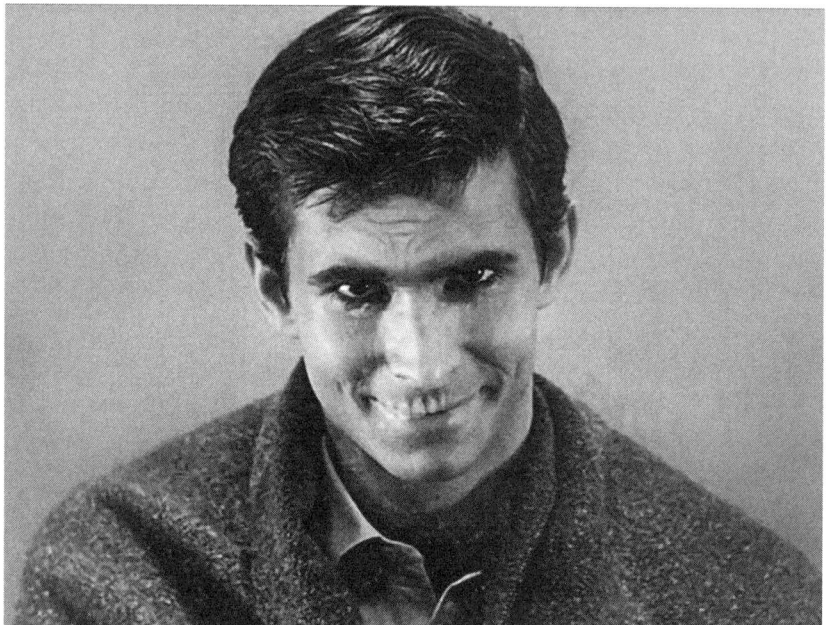

Example 9.4 An end without resolution: Norman, and a hint of the superimposed Mrs. Bates.

Herrmann could be describing his closing music for *Psycho*. As "Mrs. Bates's" voice-over ends, Norman breaks the fourth wall: his eyes raise, and look directly at us. He grins. A dissolve superimposes Marion's car, dredged by chains from the muck of the swamp, and then—*did I see that?*—a near-subliminal glimpse of Mrs. Bates's skull, layered over Norman's smiling face. "The Madhouse" blasts *fortissimo* as if the horror is starting over. Then *Psycho* ends with fifty musicians holding a brutal, strident chord—"a low, heavy, acidulous dissonance," wrote Christopher Palmer, "a chord without a resolution, a finale without an ending."[13]

March 16, 1960, was the kind of California day George Tomasini loved: 66 degrees and clear, as he and his assistant, Terry Williams, strolled from their edit bay to Paramount's scoring stage. After two months of cutting and re-cutting *Psycho*, both editors were eager to hear the score Benny had enthused about for weeks. It took seconds for Williams to reach a verdict.

"It scared the shit out of me. My God. Scared me at Paramount the first time I heard it, just watching the orchestra. I was there for a very short time, until Benny Herrmann threw his baton at one of the fiddle players. I thought it was time to leave. And George said, 'I think we best go over to Nicodell's'—a restaurant across the street—"and have a couple drinks."[14]

True, *Psycho*'s three days of recording were infused with familiar agitation. But the sound mixing sessions that followed were unprecedented, giving Herrmann his peak career triumph when it came to having final say. Hitchcock had not yet heard the cue Benny wrote for the shower scene. When the session reached that sequence, Hitchcock listened to a sound blend that reflected his instructions: Marion's screams, running water, and the slashing knife (made using "a big roast with gristle on the side," according to sound editor Danny Greene).[15] Then Hitchcock stated what was evident to all. The soundtrack wasn't powerful enough.

It was the moment Herrmann had waited for. "I said, 'I really do have something composed for it. And now that you've seen it your way, let's try mine.' We played him my version with the music. He said, 'Of course, that's the one we'll use.'"[16] In his excitement, Herrmann couldn't simply take the win—he needed to hear a concession. "I said [to Hitch], 'But you requested that we not add any music!' 'Improper suggestion, my boy, improper suggestion,' he replied."[17] The exchange became one of Herrmann's favorite anecdotes.

At mix sessions, audio was often played at high volume for maximum clarity. During the shower scene, recalled Danny Greene, "Hitchcock would say 'Okay, just have a hint of that, and keep the music up,' because the music was the thing that really made the scene. It enhanced it so much."[18]

> 2017. A weapon is raised, and a voice shrieks. Violins pierce the soundtrack as we see. . . . Bugs Bunny. Homer Simpson. M&M candies. Kittens. By the time the website TIFF Originals posts its "Psycho Shower Scene Mashup" on YouTube, featuring some of the scene's imitators, it is impossible to count the times that Hitchcock and Herrmann's creation has been parodied. The most abrasive sound in film music history has become internationally recognized shorthand—a way to laugh at our own vulnerability.
>
> Daniel Noah, film producer: My seven-year-old daughter knows that. She doesn't know what it comes from, but she's made that joke. [imitates violins] Nyeek! Nyeek! Nyeek! I don't know where she got it. It's evolutionary. We're just born knowing the shower scene.[19]

For Alfred Hitchcock, weeks of fear—of financial loss, and failure of creative vision—were replaced by excitement as post-production neared an end. Herrmann's score had transformed the film. Hitch loved the shower music so much that he replaced Benny's music for the reveal of Mrs. Bates with a third use of "The Murder." It was an effective choice, although the high violins buried a line of dialogue that few audiences ever hear. "I am Norma Bates!" Norman shouts as he appears in the cellar. The words once seemed important; music and visuals made them unnecessary.

"He called me when it was in its final cut with Bernard Herrmann," recalled Joseph Stefano. "I could hardly believe the greatness of that score. Heartbreaking music. So heartbreaking."[20] And "I had never heard of anybody doing a movie score with all strings. And when I heard it, of course, I realized what he had done. He had just taken everybody's guts and used them for music."[21]

In late spring 1960, a congregation of Hollywood power assembled for a screening of *Psycho*. Those present included Hitchcock, Janet Leigh, her husband Tony Curtis, Bernard Herrmann, Robert Bloch, *Psycho*'s crew and their partners, and Lew Wasserman.

For assistant director Hilton Green, the final version was astounding. "When the music came in, it just knocked people out of their seats."[22]

For assistant editor Terry Williams, it was "one of the most dramatic screenings I had ever been to. When Bernard Herrmann's score hit—Jesus, there were grown-up people, cast people that had been on the stage when that stuff had been shot, up and screeching." Script supervisor Marshall Schlom "was sitting in the back row with my wife, Mr. and Mrs. Hitchcock, and Hilton [Green] and his wife. . . . When Marty [Balsam] starts up the stairs and the camera pulled back, Mother's knife came in and Bernie Herrmann's music started shrieking, everybody came off their seats a good six inches! [Hitchcock] leaned forward and looked over at me. And in the darkness, with a little bit of twinkling light from the screen . . . he smiled."[23]

Even *Psycho*'s originator, author Robert Bloch, was shaken by the score. "I simply didn't know how to take it. It was . . . not the sort of thing one usually expected to accompany that kind of motion picture. It threw me for a loop. I was not prepared for such *screeching*."[24]

After the film, Bloch gave Hitchcock an ambivalent review. "I told him, 'I'll be frank. It's either going to be your biggest success or your biggest flop.' . . . Nobody could tell at that juncture how the public would react to something that graphic."²⁵

Lew Wasserman shared Bloch's opinion. To maximize profits—or mitigate failure—he suggested a novel release strategy: have Paramount book *Psycho* in a "pre-release engagement" in two New York theaters. After that, open the movie simultaneously in thousands of theaters. *Psycho* historian Stephen Rebello summed up the thinking: "If word of mouth buried the picture, it was reasoned, the Hitchcock name would at least lure in the faithful for a week or two."²⁶ Paramount followed Lew's advice, and Hitchcock built on it by forbidding pre-release screenings for critics. The ban was sure to trigger some negative reviews, but Hitch considered those preferable to plot spoilers from critics. *Psycho*, if it was anything, was an audience picture.

For decades it had been common for moviegoers to arrive midway through a showing, then stay through the next screening to see what they missed. To do so would undercut *Psycho*'s biggest surprise: Marion's murder. What began as a storytelling problem led to Hitch's most famous ad campaign. "No

Example 9.5 Hitch and Lew Wasserman confer outside the Bates Motel.

one ... BUT NO ONE ... will be admitted to the theater after the start of each performance of *Psycho*," read the edict on thousands of posters and theater standees.

If its content and its posters weren't radical enough, Hitchcock went a step further: *Psycho*'s trailer has no scenes from the movie. Instead, the director filmed an original six-and-a-half-minute preview in which he, in the style of his TV host intros, gives a wry but mysterious tour of the Bates house and motel. "In a flash there was the knife. And in no time, the victim fell with a horrible crack ... it was ... well, I won't dwell upon it. Come upstairs." On the soundtrack, cheerful stock music is gradually replaced by Herrmann's queasy underscore, culminating in the first public hearing of the shower music, as the film's title graphic appears.

In every part of *Psycho*'s promotion, Hitchcock made himself, and his three-decade track record as a storyteller, the main attraction. On June 16, 1960, he would find out if his bravest experiment had been worth the risk.

It opened in New York. The next morning, we got these stories from theater owners who were calling the distribution exchanges, telling them about people going berserk in the audience, running up and down the aisles. It was mayhem. They had to call the cops. —Marshall Schlom, script supervisor[27]

Must report three faintings at Paramount Theater and expect many more among trade when weeks' [box-office] figure published. —Boston film exhibitor[28]

A theater manager told me about a little boy who went to the first showing the day it opened. They emptied the theater and the little boy went back to every show that day. He kept running up and down the aisles yelling, "Oh my gosh, oh my gosh—wait till you see what's going to happen!" —Janet Leigh[29]

I saw people grabbing each other, howling, screaming, reacting like six-year-olds.... I couldn't believe what was happening.... When the shower sequence was over, paralysis set in. Nobody knew quite what to do. —Joseph Stefano[30]

The minute the [shower] curtain opened ... there was a sustained shriek from the audience. Psycho *is the moment in movies when, for the first time, movies weren't safe. —Peter Bogdanovich*[31]

Hitchcock was flummoxed by reports of hysteria. Furious letters poured into his office. Later, real-life killers claimed inspiration from *Psycho*. Recalled Anthony Perkins, "He was confused at first, incredulous second, and despondent third."[32]

By year's end, despondency changed to delight. The film that cost just over $800,000 had grossed $15 million—over $161 million today.[33] Most of that went to Hitchcock. True, many reviews were bad. "A blot on an honorable career," wrote the *New York Times*' Bosley Crowther—before Crowther reversed himself that December, putting it on his list of Ten Best Films of 1960. That year, *Time*'s reviewer lamented having to watch "one of the messiest, most nauseating murders ever filmed." In 1966, a different *Time* critic hailed *Psycho* as "superlative" and "masterly."

French critics-turned-filmmakers François Truffaut and Claude Chabrol hailed *Psycho* as a masterpiece. But pleased as Hitchcock was to be pocketing millions, he was puzzled that a movie made for so little, in haste, and without stars like Cary Grant or James Stewart outgrossed and overshadowed every film he'd ever made. According to its camera operator, Leonard South, *Psycho* "embarrassed" Hitchcock, who told him, "Here's this bloody piece of crap, and the money doesn't stop coming in."[34]

According to Dorothy Herrmann, Benny expressed a similar feeling in 1960. "When it first came out, I went to a showing with him. And he said, 'Did you ever see such crap?' Then when it became successful, he was really proud of it."[35] Herrmann, as ever, was a walking contradiction. His emotional connection with *Psycho* is inarguable: just listen to the score. And as Joseph Stefano observed, Benny "was the first person . . . who dug the movie, the first who said 'Oops—we've got something else here.'"[36] But as with Hitchcock, the hysteria it inspired, and its success relative to the cheapness of its production, initially stunned its composer.

So what changed minds between 1960 and 1970? Everything. With eerie prescience, *Psycho* anticipated the horrors of the decades ahead. Americans would witness real murder, captured live on TV. Government and other authority symbols could no longer be trusted, in the age of Dealey Plaza and Vietnam. And as homicides increased and nuclear weapons proliferated, the world feared what lay ahead. In *Psycho*, "Beneath the shock and suspense tactics lies a reservoir of profound understanding of the fragility of life," Stephen Rebello wrote.[37]

The same author perceptively wrote that Herrmann's music "would prove to be a summation of [his Hitchcock work] . . . conveying as it did the sense of the abyss that is the human psyche, dread, longing, regret—in short, the wellsprings of the Hitchcock universe."[38]

On February 27, 1961, Hitchcock received his fifth and final Best Director nomination from the Academy. He lost. Herrmann was not even nominated, nor were any of his Hitchcock scores. His lack of a single nomination since 1947 suggests the degree of enmity felt toward him by other composers and browbeaten producers. At least Hitchcock appreciated his contribution. The director who rarely praised collaborators told Joseph Stefano that "the music raised *Psycho's* impact by 33 percent." For Stefano, "it raised it for me by another 30."[39]

It has been written that Hitch was so pleased with Benny's work, he doubled Herrmann's salary, paying him an additional $17,500. Alas, that did not happen. *Psycho's* final cost report does show $17,500 in music fees on top of Herrmann's salary. But that extra amount went to the cost of musicians and recording.[40]

Even without bonus salary or awards, Herrmann's music for *Psycho* marked a turning point in his career. "The Murder" has become the best-known piece of film music ever written. But success had a shadow. Seldom would Herrmann be asked again to score a movie that wasn't a thriller or lacked an element of the macabre. And his separate resentments—the scarcity of symphony conducting offers, the ignoring of *Wuthering Heights*—festered and grew.

Lucy Anderson bore the brunt of his tirades, but they also cost him a daughter's affection. Wendy Herrmann, age fifteen, was so traumatized by her father's outbursts that she chose to remain each summer in Maryland with her mother Lucille and her stepfather, Douglas Wallop.[41]

Hollywood had undergone massive change in the five years since Benny and Hitch began their partnership. In 1956, Darryl F. Zanuck stepped away from the studio he founded, Twentieth Century–Fox. That same year, RKO closed, after years of mismanagement under Howard Hughes. Louis B. Mayer died in 1957, Columbia chief Harry Cohn in 1958. Of the moguls who built Hollywood in the 1920s, only Jack L. Warner remained.

For Herrmann, the most painful exit was that of Alfred Newman, who in 1960 ended his two-decade reign as Fox's musical director. Since 1943, Al had given Benny a safe space to compose seventeen scores, his most for any studio. Replacing Alfred was his brother Lionel, a talented, vulgar company man who liked his movie scores tuneful. "Benny couldn't write a tune to save his ass," Lionel said in 1984. "He was Charley Ostinato. After Al left Fox, Benny couldn't imagine being out of a job. But times changed."[42]

In 1960, that future was not yet apparent. Herrmann was relishing what he considered his rescue of *Psycho*, first by talking Hitch out of a radical cut-down for television, then by giving the shower scene such emotion that the sequence became a worldwide cause célèbre.

Hitchcock also spent 1960 reveling in success. *Psycho* inspired him to break his two-decade pattern of starting a new film as soon as its predecessor was delivered. Instead, he spent much of the year promoting his surprise blockbuster, on a four-continent press junket. But jocular interviews—*Psycho*, he now claimed, was a comedy—and lavish meals in Sydney, Tokyo, Paris, and Rome couldn't make him forget the question that Lew Wasserman asked, in what was meant to be a congratulatory telegram.[43]

"What will you do for an encore?"

10

Electronic Assassins

Ten P.M. was late for a phone call at the home of Miklós Rózsa. The Oscar-winning composer typically preferred his evenings quiet at his Spanish-style home in the Hollywood Hills. But after years of friendship with Bernard Herrmann, Rózsa knew that little about his caller was typical, or quiet.

Benny had returned from England. He "said he had a fantastic record and I had to hear it," Rózsa recalled. "I thought it would be Arthur Bliss or William Walton. He came over, put on the record, and I heard this inane stuff with guitars. I said, 'Benny, this is nonsense.' He said, 'No, no, don't say that. Listen to this modulation!' He was in ecstasy."[1]

In spring 1961, during a trip to conduct the BBC Northern Orchestra, Herrmann visited a nightclub in Liverpool, where he heard the pop musicians he later extolled to Rózsa. After the show, he met the band: Paul McCartney, John Lennon, George Harrison, and Pete Best.[2] Herrmann returned to Los Angeles with a demo by the group, which he also played for Norman Lloyd. "Benny said, 'This is worthy of Beethoven.' I remember that specific quote. He had great recognition of their extraordinary gifts."[3]

"I thought the Beatles had something new and different to offer," Herrmann recalled. "I took them to all the big powers in town—and they all laughed at me. I took it to Universal and CBS, and they said, 'There's nothing in that crap.' They could've had them for a slight sum of money, but no one was interested."[4]

That Herrmann was among the Beatles' first champions in America is ironic, given his own career status in 1961. Few in Hollywood associated him with commercial viability, or for that matter basic civility. On June 11, Herrmann turned fifty. The gap between his youthful ambitions—a life of conducting, a substantial body of concert music—and the path his life had taken exacerbated his hair-trigger temper. "Benny would watch run-throughs of pictures," Norman Lloyd recalled, "and afterwards he would say, 'Not me! I won't score this shit!' He could have turned it down, but he made a point that no one misunderstood his turning it down. I would say, 'Benny, you're going to run out of studios.'"[5]

Example 10.1 Herrmann, early 1960s.

By 1961, the composer once considered a film pioneer now received few offers outside of Hitchcock and Harryhausen. And even those two supporters couldn't escape his rages about the system. "Benny didn't spare Hitch when it came to yelling and screaming," observed his friend Joan Greenwood.[6]

At the same time, more amenable composers like Max Steiner, Franz Waxman, and Hugo Friedhofer also were finding themselves sidelined. A new generation of directors, like Blake Edwards, Sidney Lumet, and Tony Richardson, preferred working with younger talent. Film music was sounding less like old-school European Romanticism, thanks to jazz- and pop-inflected scores from such innovators as Elmer Bernstein (*Sweet Smell of Success*), John Barry (the James Bond series), and Henry Mancini (*Peter Gunn, Breakfast at Tiffany's*).

As work offers dwindled, Herrmann complained loudly and often about what he saw as the debasement of cinema. His state of mind was reflected in the sad saga of *Tender Is the Night*. Fox's screen version of F. Scott Fitzgerald's novel starred Jennifer Jones, a decade too old to play an emotionally troubled flapper. Directing what would be his final film was silent-era veteran Henry King, age seventy-five. A friend of Herrmann, King asked him to write the score. Benny said yes. But when producer Henry T. Weinstein insisted that he incorporate a title song by Sammy Fain and Paul Francis Webster, Herrmann resigned.

The job then went to Lyn Murray, the composer who had recommended Benny to Hitch for *The Trouble with Harry*. Murray had been a Herrmann disciple since the two worked side by side at CBS Radio in the 1940s. He was a frequent guest at Bluebell Avenue, where the pair watched TV wrestling while discussing Debussy. But one afternoon in 1960, Lyn was stunned when his friend of two decades launched into a spittle-spewing evisceration of a Murray composition. The friendship finally broke after a phone call that November: Herrmann was enraged that he hadn't been invited to an election-night party at Lyn's celebrating JFK's victory. (Murray knew Herrmann was politically conservative.)[7]

Benny's unkindest act came when Murray was assigned *Tender Is the Night*. Lyn had just begun work on the score when he learned that he was suddenly off the picture. A desperate Herrmann had met with Henry King, and begged "with tears in his eyes"[8] to be reassigned. He got his wish—but the lumbering drama was dead on arrival when it opened in 1962. (Around the same time, Benny turned down what might have been a game changer: *Lolita*.[9] Its thirty-three-year-old director, Stanley Kubrick, had been a Herrmann fan since *Citizen Kane*. But the composer refused to incorporate a love theme written by Bob Harris, brother of Kubrick's producing partner, James B. Harris.)

Herrmann never worked at Twentieth Century–Fox again. When its new music director, Lionel Newman, bluntly told him that directors didn't want him—that Fox was "running with the kids now"—Herrmann answered with obscenities, and a slammed door. Outside Newman's office, he saw music editor Richard Berres, with whom he'd had a long, friendly relationship. "You guys don't wanna work with me?" Herrmann snarled at the puzzled Berres. "Fuck you."[10]

According to Elmer Bernstein, the attitude of studio music heads "was never lack of respect. But they'd prefer not to get involved with him. I don't think Benny meant to alienate anybody—but you just don't tell a director his film is a piece of crap. What's the point? You're just going to make an enemy of someone who may make a really good film next time. But Benny couldn't do that. It was almost as if he couldn't stand emotional prosperity. Any time he became emotionally prosperous, he would do something to bring him down."[11]

For Taffy, Herrmann's outbursts were a sign of an inferiority complex. "I don't think my father ever forgot the words of *his* father to Daddy's brother: 'Louis, you will always have to take care of your brother, because he will never be able to take care of himself.'"[12] For his part, Louis believed that his brother suffered from porphyria. A disorder caused by the buildup of various chemicals in the body, its symptoms included irritability, anxiety, and paranoia.[13]

Accurate or not, each of those qualities would be manifest in Herrmann's behavior during the next five years, with disastrous results.

By the autumn of 1961, Herrmann's pessimism was echoed by a nation on edge. The US invasion of Cuba had ended in disaster, emboldening Nikita Khrushchev. On August 13, Soviet-controlled East Germany began building the Berlin Wall.

Five days later, a curious incident in California caught the attention of Alfred Hitchcock. Along the coastline south of San Francisco, locals in Santa Cruz were alarmed by the sight of thousands of seabirds slamming into homes and other buildings. "Dead and stunned seabirds littered the streets and roads in the foggy early dawn," the local paper reported.[14] No reason for the birds' behavior could be found.*[15]

The news bolstered Hitchcock's recent decision that a short story he'd optioned—"The Birds" by Daphne du Maurier—would be his next film.

Unusually, Hitch had been flirting with several science fiction titles, in his quest for material that could somehow top *Psycho*. After selecting *The Birds*, he turned to one of sci-fi's most popular authors. "Hitchcock offered me *The Birds*," Ray Bradbury recalled. "I went to see him at Paramount, and I said, 'I like it very much. I think I could do a good job for you.'" But Bradbury was fully booked, on projects that included writing for Hitch's TV show. "I asked, 'Can you wait for me?' Well, Hitchcock couldn't wait for Hitchcock. And I'm really sorry, because the film is not everything it should be."[16]

The writer Hitch finally chose, Evan Hunter, had hit a bullseye with baby boomers in 1955, with his script for *The Blackboard Jungle*, a juvenile

---

* At least not until 2012, when scientists deduced that the birds had eaten a plant organism that can cause "confusion, disorientation . . . and even death."

delinquent drama that introduced Bill Haley's "Rock around the Clock." Hitch liked Hunter's idea of starting *The Birds* as a romantic comedy, then gradually escalating the menace. They moved its setting from the British seacoast in du Maurier's original to Bodega Bay near San Francisco, an area Hitchcock loved, and close to the Santa Cruz bird "attack." But despite months of meetings between director and writer, Hunter's characters—spoiled socialite Melanie Daniels, handsome lawyer Mitch Brenner, Mitch's over-protective mother Lydia—refused to come to life. Hitchcock needed what Ernest Lehman, Joseph Stefano, and John Michael Hayes had given him: engaging characters, and a compelling story to link Hitch's set pieces—here, the attacks by his avian stars.

By 1961, more than *The Birds* was on Hitchcock's mind. Paramount was scaling back, after a string of flops that echoed the downturns of MGM and Fox. In 1958, Paramount sold most of its pre-1950 movies to an eager buyer: MCA.[17] The talent agency–production company quickly monetized those films with sales to television. In 1959, Paramount had urged Hitchcock

Example 10.2 The "only stars" of *The Birds*. Publicity still, 1963.

not to make *Psycho*. Wasn't that proof, Hitch wondered, that it was time to move on?

Lew Wasserman thought so. During *The Birds*' pre-production, the executive considered by many "a messiah at the time when the original movie moguls were literally dropping dead"[18] urged Hitchcock to make another bold move. Come to Universal, Wasserman told his friend. The studio was already producing Hitch's television series, and MCA owned the entire backlot. It's likely that over a Dover sole at Chasen's, Lew also confided to Hitchcock his ultimate goal: to have MCA buy Universal in its entirety.

Psycho convinced the director that he had begun a new golden age in his career.[19] With a fortune amassed in savings and stock, Hitchcock knew he need never worry about money again. What mattered now was retaining his power and freedom as a filmmaker. After months of indecision, Hitchcock finally agreed with Wasserman. Universal was his future.

If the 400 acres of Universal Studios was a city within a city—an incorporated municipality, Universal City had its own police station and hospital—Hitchcock's new offices would be a fiefdom within it. Lew agreed to build Hitch a private compound. It encompassed, as Stephen Rebello wrote, "a capacious suite of offices filled with antiques; rooms for editing, art, costumes, and conferences; a twenty-seat screening room; a kitchenette and private dining room."[20] Universal would pay for it all.

Assistant Peggy Robertson was at her boss's side as he planned each room. "Hitch said, 'That'll be good for the art department. . . . There's the cutting room all ready.' . . . There was a little office in the front. He said, 'Let's take this wall down and have a secretary there, answering the telephones and greeting people as they come in.' "[21] Peggy would have her own office next to Hitchcock—even her own private bathroom, accented in beige marble.

The director who dreaded walking through a crowded studio commissary could now enjoy meals in a private dining room, prepared by a gourmet cook. The décor was antique English, an extension of his home on Bellagio Drive.

In February 1962, Hitchcock, Peggy, and Sue Gauthier officially moved into what would be their creative home for the rest of their careers. Five months later, after months of antitrust negotiations in Washington, MCA agreed to sell its talent agency, in order to attain full ownership of Universal Studios.[22] The deal marked a new era in Hollywood—one in which studios

Example 10.3 Assistant Peggy Robertson takes careful notes as usual, 1968.

like Universal, founded in 1912, became mere assets for sale, their value a fraction of a corporation's vast portfolio.

Hitchcock's new position seemed a boon for all around him. But there was one dissenting voice.

On February 21, 1962, Herrmann visited the new offices for lunch with Hitch. He had just scored *Cape Fear* for Universal; that film's producers also used George Tomasini, to make their thriller as Hitchcockian as possible. But Herrmann regarded Hitch's move to Universal with suspicion. To him, Lew Wasserman was an ice-blooded adding machine whose sole talent was making money.[23] His concern added a fresh source of pessimism to Herrmann's darkening worldview.

At Universal, Hitchcock continued developing *The Birds*. He was unnerved by its swelling budget, mostly for special effects. To keep costs under

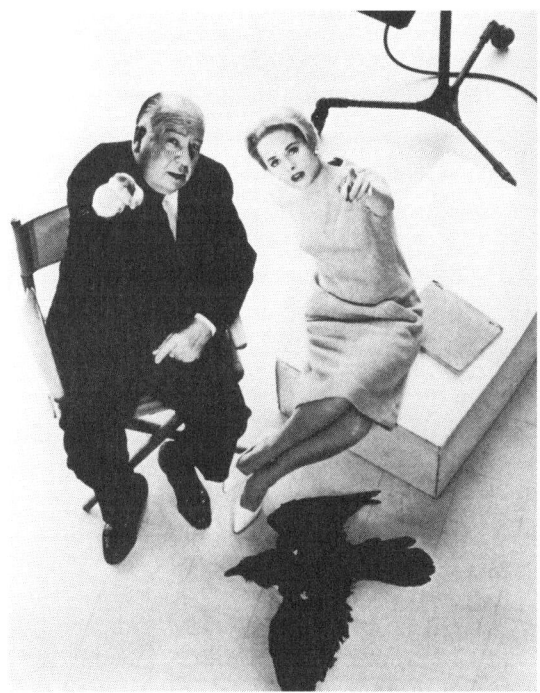

Example 10.4 The ultimate filmmaking course: Hitch and Tippi Hedren, c. 1962.

Example 10.5 Filming *The Birds*' finale, 1962.

$3 million, Hitch dismissed his early casting ideas of Audrey Hepburn and Cary Grant. He decided that "the only stars in this movie are the birds and me."[24] That led Hitchcock to gamble on an experiment he'd long pondered. Could he take an unknown actress, preferably one with few preconceptions about the craft, and mold her into another Bergman or Kelly, minus the demands that came with a star?

After Hitch spotted an attractive blonde in a TV commercial, he had his chance to find out. His decision in 1961 to put thirty-one-year-old model Nathalie Kay Hedren under contract hardly seemed momentous. But over the next three years, it would impact his work, his personal life, and his relationship with Herrmann.

Assessing Hedren's performance in *The Birds*, Benny did not share the director's enthusiasm for the Eileen Ford model, whose family nickname was now her acting name: 'Tippi' Hedren (Hitchcock added the single quotes). But Herrmann *was* intrigued in the spring of 1962 when Hitch shared with him a radical idea for *The Birds*' musical score.

There would be no musical score.

Months earlier, Hitch's most vocal admirer in France, director François Truffaut, released *Jules and Jim*. Its jump-cutting freshness, and critics' evaluation of it as a work of art, fueled Hitchcock's desire to take more chances. *The Birds*' soundtrack, one in which bird sounds took the place of score, gave him a way to do so.

By April 1962, he had found a way to achieve his aim. A letter had arrived from Remi Gassmann, an American-born composer who specialized in writing for electronic instruments.[25] Gassmann and his colleague, Oskar Sala, followed a path begun in the 1920s, a time when machines offered new musical colors and abstract sounds. The most famous of these was the theremin, invented by the Russian Leon Theremin. His instrument emitted buzzing pitches when a player moved a hand between two antennae. By the 1950s, electronics were also expanding the sonic possibilities of familiar instruments—most notably electric guitars.

Encouraged by his friend, designer Saul Bass, Gassmann urged Hitchcock to use one of these experimental devices: the Studio Trautonium. "Familiar sounds—from common noise to music and esoteric effects—as well as an almost limitless supply of completely unfamiliar sounds, can now be electronically produced, controlled, and utilized for film purposes. The result is much like a new dimension in film production."[26]

The trautonium had been devised three decades earlier by Dr. Friedrich Trautwein in Berlin. In 1961, Sala and Gassmann used it to compose a stage work for the New York City Ballet. "The future is here," wrote critic Louis Biancolli of the result. "This stuff is really terrifying in its potentialities."[27]

Ideally, Hitchcock thought, electronic sounds could provide the precise sounds he wanted. The birds' shrieks and caws could be manipulated, to give rhythm and shape to a sequence instead of music. It's hard not to wonder if there was another agenda in Hitchcock's mind. His previous film had been saved by music. As grateful as he was for the *Psycho* score, pride may have led him to prove that he didn't need music to have a hit.

At Hitch's instruction, Peggy Robertson sent Gassmann's letter to Herrmann. Rather than feel threatened, Benny was enthusiastic. After all, when it came to electronic music, he too had been a pioneer.

January 1938. A microphone hovers over the players assembled for this week's live broadcast of The Columbia Workshop, *CBS Radio's most experimental series. The "orchestra" consists of saws, hammers, and nails. Their electronically recorded rhythms make up Herrmann's score for "The House That Jack Didn't Build," the* Workshop's *poetic dramatization of Depression-era housing problems. Notes a columnist in 1938, "Herrmann is not satisfied with his accomplishments hereto. And now he is planning to write a musical score to portray 'silence.' "*[28]

May 1941. On RKO's cavernous music stage, a lone violinist sits under a mic, his ears focused on the steady rhythmic "click" heard in the headphones he wears. He plays a tune sprightly and familiar: "Pop Goes the Weasel." Nearby, twenty-nine-year-old Benny Herrmann signals approval, and the violinist swaps his pages for new ones. From the booth, an engineer slates a new take. The violinist again plays "Pop Goes the Weasel," but not its melody. Instead, he plays an accompaniment for the tune: dancing triplets and flashy, upward-sliding glissandos. The violinist then plays another set of variations. And another. The "click" in his headphones ensures that all four recordings will perfectly synchronize. Days later, Herrmann is delighted as he listens to the four violin tracks, now combined.[29]

In All That Money Can Buy—*the supernatural fantasy that will win Herrmann an Oscar—Mr. Scratch, aka the Devil, haunts the life of Jabez Stone, the New Hampshire farmer whose soul he has bought. On the night*

Example 10.6 Benny experiments, with director William Dieterle, on *All That Money Can Buy* (1941).

Jabez becomes a father, Mr. Scratch "celebrates" with townsfolk at a barn dance. Perched in the rafters, the Devil plays the fiddle. "We had to have something that Mr. Scratch could play, a fiddle reel that nobody else could play," Herrmann explains. "So I had what I thought was a pretty brilliant idea, because since then it's become very popular. I simply imposed a series of tracks on top of each other." *He explains how the four tracks were combined* "to make one violin, playing the most impossible things that no one violinist could ever play."[30]

Weeks earlier, he captures an even more innovative sound: the music of electricity. At 4 A.M., he and a recording engineer stand in darkness under a telephone power line in the San Fernando Valley. After a few minutes, the engineer turns off his machine. He has recorded the sound of "singing" phone wires. The sound will be used in All That Money Can Buy: *the wires' soft, eerie hum provides the "score" for the first appearance of Mr. Scratch in the barn of Jabez Stone, where Jabez will sign the contract for his soul with his blood.*[31]

July 1951. Having recorded two theremins, electric violin, electric bass, and other offbeat instruments for the main title of The Day the Earth Stood Still, *Herrmann moves on to something even more unusual. Brass and vibraphone dissonances are recorded. Then the track is played backward, to evoke the stoppage of electrical power on earth. Fifteen years later, the Beatles will use similar techniques on* Revolver, Sgt. Pepper's Lonely Hearts Club Band, *and other albums.*[32]

"Bernie had a thing he used to say about motion picture music," recalls James G. Stewart, sound recordist on Citizen Kane and All That Money Can Buy. "He'd say, 'It isn't music. It's just musical sound effects.' "[33]

Hitchcock and Herrmann wanted a test of exactly what the trautonium could offer *The Birds*. In May 1962, the director sent 750 feet of film to Gassmann and Sala. It was one full sequence: the bird attack on Lydia Brenner's home, which sets the story's final act in motion. The choice was perfect since the birds are only heard, never shown. Sound would be the sequence's most critical element.

As Gassmann and Sala began their audition, Herrmann looked forward to a brief vacation from thrillers. That spring he traveled to London, to conduct the BBC Concert Orchestra and the Royal Philharmonic Orchestra. In autumn, the Philharmonic would be used to record Herrmann's *Jason and the Argonauts* score for Harryhausen. In a likely act of reciprocity, Herrmann conducted the Philharmonic on May 18, in a well-received concert featuring his beloved Elgar's *Enigma Variations*. Herrmann's film music of the time was usually charged with dread. In Elgar's score—a tribute to the composer's friends, whom Elgar depicts in a series of variations on a theme—Herrmann found escape from tension, achieving the closest thing in his life to ecstasy.

In Benny's absence, Hitchcock deemed Oskar Sala and Remi Gassmann's demo a success. By late October the pair were hired to work on *The Birds* in its entirety. Hitch's usual "sound notes" were unique, as they detailed each sequence's bird sounds to ensure a changing palette of audio textures.

For the main titles, he suggested trying "wing noises only with a variation of volume and a variation in the expression of it in terms of rhythm."[34] For the attack on a children's birthday party, he urged Sala and Gassmann "to watch that the screams of the children and the screams of the gulls do not sound the same." The sparrows that fly down the chimney into the Brenner home "should have a quality of shrill anger as though the birds [were] almost screaming at the occupants." For the attic sequence in which Melanie (Hedren) is attacked, he was most specific. "It is very essential . . . that we give the sound a quality that gives this volume but is not of such a serious quality as to cause the people downstairs to be awakened by it." Perhaps most challenging was sound for the unresolved ending, in which the protagonists escape by car from a screen-filling army of birds, seemingly waiting to attack. For this, Hitchcock wanted "the equivalent of a brooding silence."

The same week that Hitchcock penned these notes, *The Birds'* apocalyptic tone was mirrored in reality. On October 22, 1962, Benny joined Hitch, George Tomasini, and Remi Gassmann for a meeting at Universal. Hours later, at 4 P.M. Pacific Time, John F. Kennedy told the world on live television that the Soviet Union had placed nuclear missiles in Cuba—and that a launch of them would lead to a "full retaliatory response" from the United States.

In 1949, the Soviets' test of an atomic bomb had sent Herrmann into an emotional panic.[35] His reaction to 1962's threat of nuclear war was likely just as strong. Anxieties eased on October 28, when Khrushchev announced that the missiles in Cuba would be removed. But the episode reinforced for Hitch and Benny that *The Birds*, with its violent, unpredictable vision of humanity under attack, was the right movie at the right time.

As the specificity of his notes shows, Hitchcock could have dispensed with Herrmann's services on the film. But friendship aside, Hitch knew that Benny would bring an astute ear to the pitch and rhythm of the trautonium's bird simulations. If the effects sounded too much alike, the result would be monotony rather than suspense.

"I hope to make a deal with Bernard Herrmann," Hitch told Truffaut that August. "Of course he's a very temperamental fellow, you know, very temperamental—to supervise the sound of the whole picture, because you often hear musicians when they compose or they orchestrate, they talk of making sounds, which is what they really do."[36]

Herrmann was delighted to be hired as "Sound Consultant." Even better was news that Hitch wanted him at his side that December when he flew to West Berlin. There they would listen as Sala, the main composer, and Gassmann played back their final effects. Herrmann loved opportunities to have exclusive time with Hitchcock, and their experience in Germany would be their happiest and closest since the shooting of *The Man Who Knew Too Much* in London.

On December 14, the pair flew together from Los Angeles to Copenhagen, then on to Hamburg, where they arrived on December 15. There, Hitch visited one of his first leading ladies, the beautiful German blonde Anny Ondra, who starred in *The Manxman* and *Blackmail*. At 4:30 P.M. the same day, he and Benny flew to West Berlin.[37] There, they were joined by George Tomasini. The genial editor had arrived on December 4, and would be the principal note-taker during the sessions.

Herrmann had just one concern about the trip: he dreaded being surrounded by ex-Nazis. "He was violently anti-German," recalled Charles Schneer, Ray Harryhausen's producer. So strong was Herrmann's feeling that he refused to ride in Schneer's German-made Mercedes.[38]

But Hitchcock's company softened those tensions. The director always traveled first class, and Benny relaxed in the plush accommodations of the Berlin Hilton. Over dinners the two men could have far-ranging conversations, more relaxed than their single-minded problem solving in Los Angeles. *The Birds* inevitably was discussed, as Herrmann shared ideas on how to enhance Hitch's goal to differentiate each attack. "It was the one Hitchcock film Benny talked about a lot," said director Alastair Reid, a later collaborator. "He regarded himself as one of its prime movers, almost a co-director."[39]

The paperwork that emerged, from four days of sessions in Oskar Sala Sound Studios, testifies to an experience unlike any that Hitch, Benny, and George had before. Traditionally, film music timings are broken down into "cue sheets." They list, to the twenty-fourth fraction of a second, what music will be heard when an onscreen action occurs. *The Birds* would have cue sheets, but these would notate electronic effects, not music.

For the main title, the sheet breaks down the entrance and exit of "vocals and flutters"—the first imitation bird sounds heard over the Universal logo. Listening to the result, it's clear what excited Hitch and Benny. The sounds are close enough to bird calls to be recognizable. But there is a cold, mechanistic quality to the cries that unsettles the listener. Soft and distant at first, the cawing and fluttering wings are *forte* (loud) and abrasive as credits appear. Black crows flap across the screen left to right, their movement motivating the forming and breaking up of each word of text in the credits. The bird calls range from low to high in timbre; and Herrmann could not have missed the similarity between the reverberant, high-pitched gull calls and the stabbing violins of *Psycho*'s shower murder.

The Birds' cue sheets confirm the complexity of sounds that were made, then blended. The most complicated sequence was the birds' attack on the diner, where Melanie becomes trapped inside a phone booth (she becomes the bird in the "gilded cage" that Mitch mockingly called her early in the film). For the attack on the Brenner home, the cue sheet lists "single flutters . . . swarm effect . . . single [bird] vocals . . . window . . . wood pecks . . . scratching . . . flutters (departure of birds)."[40] Benny's input is reflected in a list of additional requested sounds. "Two low tones for Bernard Herrmann . . . one very high effect, for Bernard Herrmann . . . one shrill motif, for Bernard Herrmann." The fluidity of the creative process is clear from handwritten scribbles on small squares of paper: "First bird over Cathy starts too late. . . . Low bass throb inaudible. . . . Cut the flutters in half—add rhythmic waves of flutters to climax at door."

During the sessions, Hitchcock the showman posed for photos in which he stands by the Studio Trautonium, wincing in supposed agony. His real feelings were conveyed in a telegram to Peggy Robertson on December 20: "WORK IN BERLIN COMPLETED TO MY SATISFACTION / HITCH."[41]

Example 10.7 Hitch and Oskar Sala find new sounds for *The Birds*, West Berlin, December 1962.

Example 10.8 Hitch "prepares" moviegoers for the trautonium.

The director left Germany for St. Moritz, Switzerland, the site of his annual Christmas vacation with Alma. For Herrmann, life at home was far less tranquil.

Lucy Anderson was growing weary, after thirteen years of Benny's verbal abuse and mood shifts. "Lucy would make us dinner," recalled musician Victor Bay, "and we'd sit down. Benny would say, 'Y'know, let's go to a movie.' She would get dressed. And then he'd say, 'On the other hand, maybe we should listen to that symphony here.' So she would take off her overcoat and sit down. Then he'd say, 'Let's go to the movie after all.' That went on fourteen times."[42]

"Lucy would do things to please him," said actress Kathryn Corwin. "She was very devoted to him, and he was very difficult to her. I wouldn't hesitate to scold him when I saw him getting sharp with Lucy. I'd say, 'Lucy, don't take that—answer back!' She was dignified and quiet. I would have been far less so."[43]

Even Herrmann's talent became a source of pain. "Since he composed at home, and always wanted me near at hand, his music became an integral part of our years together," Lucy told the author in 1984. His intensity during the process of creation left her "emotionally distraught."[44]

In a reversal of the events that brought them together, Herrmann was finding greater peace in the company of Lucy's cousin—his first wife, Lucille Fletcher. Benny would visit Fletcher and her husband in their Maryland home. Returning to Bluebell Avenue, he was often depressed and resentful. One day, while daughter Taffy was visiting, she found herself in "one of the few deep talks that I ever had with my father. It was in his garden, as he was tending to his roses. He confessed that it was a terrible mistake for him and my mother to have ever gotten a divorce. And she also confessed the same thing to me. That was the tragedy of both people's lives, that they gave up a marriage in which they really understood each other."[45]

Herrmann's gnawing sense that his life had gone off track, and that the future offered slim hope of change, was uncannily reflected in the tone of his film and TV projects. And while *The Twilight Zone* offered the most poetic outlet for his ruminations, another television series—overseen and hosted by Alfred Hitchcock—gave him seventeen opportunities to translate his pessimism into music.

Those scores remain the most neglected part of the Hitchcock-Herrmann canon. An exploration of them reveals gems worthy of a Hitchcock feature, created at a time when Benny's career options were becoming ominously few.

11
Murder by Television

In 1963, Bernard Herrmann composed no film scores. A conducting career in America seemed a hopeless dream, as did a staged production of *Wuthering Heights*. Any interest shown by producers in the over-three-hour opera was squelched by Herrmann's refusal to cut a single bar.

Instead, he found other creative outlets. Spring brought concerts with the Royal Philharmonic, at one of London's most prestigious venues, the Royal Festival Hall. And in Los Angeles, Benny and Hitch met for lunch, to discuss a new project—their first that was not a film.

In the eight years since *Alfred Hitchcock Presents* bowed on television, producers Joan Harrison and Norman Lloyd, who joined Harrison during Season 3, brought racehorse skill to the workhorse task of making 268 episodes. After seven seasons, the half-hour show expanded in 1962 into *The Alfred Hitchcock Hour*. "It was greatly to MCA's advantage to have us go to an hour," Lloyd recalled. With more minutes for ads, "they got more money."[1]

The expansion altered more than running time and ad dollars. The half-hour show specialized in darkly comic irony; depth of characterization was secondary to a strong twist ending. No episode reflected that tone better than "Lamb to the Slaughter," in which Barbara Bel Geddes's frustrated housewife kills her straying husband by clobbering his skull with a frozen leg of lamb. Her guilt goes undetected by investigating police, who accept her invite to stay for dinner. The entrée she serves is the murder weapon, eliminated bite by bite by her guests. As one cop discusses the mysteriously missing instrument of death, he remarks, "It may be right under our noses." Bel Geddes smiles. Fade-out.

While some episodes had pathos, the switch to one hour let Harrison and Lloyd tell stories that, at their best, rivaled feature films in their suspense and nuance of character. The content also grew darker. Airing from September 1962 to May 1965, the *Hitchcock Hour* was a mirror of existential fears, like the Cuban Missile Crisis; the assassination of a US president; the murder of his apparent killer on live TV; and a growing distrust of government, as

American involvement in Vietnam escalated. Violent crime jumped 126 percent during the decade. From 1962 to 1964, a serial killer dubbed the Boston Strangler murdered thirteen women in their homes. And by the mid-1960s, over half of the US population was under thirty. For them, *Psycho* was Hitchcock's defining work. Since its release, onscreen violence had been normalized by that movie's endless imitators.

Despite its star-filled guest roster, the Hitchcock TV show was tightly budgeted for maximum profit. Underscoring was minimal in the half-hour shows; to save costs, MCA hired composer Dave Kahn to create a library of reusable cues.[2] His dramatic music was, at best, serviceable. And his comic cues—often used after the final twist is revealed—were cartoonishly broad, down to a trumpet "wah-wah" better suited to a sitcom. (Kahn also scored MCA's *Leave It to Beaver*.)

But one choice of music was perfect. Each episode opened with the image of Hitchcock's famous self-caricature in profile. The series title appears over it—then from screen right, Hitch's corpulent shadow steps into the caricature. On the soundtrack we hear a fanfarial arrangement of "Funeral March of a Marionette," written in 1872 by Charles Gounod. Just as Rossini's "William Tell" was co-opted by *The Lone Ranger*, Gounod's tune became Hitch's musical signature. Norman Lloyd believed that Herrmann suggested the piece, but the choice may have been the boss's. In 1966, when arts critic Christopher Frayling spotted the director standing near him, Frayling hummed Gounod's "March." Hitchcock "turned and said, 'Sunrise.'"[3] Frayling understood: the "March" was used in the score for F. W. Murnau's 1927 silent drama *Sunrise*, an influential film for Hitchcock. (*Sunrise* premiered just as talkies became popular, and was released with an orchestral soundtrack.)

With its cinematic montages, wordless suspense sequences, and often complex characters, *The Alfred Hitchcock Hour* needed original musical support. Also, MCA and Hitch's TV company, Shamley Productions, were facing pressure from the musicians' union.[4] The result was an extraordinary flowering of composing talent at Universal.

Heading its TV music department was forty-five-year-old Stanley Wilson, a soft-spoken man of exceptional taste when it came to hiring composers. Wilson used the rise in TV music to help launch the careers of many future A-listers. Inside his department "there were five or six rooms, little rooms with no windows," recalled John Williams, then at the dawn of his career. "Each room had a little piano. And on any given day I would be in one room, Jerry Goldsmith in the next one, Lalo Schifrin in the next one, Quincy Jones in the next one . . . and the late Bernard Herrmann, who made it his home for a couple of years and wrote some great music and drove everyone crazy. It was a situation where we taught each other and learned from each other."[5]

Wilson was delighted when Hitchcock's TV team began commissioning several original scores for each season. Lyn Murray rejoined the fold to compose Season 1's opener, "A Piece of the Action," co-starring Robert Redford. Murray would be the *Hour*'s busiest composer, scoring twenty-three of its ninety-three episodes.

By 1963, a year into the *Hour*'s run, Herrmann's calendar was nearly blank. "He was persona non grata almost everywhere," said Lloyd,[6] who, like Hitchcock, saw opportunity. From summer 1963 to spring 1965, Benny wrote scores for seventeen episodes, all for Seasons 2 and 3. His music, like the other composers', became part of a new, superior library, to be reused on episodes without original scores. Herrmann was proud to be part of what he called "one of the greatest television shows ever done."[7] His iconic brand of brooding menace would raise several episodes to the rank of classics.

He was delighted to work again with the witty, multitalented Lloyd, a former actor in Welles's Mercury Theater who had met Herrmann in 1937. "I loved Benny, and we had a long history together. He made me laugh, and my experiences with him were always good ones."[8] After being directed by Welles, Hitchcock, Chaplin, and Renoir, Lloyd would helm several of the *Hour*'s best episodes.

Hitchcock did not direct any of the Herrmann shows, but his involvement as producer made them true collaborations. The process of Hitch's participation was consistent. First, Harrison and Lloyd gave him synopses of the episodes they wanted to produce, most of them based on existing stories. (Those had an edge since their dramatic problems were already solved.)[9] Hitchcock had known Harrison since 1933. She "was like his daughter," Lloyd recalled. "She was a lovely lady, immaculately coiffed, she had beautiful clothes all the time. She'd offer people a cup of tea. [Being with her] you felt like you were civilized for a moment."[10] Lloyd was a friend of Hitchcock since 1942, and the trio's shared sensibility led Hitch to approve most of their synopses.

Recalled Lloyd, "When I was acting in *Saboteur* [as the spy who falls off the Statue of Liberty], he was always very giving of the reasons behind everything he did. Why this shot, and what the edits would be." As a result, Lloyd and Harrison developed "what you might call the Hitchcock point of view on material."[11]

Example 11.1 Hitch with Joan Harrison, chief producer of *Alfred Hitchcock Presents* and, with Norman Lloyd, *The Alfred Hitchcock Hour*.

A story synopsis might inspire additions from Hitch—one extra plot twist, or how to film a scene for maximum shock. Scripts were then written, and shot in six days. When a rough cut was ready, Hitchcock viewed it in his projection room. "Everything went by him," Lloyd said. "You never took a rough cut in for scoring or dubbing until he saw it. And he was never rude. If the rough cut was very good, he would say, 'It was good.' And if it was very bad, he'd say, 'It's okay. All right. Fine.'"[12] As with his features, he left music to his composers, and was happy to have Herrmann in the fold. "We knew Benny was his favorite composer. [Herrmann] had a sense of the theatrical in relation to story—this, plus exquisite taste."[13]

Due to the pace of television, Benny had only days to write each score; and each would be recorded in a single, four-and-a-half-hour session. "He did feel the pressures of the schedule," recalled John Williams. "He orchestrated everything himself. [But] his technique was solid. You could say the music is very 'vertical' in the way it's constructed, very repetitive and rhythmically simple, so that the 'horizontal' [forward-moving] aspect of it could be very insistent; it could drive a film in a very powerful way."[14]

Herrmann was given an ideal launch with Season 2's premiere, "A Home Away from Home," written by Robert Bloch (*Psycho*). Ray Milland starred as a sanitarium inmate who locks up the staff, deputizes patients, and kills the

Example 11.2 Benny in the studio, 1960.

head administrator. He then impersonates the man he murdered when the dead man's niece (Claire Griswold) pays an unexpected visit. Herrmann uses twenty strings, one harp, and a timpanist to create a throat-grabbing score, both lush and astringent, that is worthy of a feature. It delivers what the series had lacked: the sound world of a Hitchcock movie.

His kaleidoscopic scoring of the doctor's murder anticipates his 1966 music for *Fahrenheit 451*. As the victim is strangled, *pizzicato* strings hop anxiously like scampering bugs; harp glissandos cascade in wave-like hysteria; and skipping chords on vibraphone sound like the mocking laugh of a deranged child.

WILLIAM STROMBERG: *Clearly he told the vibraphone player to nail the hell out of that instrument with a hard mallet. It makes it sound clunky, like a xylophone, and it has a very fast vibrato [echo]. The music itself is crazy. And like* Psycho, *you've been introduced to a new character—the killer—with this music.*[15]

Later, as niece Natalie walks alone in the estate gathering clues, timpani and harp whisper a steady heart pulse, while muted violas and cellos evoke a sonorous, mournful beauty that Herrmann often conjured to depict isolated settings. Like the moments before Arbogast's murder in *Psycho*, the softness and unsettling allure of this music makes us lean in—and then leap, when *sforzando* horror occurs.

Herrmann's delight in creation is clear from the unique instrumentation he gave each score. For *Terror at Northfield*, written by Leigh Brackett (*The Big Sleep*), he employs eight bassoonists, to create the sonic equal of the color black. Their low growls and froglike croaks intensify the grimness and claustrophobia of the tale, in which a religious-zealot father hammers to death his townsfolk, convinced that one of them killed his son. Adding to the score's impact is Herrmann's close miking of the players: listening to the music tracks, you can hear the flapping of their fingers, and hear them breathe. At this session, Herrmann also recorded a new version of "Funeral March of a Marionette," used for the main titles of Seasons 2 and 3. His all-bassoon arrangement is more droll, and the instruments' low pitch and sound resemble Hitchcock's voice.

The value of expanded story time was clear in the moving episode *Body in the Barn*. Half a century after starring in silents for D. W. Griffith, Lillian Gish was an icon of American strength, belying her small, birdlike form. Her two best films, *The Wind* (1928) and *The Night of the Hunter* (1955), juxtaposed bucolic settings with the evil that feeds on the insularity of small towns. In cities, people can hear you scream. *Body in the Barn* continued that tradition, pitting a killer's clever scheme against Gish's unswerving moral compass.[16]

Herrmann adds a cinematic layer using his favorite ensemble, strings and harp, augmented by a solo oboist. The oboe becomes the musical voice of Gish's Bessie Carnby. Strings and harp conjure a pastoral setting, inflected with hints of darkness. The episode opens after Bessie's death, as auctioneers assess her possessions. A vase breaks. In it is a piece of paper, and Herrmann's wistful theme for oboe begins over hushed, tremulous strings, as Gish's voice-over shares the paper's content: "By the time this is found, it will all be over. Justice will have had its day."

Without music, we would be intrigued. *With* music, we feel in seconds Bessie's strength of character, and her acceptance of imminent death. We are also pulled into a mystery, slowly revealed: Bessie has been tricked by a neighbor, Henry Wilkins, to wrongly implicate Henry's wife in a murder she didn't commit. The wife is found guilty and executed. Only then does Bessie realize the wife was innocent; Henry wanted freedom. To make amends, Bessie poisons herself at the climax, leaving clues that implicate Henry in her demise and lead to *his* execution.

Eight minutes of the episode play without dialogue. Here, like in a Hitchcock feature, Herrmann steps forward to provide the type of underscoring Sondheim loved: music without resolution but which keeps us engaged, hinting through artful variations that answers lie ahead. One example: just before Bessie realizes she's been duped by Henry, a solo harp plays steady quarter notes in the instrument's low register. Over this palpitating rhythm, muted violas quietly throb with repressed emotion. The phrase they play is then repeated by violins, *pianissimo*, in their top register—a chilling, beautiful sound.

> JOHN MORGAN: *It's a searching kind of music. It has motivation. And the oboe theme for Bessie that we hear at the beginning has a sense of loss and regret, of saying farewell. He did "reminiscence" so well in music. Then her theme is played again at the end, as the last part of her letter is read. We've come full circle.*

Billy Wilder's *Sunset Boulevard* never had a sequel, but the episode "Behind the Locked Door" channels its spirit, casting Gloria Swanson as an icy, black-veiled woman of means, in a tomblike mansion where murder occurs. But this time, Swanson's "Mrs. Daniels" proves the hero—or at least, an avenging angel. She suspects that her daughter Bonnie's charming fiancé is after the Daniels fortune. The gentle Bonnie disagrees. After they marry, husband Dave arranges Bonnie's "accidental" death. He then heads to the family's long-shuttered estate, to learn what is behind a mysterious locked door.

He learns after stepping through it—falling two stories down an empty shaft. As he cries for help, Mrs. Daniels appears above him at the door; she knew he'd come here. Her eyes glare with Norma Desmond fire, as she raises her veil and tosses the keys he dropped, down to his crumpled, still-living body. Lowering her veil like a curtain, she steps back into darkness as the door slowly closes. Fade-out.

As he often did for short dramas, Herrmann erects his score around a single concept. Here, it's a stabbing five-note phrase built on a minor third. Think the opening four notes of Beethoven's Fifth Symphony, then reverse the notes into an upward run (instead of Beethoven's "down"), and you're close to Herrmann's pattern. It can be murmured softly by muted strings, as when Dave first explores the family home at night with a flashlight—two and a half minutes of music without dialogue. The same theme can pound with thundering finality, as it does when Mrs. Daniels seals her son-in-law in the shaft that becomes a tomb.

Of the twenty-four musicians, just two are brass—French horns—but theirs is the standout color of the score.

STROMBERG: *The two horn players are playing stopped—they put their hand all the way up the bell to make them buzz. Herrmann is telling us that we're not watching a love story—that this is pure evil.*

MORGAN: *But then, in what we think is a tender scene, the horns become beautiful. We hear low chords similar to what Vaughan Williams uses in his symphonies.*

Indeed, Herrmann's music for the doomed Bonnie is among the most tender he wrote for the *Hitchcock Hour*. Score invites us to see the world through her trusting eyes, making her death poignant, and her mother's final vengeance both triumphant and tragic.

Herrmann would score the *Hour*'s most extreme experiment. "Consider Her Ways" is a science fiction nightmare, based on a story by John Wyndham, author of the novels *The Day of the Triffids* and *Village of the Damned*. Barbara Barrie is Dr. Jane Waterleigh, who awakes to find herself a patient-prisoner in an alternate world. Her face is unchanged, but her body is bloated to grotesque proportions. An all-female staff explains that men are now extinct. Decades earlier, a Dr. Perrigan developed a virus to control rats, but it mutated and killed all men. "Mother" patients like Jane are forbidden to read or write—their sole purpose is to give birth.

For three of the story's four acts, director Robert Stevens keeps us trapped like Jane, using canted angles and visual grotesquerie, as the script explores ideas about the suppression of women. Then the episode swings for the fences with a series of fast-moving shocks. Jane awakes to find herself in our world, at home; her visions were triggered by a test study of a narcotic. Then she learns that a real Dr. Perrigan is working on a rat-killing virus—her nightmare will soon come true. She goes to the doctor's laboratory, and when he refuses to stop his research, Jane shoots him dead and burns down the lab. The end? Not quite. Jane's mission has failed: Dr. Perrigan had a son, who vows to continue his father's work.

Herrmann probably saw this bold episode as a companion piece to one of his finest *Twilight Zone* assignments, "Eye of the Beholder," in which a beautiful hospital patient is deemed repellent, in a world where "normal" citizens look like pig-snouted monsters. For "Consider Her Ways," Herrmann draws a demarcation between the two worlds. The "fantasy" portion is scored with poetic, yet dissonant, beauty with four harps and two vibraphones. For the "real world," instrumentation shifts harshly to four muted trumpets and four muted trombones. It's a strident change in sound, like Technicolor turning to gritty black-and-white.

STROMBERG: *He uses the four harps to create bitonality. Two harps are going in contrary motion [two musical "voices" moving in opposite directions] in one key. The other two harps are going in contrary motion in another key.*

MORGAN: *The harps are played very roughly. It almost sounds like they were using picks on the harp strings—it's a very brittle sound.*

STROMBERG: *And the music when she is destroying the lab—it's so audacious. No other composer would use just trumpets and trombones, playing in cup mutes, which create a darker, more muffled sound. Most composers would want to have strings, woodwind, percussion. But that's how he defines this world. Going from harps and vibraphone in the nether world to just brass creates a stark nastiness.*

MORGAN: *Then in the last seconds, when she learns that the deadly virus research is going on, the music goes back to harps and vibraphones. Because it tells us what's going to happen in the future.*

As the *Hour* entered its final season in 1964, Norman Lloyd, now the chief producer,[17] pushed the envelope of content. Some episodes sailed past "dark" to be downright nihilistic—a reflection of the national mood. On November 22, 1963, Benny and Lucy were attending a concert at London's Royal Festival Hall. By its conclusion, patrons were sharing the news that John F. Kennedy was dead. Attendees who overheard the Herrmanns' American accents offered condolences to the stunned pair.[18]

Horror and the sense of encroaching evil characterize two of Herrmann's last three masterworks for the Hitchcock series.

Hitch himself considered "The Jar" the *Hour*'s finest episode.[19] Based on a story by Ray Bradbury and directed by Norman Lloyd, it is a masterpiece of

Example 11.3 A Ray Bradbury nightmare comes to life: "The Jar" (1964).

suggestion that disturbed even Stephen King: "I've never forgotten the effect of 'The Jar.'"[20]

The Emmy-nominated teleplay by James Bridges (later director of *The China Syndrome*) opens in the kind of dark carnival where Stephen King's clown Pennywise would feel at home. It's night... closing time... but sweet-tempered bumpkin Charlie Hill (Pat Buttram) can't leave the booth of a dwarf barker. Charlie's eyes are transfixed by a large jar filled with... And there is the story's mystery. Jostling slowly in a liquid, the jar's contents are ambiguous, but suggest a demonic creature with a penetrating eye. Even before we see the jar, Herrmann transports us to a nightmare circus. A solo organ evokes a calliope; its waltzing little phrase repeats and repeats. Studio reverb gives a dreamlike wash to the organ, and to the soft muted trumpets and trombones that punctuate it with eerie bitonal fanfares.

When Charlie buys the jar and brings it home, the isolated residents of Wilder's Holler share his obsession. (They include Jane Darwell, Ma Joad in John Ford's *The Grapes of Wrath*.) A nightly ritual begins, as the locals gather in Charlie's shack to stare at the jar and describe what they see in it. No two accounts are the same. The jar inspires confessions, religious imagery, and the vision for one woman of her dead child. Charlie sees in it someone lost in a swamp "for years and years... shrivelin' up and witherin' away. Finally he'd maybe sink down in one of them old muckholes, and lay there like the maggot skeeters, sleepin' in all that old sump water." For a pigtailed little girl, the jar's contents are obvious: "It's the Boogeyman."

During these trancelike reflections, Herrmann's solo organ subtly evolves. Its notes now play a dimly familiar phrase. It is the *Dies irae*, the medieval Gregorian chant that describes the Last Judgment, used in rites for the dead. Listeners today know it best from its use in *The Shining* (1980), another tale of gradual possession. In *The Jar*'s final third, the "calliope" organ gives way to six trumpets and six trombones, all muted—the sound of a satanic mass.

The teleplay's ending over-literalizes a resolution done more subtly in Bradbury's short story. Charlie's cheating wife enrages him by dumping the jar's contents in their home. Charlie replaces them with her head. Despite this conventionally Hitchcockian turn, Herrmann's malevolent brass and a final return of the "calliope" theme retain a tone of supernatural evil to *The Jar*'s last frame.

Much of the same talent re-teamed in fall 1964 for an episode that, while shrouded in darkness, ends more hopefully. "The Life Work of Juan Diaz" was directed by Norman Lloyd, with Ray Bradbury adapting his own story. Set in the graveyard of a Mexican village, it aligns us with Juan Diaz (Alejandro Rey), a poor, dying man who in his final days seeks security for his family, and a grave for himself. He rents a burial spot from Alejandro, the imperious local cemetery owner, and dies soon afterward. When Alejandro removes Juan's mummified body a year before the agreed time, propping his remains with other unlucky "tenants" in a catacomb, Juan's widow Maria and son Jorge plan to rescue him.

Bradbury's evocative language, Lloyd's shadow-filled visuals, and Herrmann's score combine to make death a character. Reflecting its cinematic ambition, Herrmann uses his largest orchestra for the *Hour*: twenty strings, four French horns, one English horn, timpani, and harp. His opening cue is a hammer—a habanera reminiscent of *Vertigo*'s "Carlotta" theme. Herrmann's pounding rhythm and high, *fortissimo* violins lay out in sound the battle between a dying man and the grave-digging "keeper of dry souls."

STROMBERG: *What's very important is that Herrmann has the strings play without vibrato. It's very cold-sounding.*
MORGAN: *And this is a perfect example of his orchestration technique. Throughout the episode it's mostly the same musical material. It's the way he puts different instruments together, emphasizing either the habanera*

rhythm or the melody ... inverting chords [playing the same notes in different ways—like E–G–C instead of C–E–G], adding high harmonics. It's interesting: if you listened to this just as music, it wouldn't mean a lot. The film helps the music as much as the music helps the film. They are equal; take away one and you don't have the whole.

Throughout, a sole English horn, which sounds similar to an oboe, captures Juan Diaz's frail but resilient spirit. That spirit is also part of the score's most haunting cue. As Juan lies dying on his bed, he asks his trio of children to take three breaths with him. The soundtrack is silent, except for each intake of breath. As Juan attempts his third, his body does not exhale. Lloyd pans to the children, all holding their breath. Then, Herrmann becomes Death: *pianissimo* low strings murmur the habanera rhythm in grave minor thirds. As the children exhale, their release of breath is matched by a muted, sustained high note for strings. In music, a spirit has traveled from one world to the next.

After the grave owner's treachery, Maria and Jorge make a suspenseful trip into the catacomb, which Herrmann's muted strings turn into a journey to the underworld. They rescue Juan's body and place it in their home, which becomes "The Juan Diaz Museum." There, the mummy draws tourist money and brings the family security. When Maria asks her husband's remains, "Do you forgive me?" a shift of sunlight makes the mummy's eyes briefly spark with affirming light, as the habanera shifts to a benevolent, major-key resolution. No doubt Hitchcock and Herrmann recognized this final shot as an upbeat inversion of another: the close-up of mummified Mrs. Bates, complete with light movement in the "eyes."

Search the internet and you'll find dozens of comments from viewers who spent the night of February 15, 1965, petrified—pleasantly or traumatically— by another Herrmann-scored episode.

I well remember "An Unlocked Window" as one of the most terrifying experiences of my life. That night, I went to bed with a butcher knife under my pillow.

We lived out in the country where there were few neighbors. I watched this and didn't even try to sleep until it was daytime.

I was too afraid to get out of bed to shut off the television set when it was over.[21]

While not his last score for the series, it was the last episode worthy of the score Herrmann delivered.²² Dana Wynter (*Invasion of the Body Snatchers*) starred as one of two nurses tending a frail young man, on a stormy night, amid reports of a local strangler who targets . . . nurses. Decades of slasher movies haven't softened "Window's" chill factor, thanks to Joseph M. Newman's claustrophobic direction, and inky-black cinematography by the great Stanley Cortez (*The Magnificent Ambersons*, *The Night of the Hunter*). Herrmann's contribution is brute force: his eccentric group of nine trombones and six double basses creates a pervasive heaviness, defining the killer we glimpse only from a distance until the last seconds. (Herrmann may have been inspired by a line spoken by the housekeeper, played by Louise Latham: "I read in a book about a man who only killed trombone players. He beat them to death with their own trombones.")

From the start we know what we're in for. The camera follows an attractive nurse, leaving a job at night and rounding a corner alone. The camera's movement reveals a man in the shadows—Herrmann's signal to begin. Plucked

Example 11.4 Viewers felt Dana Wynter's fear in "An Unlocked Window" (1965).

double basses imitate, but do not exactly match, the pursuer's footsteps. Tempo accelerates, as do the cross-cuts between the stalker's gait and the nurse's anxious footfalls. Muted trombones join the double basses: mass is moving in on her. Instruments engage in a sinister call-and-response, then swell with snarling chords. Finally the music stops as the nurse is cornered, and we hear an offscreen voice. "Frieda? You're such a pretty nurse. . . ." A gloved hand covers her screaming mouth; the man laughs. Bitonal chords wail, as storm clouds unleash a downpour, and a zoom takes us into the rain-swept house we never escape until episode's end.

MORGAN: *This gets my nomination for the most bizarre instrumentation he used for Hitchcock. When the basses and trombone players walked into the recording, I'll bet they all looked at each other and said, "Ah, we're doing a Herrmann score today!"*

STROMBERG: *He loved having three trombones with one kind of mute, then three trombones with another kind, then three trombones open [without mute]. He could do big minor chords that sounded unusual because of the differing mutes. For example, straight mutes make trombones sound like a trumpet. As for the double basses . . . it's not so unusual to have cellos and basses. That creates a more standard, homogenous orchestral sound. But if you ever listen to just the basses rehearsing in the orchestra, they have a stark, cold quality . . . an ugly quality.*

MORGAN: *Then he takes the double basses way up in the viola register, playing high notes to get a different sound, like when the housekeeper drinks. And in some cues, he has chords with all the instruments playing in their low range, while every orchestration book on the planet will tell you that's a no-no.*

STROMBERG: *Exactly. The lower you get, the more spread-out the chords should be. Double basses are the most "muddy" instrument to have in the lower register. Herrmann does that on purpose.*

MORGAN: *It sounds like the bottom of a pit.*

STROMBERG: *He also uses contrary motion, where the top chord in the double basses goes downward and the bottom chord goes up. They merge together to create a new dissonance. Something he also did brilliantly in* Cape Fear.

MORGAN: *I think he chose these wild instrumentations not only because they fit the story. I think he chose them because the scores aren't long. He knew the sound wouldn't outstay its welcome. But listening to the scores, we don't feel like we're missing any part of the orchestra, because you get caught up in the sound and in the drama. It feels full. As a matter of fact, I always thought there were other horns and woodwinds, like bassoons, in the score.*

Trapped in the house, Stella (Wynter) discovers that fellow nurse Betty is actually a man—the strangler. (T. C. Jones, who played Betty, was a busy female impersonator.) Hitchcock loved the twist, and told producer Lloyd to add a detail. "When Wynter fights Jones and rips off his wig, she also rips his garment, baring his *chest*, so that you can see there are no breasts." The image of Jones's barrel-shaped, hairy chest seems almost obscene in the context of a TV show of the '60s.

Hitchcock made his name with films about vulnerable women who emerge victorious. Here, darkness is triumphant. Wynter—the audience surrogate, whose intelligence has kept her alive—is last seen bent over, screaming, as hands move toward her throat. Cut to a close-up of her killer, his bulbous face caked in women's makeup, as he strangles her to death. Herrmann's final flourish of octave-leaping trombones is the voice of his inner monster.

For all of its run, Hitchcock's TV series enjoyed a creative freedom given to few. "We were an MCA baby that got the care and attention that all others desire and never receive," said Lloyd, "because of Hitchcock's close association with Wasserman. Lew adored Hitch, and reveled in the fact that he had this major star working in television for him."[23]

But after a decade, Hitchcock sensed that the time was right to end it—and ten was such a nice round number. Some at MCA tried to save its golden calf from execution. According to Lloyd, studio executive Taft Schreiber "came in and said, 'What the hell—what we should do is go back to the first year and do all the shows as westerns!' MCA never wanted to let go of anything."[24]

For Hitchcock and Herrmann, the final two seasons had been a way to maintain their relationship from 1963 to 1965—a two-year period that, away from the series, found both men facing significant crises.

For each, the result would be misfortune, professionally and personally.

12

Torture the Women

Marnie

> ALMA: *Something wrong, my dear? You were a bit quiet at dinner.... I presume he's having a bad patch with his music? I'm sure things are harder on you when the work isn't satisfying?*
>
> LUCY: *He hardly conducts any more. No one will take the risk. Who wants World War Three the afternoon before a concert?... And he's lost! Lost when there isn't a project he's passionate about, something for him to pour his love into.... There's just so much ambition in him—unfulfilled. You set your career aside for Hitch—you must feel it, too.*
>
> ALMA: *Well, no, not at all. I share Hitch's work with him—his passions, his choice of projects, choice of casting.... My ambitions are his. And his mine... I'm fortunate. My work and my love reside in the same place. With Hitch. That isn't possible for everyone.*
>
> LUCY: *Work and love! Benny can't seem to take care of both in his life at the same time.*
>
> [*The two women now stand outside of time, looking back at their lives—specifically the events of 1964.*]
>
> ALMA: *Lucy, my dear, we shall never meet again after that walk in the garden. So this is goodbye.... Who was to blame? I'll tell you one thing for certain. It was never us.*
>
> —Andrew McCaldon, "Benny & Hitch" (BBC Radio 3)

By 1963, the fissures in Bernard Herrmann's marriage were ready to burst.

"He would shout at Lucy at the slightest provocation," Miklós Rózsa recalled. "I don't know how many women could take that."[1] Lucy's anxiety manifested itself in a facial tic. "She would die a little each time he got into one of his tantrums," observed violinist Henry Greenwood. "Lucy was too gentle and sweet to live with Benny."[2]

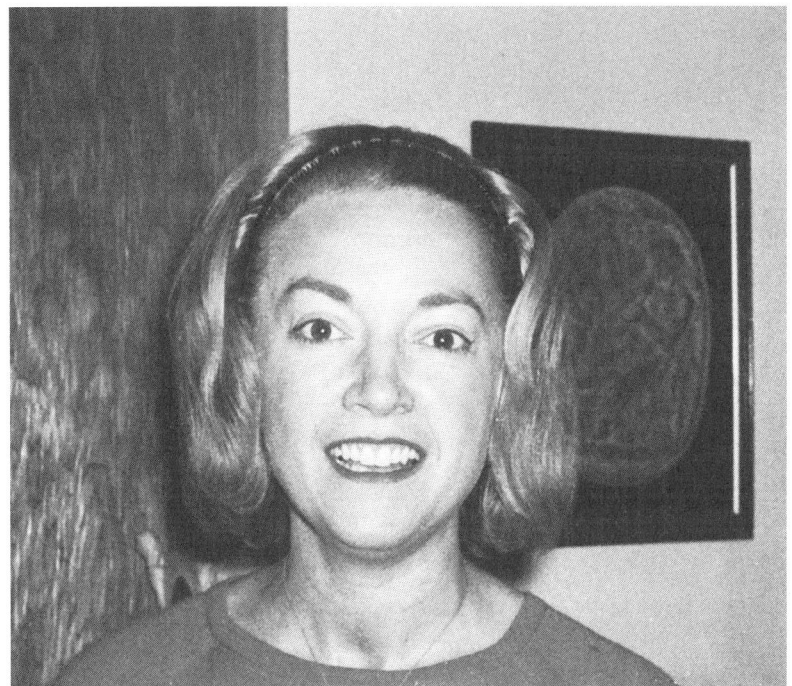

Example 12.1 Lucy Anderson, c. 1963.

Consumed with his own frustrations, Herrmann failed to recognize his wife's pain. He became more controlling. And his jealousy of time Lucy spent with friends turned to paranoia. "Daddy accused her of having an affair with her best friend Jane, which was so ridiculous," daughter Taffy recalled. "It couldn't have been further from the truth. I think that Lucy also felt that her life was wasted. She didn't have a career of her own."[3] The rare quiet moments in Lucy's home came in the dead of night—when she sat alone in the living room, drinking gin.[4]

In spring 1963, after fourteen years of marriage, Lucy summoned the courage to leave her husband for a trial separation. Herrmann was stunned, and pathetically uncomprehending. From London, where he conducted three concerts, he sent letters that seemed to come from a different person—the man she fell in love with in 1947.

> *My suffering is only because of my deep love for you—and if I must let you go—in order to give you happiness—I love you deeply enough to do so. So*

please dear heart—allow all pressures to be lifted and bask in the sun and enjoy our dear pets and have a triumphant life.

You can come to me at anytime and I will be there with open arms and heart to welcome you.

We have had a wonderful fifteen years together and I [would] like to spend the rest of my life with you. I married you in happiness and I cannot bear to leave you in sorrow and torment.[5]

Lucy returned to him. But so did his abusiveness, sparked by grievances against enemies real and imagined. They included film producers, music department heads, other composers, and two studios: Twentieth Century–Fox, for its rejection of him, and Universal-MCA, for what he feared it would do to Alfred Hitchcock.

Herrmann had been an MCA client years before his work with Hitch. He ended ties with the agency by the 1960s. The composer was incensed that on each film project, MCA took ten percent of his earnings "for doing nothing," he wrote a friend in 1952. "It is an evil thing to have to pay these leeches and brigands.... My blood boils when I even think of them."[6]

For Hitch, 1963 was a year of prosperity. *The Birds*' startling premise, and the Hitchcock brand, made it another cultural event and commercial hit, albeit not on the scale of *Psycho*. (*The Birds* was much more expensive, topping $3 million.)[7]

Most gratifying was recognition abroad from critics like Truffaut, Claude Chabrol, and Eric Rohmer, who insisted that Hitchcock was no mere entertainer, but one of cinema's supreme artists. In 1962, Hitch began what would be over twenty-five hours of interviews with Truffaut. The resulting book, *Hitchcock/Truffaut* (1967), did more to elevate its subject's standing than any other volume.

But if Hitchcock was lionized overseas, something subtle and troubling was happening at his home studio. By 1963, MCA-run Universal was the top in its field—if that field was television. "If your family watched television 15 hours a day for one full year, they still would not see all the 5,840 hours of filmed programming distributed annually by MCA-TV Ltd," the company's annual report boasted.[8] Movies were secondary to its corporate bottom line, and many of those movies looked like TV shows.

Hitchcock's deal with Universal was proving even more profitable than his contract at Paramount. But it wasn't long before he faced pressures to economize. During shooting on *The Birds*, a studio representative "showed up on location in San Francisco asking such questions as, 'Do you think you're going to be out of here by Friday?'" recalled assistant cameraman Leonard South. "Hitch said, 'When Friday comes, if we're ready to come back to the studio, that's what we'll do.' There was never any of that from Paramount."[9] MCA never stopped encouraging its star director to work less like an artist, and more like a man who owned millions of dollars' worth of studio stock.

Creatively, Hitchcock faced a crossroads. He hoped to lure Grace Kelly back to movies for *Marnie*, based on Winston Graham's novel about a beautiful thief who is sexually frigid. But Kelly's real-life role as Princess Grace of Monaco forced her to decline. Instead, Hitchcock chose an expedient Plan B. Tippi Hedren, already under contract to him, would play the challenging role in her second film.

Herrmann considered the casting a mistake. "It wasn't a personal thing," according to Taffy. "My father just thought she was talentless. He didn't understand what Hitchcock saw in her."[10]

Benny's concern for his friend ran deeper. As he and others saw, what began as a warm mentorship between the sixty-one-year-old Hitchcock and thirty-one-year-old Hedren had become, for the director, an obsession. It was equally clear that his controlling impulses were pushing Hedren away.

Ingrid Bergman and Grace Kelly were earlier subjects of his obsession. But the non-romantic love they showered on him, plus their established status in the industry, ensured that those relationships stayed mutually respectful. Hedren's background was different. Hitchcock had lifted her from obscurity, giving her a two-year course in acting and film production, and risked his reputation by casting her as the lead in *The Birds*. All that, he believed, entitled him to have a say in both her work and her personal life.

By the start of *Marnie*'s shooting in November 1963, Hedren was tired of playing Trilby to his Svengali. It didn't help that in *Marnie* he would direct her in a rape scene. "I always believe in following the advice of the playwright Sardou," Hitchcock told the press. "He said, 'Torture the women!'"[11]

Herrmann believed that the director's feelings toward Hedren reflected his need for ego reinforcement, not sex. "Benny said that Hitchcock was not after her romantically or sexually," one intimate recalled. "He said that Hitch admired her beauty, and he desperately wanted her to adore him. Hitch said to Benny, 'She's ungrateful.' He was a great director, and she should treat him as such. Alma knew about it and didn't worry. Benny said that if Tippi Hedren had ever said to Hitch, 'Let's go to a motel together,' he would have run a mile in the other direction."[12]

Example 12.2 A relationship sours on the set of *Marnie* (1964).

Hitchcock's fixation on Hedren coincided with, or resulted from, an expanding list of fears. Most directors of his generation were making their final films. His obese body was often crippled by pain. During *Marnie*'s shoot "he was drinking more than ever," wrote biographer Peter Ackroyd, "and often fell asleep after lunch. He had a general sense of ill health, and often seemed disturbed or anxious.... He started receiving injections of cortisone, which can induce insomnia, sweating and sudden changes of mood." One day, he turned to Norman Lloyd and said, "You might have to finish this one for me."[13]

In February 1964, Hitchcock's anxieties collided with Hedren's sense of entrapment. When she asked for time off during the shoot, to accept a "Most Promising Newcomer" award in New York, Hitchcock erupted. Only he and Hedren ever knew what they said to each other. Hedren later claimed that he threatened her for sex; Hitchcock told his biographer that "she did what no one is permitted to do. She referenced my weight."[14] Whatever their exchange, the outcome was certain: their working relationship was over.

But five weeks of filming remained. Director and star spoke through intermediaries. Hitchcock often seemed less engaged in production. When production designer Robert Boyle urged him to reshoot a painted background, after dailies confirmed that it looked unconvincing, Hitchcock said no. The footage arriving in George Tomasini's edit bay was wildly uneven: moments of visual invention, but too many takes of what Hitch often said he hated: "pictures of people talking."

Herrmann was eager to boost the picture. He had viewed the movie-in-progress on January 15, weeks before the on-set blowup, and discussed the score with Hitchcock over lunch the next day. One can only guess how candid he was about Hedren; but after nine years with the director, he was probably blunt. "Benny liked to say, 'Don't worry—I'll fix it!'" recalled Buck Houghton, producer of *The Twilight Zone*. "He looked upon every picture as a cripple that needed his fine hand to make it work better."[15]

BENNY: *The emotion isn't reaching through the screen. There's your problem.*
HITCH: *You know, there's only one other person who used to speak to me that directly—and I married her.*
BENNY [REFLECTING BACK IN TIME]: *Everyone tiptoed around you. Being candid with Alfred Hitchcock was like defecating in front of the Pope. But what did you want from me? I respected you—you were owed the truth.*
—Andrew McCaldon, "Benny & Hitch" (BBC Radio 3)

The Score

Director and composer agreed that the character of Marnie should have a lyrical main theme. Since the movie was a psychological jigsaw puzzle—the search for the cause of Marnie's fears—Herrmann proposed sub-themes reflecting other aspects of her character.

Benny advocated for music of heightened, neurotic emotion, an approach Hitchcock agreed with. In the final score, the composer "uses the word *agitato* a great deal," notes William Stromberg.[16] "The music is all emotional and agitated." John Wilson conducted Herrmann's 1968 suite from the score to a sold-out audience at the BBC Proms. He called it "the most dramatically intense score of his that I know. I love the unrestrained romanticism of it. In a lot of Herrmann's writing you hear a string sound with really searing intensity. The best example of this for me is *Marnie*. He's almost drawing blood from the players."

Fate gave Herrmann the perfect project for the time. He may have disliked Hedren's performance, but his own romantic disconnect—with a woman he loved, but couldn't stop driving away—mirrored aspects of the film. *Marnie* is about a woman alone in the world. Her emotional vulnerability has led to a self-destructive life. As Herrmann scholar Christopher Husted observed, "It is easy to imagine how the troubled relationship in *Marnie*, marked by its obsession and complexity, would have given vent to very personal expressions on the composer's part."[17]

Herrmann also had character aspects to explore that were separate from his experience. Marnie feels unloved, and distrusts men. Her sex drive is blocked by memories of her mother's prostitution. And her phobia over the color red has an explanation in childhood: while defending her mother from a client, Marnie accidentally killed the man. His flowing red blood triggered lifelong trauma.

To capture those extreme states, and to compensate for what he felt was a lackluster performance, Herrmann delivered his biggest sound for Hitchcock since *North by Northwest*: a full string section, four horns, and nine woodwinds (but no percussion).

The main title "Prelude" combines the major themes. First comes the "red" motif. Its angry, fluttering *tremolo* is the sound of mental seizure, its leap to a phrase for high violins a scream. Then, after a chromatic swell for full orchestra, strings exclaim Marnie's theme, the most lushly romantic one that Herrmann had given Hitchcock since *Vertigo*. A foreshadowing of the story's pivotal hunt sequence follows, as a variant of Marnie's theme is heard as a gallop.

WILLIAM V. MALPEDE, COMPOSER: *The "Prelude" plunges us into the angst of Marnie's trauma—the "red" motif is the first thing we hear. Then it goes into her rhapsodic main theme, to a time when she isn't feeling like a damaged child. It's usually when she's riding her horse, Forio, that we hear her theme in this passionate, yearning way. That's a Herrmann trademark—this heavily accented, beautiful, but tragic longing.*

Hitchcock withholds our first sight of Marnie for minutes into the film. First we witness the aftermath of her latest burglary, from a business she infiltrated as a worker. Then music enters mysteriously, as Marnie—shades of *Vertigo*—appears and undergoes a transformation. This wordless sequence is classic Hitchcock. Safe inside her hotel room, a woman counts her stolen money ... selects one of many false Social Security cards ... then rinses her dyed-black hair in the sink. An orchestral crescendo climaxes into the Marnie theme, exultant, as we finally see Hedren, in a *Gilda*-like head toss, revealed as a classic Hitchcock blonde.

MALPEDE: *This is as charged as any Herrmann cue I can think of. It's on the level of the* Vertigo *revelation scene, of Judy stepping out of the green light. Minutes later, when Marnie is with her horse Forio, the same theme sounds lovely played by woodwinds, with solo oboe. That instrument is often marked "Dolce" [sweet, soft]. It's used to convey her true emotions or longing.*

LAURENT BOUZEREAU, FILMMAKER: *The thing that Herrmann's music accomplishes in a lot of Hitchcock movies is giving characters who are not fully fleshed out a real backstory. In* North by Northwest, *the love interest only exists as a hint in the story. It evolves through music. And Marnie's theme opens up the film. It gives her a voice, it gives her depth.*

Marnie's most controversial aspect is the relationship between Marnie and Mark Rutland (Sean Connery, hot off the first two Bond films). The wealthy Mark is her latest target for theft. But he catches her, falls in love with her, makes her marry him, and forces sex on his bride. After the rape, Mark switches to become her therapist/detective, solving the mystery of her phobias.

In the book, Marnie sees a psychiatrist. Hitch insisted on combining that character with Mark. Writer Evan Hunter was fired after protesting this change, as well as Mark's rape of Marnie on their honeymoon. Playwright Jay Presson Allen (*The Prime of Miss Jean Brodie*) gave Hitchcock what he wanted. Musically, Herrmann tries to smooth the troubling shifts between Mark as sexual blackmailer and Mark the savior. When the character first kisses Marnie during a lightning storm, Herrmann introduces a love theme shaded with darkness.

MALPEDE: *I love this theme. It has the contour of Rochester's motif in Herrmann's score for* Jane Eyre *[1943]. It also has an old-fashioned lushness. Later, at the start of the rape scene, when Mark's theme comes in, it's got a muted sadness. Mark does love her, and the music tells us his feelings for her.*

In shooting the rape, Hitchcock uses tight close-ups to create a sense of intense audience identification. The close-ups cross-cut from Mark's point of view of Marnie to Marnie's point of view, as Mark's face looms down on her, inescapable. So how does Herrmann score the scene? As Marnie floats backward toward the bed—she has surrendered, her face a blank mask—her main theme is played skippingly, lightly. Herrmann is reminding us of her childhood self, when her traumas began. Hitchcock then cuts to his tightest close-up of Mark. Connery's eyes fill the frame, coming at us like a predatory animal. On this shot, Herrmann gives us the most dominating version of the love theme imaginable. It continues as we cut back to Marnie. In doing so, Herrmann ultimately emphasizes the darkness of the scene.

The composer's favorite sequence was "The Hunt," in which Marnie rides her precious horse Forio in a fox hunt. A rollicking gallop motif starts the sequence with optimism and excitement, until Marnie fixates on the red jacket of a fellow rider. After a burst of the buzzing "red" motif, Herrmann delivers the score's most exciting passage, as Marnie rides Forio away from the other hunters, and the dead fox they are celebrating. Against the furious gallop rhythm, Herrmann adds a hysterical version of the Marnie theme. The gallop theme returns, now suffused in bitonal dissonance. This hard-charging music is thrilling. It also tries to distract us from the poor rear-screen projection throughout the sequence.

More than any other of his Hitchcock scores, Herrmann returns scene after scene to a single theme: Marnie's. Its frequent appearance, to the point of overuse, may reflect a Hitchcock directive.

The screenplay for *Marnie* contained descriptions of possible underscoring. On October 10, 1963, a month before shooting began, Universal publicist Dave Golding wrote Hitchcock, "I have noted the reference to the *Marnie* theme in the script. I don't have to tell you what [Miklós Rózsa's] *Spellbound* theme meant for the exploitation of your picture.... The *Marnie* theme could likewise work for us very effectively."[18]

Hitchcock had hired songwriters to deliver a hit tune for *The Man Who Knew Too Much*. On *Marnie*, he was so taken with Benny's principal theme that he decided it had commercial potential. But Herrmann wasn't flattered. For one thing, the theme served a different purpose in the film from inspiring romantic relaxation.

LAURENT BOUZEREAU: *The Marnie theme is like a scream for a character who keeps it all inside. Only at the very end, when she has a flashback, does her scream blend with the music. It's interesting that music and her phobias get resolved at the same time, almost as a hand-over. It signifies that the music is all about the character, not a backdrop to the story.*

Instructed to turn his melodic but short motif for Marnie into a song, he exploded. "What the hell do I care about songs?" he shouted at MCA executive Lou Levy. "I'm trying to do a picture!"[19] His protests were repeated at home. "The studio was anxious to have a popular song, a hit song," recalled Lucy Anderson. "They were stressing Hitchcock at the time, and he didn't seem able to refuse them."[20]

HERRMANN: *I want to send audiences out of a movie theater feeling the story in their guts, in their bones—not whistling a happy tune.*
WASSERMAN: *Hitch! Do me a favor—make the man see sense.*
HITCHCOCK: *I, I, I just need to check an appointment with Peggy. One moment.*
HERRMANN: *I'm someone of standing, with respect for Hitch, respect for film. I worked with—*
WASSERMAN: *Orson Welles. I know. We all know. You're the New York wunderkind, Mr.—Benny, look, no one's trying to screw you here. I'm just the messenger. I also happen to have Hitch's best interests in mind.*
HERRMANN: *So do I.*
—Andrew McCaldon, "Benny & Hitch" (BBC Radio 3)

With Herrmann unwilling or unable to deliver, songwriters Peter Jason and Gloria Shayne were hired to do the job. They reshaped Herrmann's theme into song form and added lyrics: "Moon and mist / Make rainbows in your hair / When I see your smile / There's sunlight everywhere / But your world is lonely / Marnie..." Johnny Mercer's lyrics for *Laura* seem to be the point of inspiration, minus the inspiration.

On Monday, March 30, 1964, Herrmann arrived at Goldwyn Studios in Hollywood for the first of three *Marnie* recording dates. He would remember the week for reasons unrelated to the music.

After a day of recording, the drained composer returned to Bluebell and found Lucy's closet empty. His wife had left him. Herrmann's panic rose when a restraining order arrived, forbidding him from contacting her.

Just as pathetic as the marriage's end was Herrmann's inability to recognize the cause. Recalled Martha Newman, "After Lucy left him, Benny called everyone and said, 'Why did she do it? Do you have any clues as to why she left?' I think he saw himself as a pure person. And basically he *was* a very good person. I don't think he realized he was his own worst enemy."[21]

Staying at Sportsman's Lodge, a frequent home for rejected husbands, Herrmann remained in Los Angeles through the end of *Marnie*'s sound mix on April 3. He then flew to Britain, finding brief escape from the wreck of his life by conducting two concerts. The first was with his favorite orchestra, the Hallé in Manchester. Its principal conductor, Sir John Barbirolli, was a loyal friend; but even he could do little to assuage Benny's torment when Lucy began divorce proceedings. "He almost had a nervous breakdown after that," said friend Diane Gleghorn. "Benny was on our doorstep every two seconds when the divorce was taking place, and you never could get rid of him."[22]

Example 12.3 Benny shows the love he gave most freely, c. 1963.

May 17, 1964

I am not trying to upset you or agitate you—but I am so exhausted from the strain of all the work—the divorce suit and its problems and the concerts—that I am slowly but surely reaching a point of no return—that is I cannot even begin to consider any work of any kind—I live in a daze and concern—for both of us. I bless you dear one—keep well—you are ever in my heart and thoughts...

Bernard

Solitude proved unbearable. To shut off his mind, the man who seldom drank turned to alcohol. "After Lucy left, Benny couldn't get in the car with us without a bottle of Scotch," remembered Henry Greenwood's wife, Joan. The Greenwoods were two of Benny's closest friends in London; but even they "asked ourselves, can we take it any longer? We had him day after day, weekend after weekend. He was always yelling about something, because he so desperately didn't want to be divorced from Lucy. He didn't want to be alone."[23]

As Herrmann unraveled that summer, Alfred Hitchcock's office buzzed with activity. *Marnie* would open internationally in early July, and every promotional opportunity was being scrutinized. In 1924, MCA had been founded as a band booking agency. Forty years later, music was still part of its operation, reflected in its purchase of Decca Records.

Lew Wasserman had hoped that *Marnie*'s score would be ripe for commercial exploitation. But he found little to mine in Herrmann's traditional approach. At a time when soundtrack albums were increasingly common, MCA chose not to issue a disc of *Marnie*'s score. Instead they promoted the song extracted from it. Aiming high, they hired Nat King Cole to record "Marnie" as a single. With Cole's track record of 14 million sales, they could hardly have done better. On June 29, two weeks before *Marnie*'s release, the record was released with an unwieldy caption: "Nat the King sings the beautiful lyrics of the tune inspired by the brilliant Alfred Hitchcock production for the Capitol Records label."

Hitchcock was aware of Herrmann's bleak state of mind. For the first time in their ten-year partnership, the director who seldom mentioned coworkers in interviews sent a memo via Peggy to publicist Dave Golding: "Mr. Hitchcock wishes BERNARD HERRMANN, who composed and conducted the music for 'MARNIE,' to be given publicity. Accordingly, would you please meet with Mr. Herrmann as soon as you can."[24]

It was a significant gift from Hitchcock to his friend, and Herrmann was grateful. But like the scorpion in the parable who stings the frog carrying him across deep water, Benny could not change his nature. Interviewed by the *Hollywood Reporter*, he turned what could have been a positive profile and a plug for the Nat King Cole record into a rant against the system, and songs in movies.

> As far as good musical scores for features are concerned, Hollywood is gradually becoming tone deaf, according to veteran composer Bernard Herrmann. . . . He says that fine musical scores are becoming "as rare as whales in telephone booths" [and] that many current producers are so anxious to hear the sound of music at the box office they pay very little attention to it on a scoring stage. . . .
>
> "There are still a handful of producers," states Herrmann, "like Hitchcock, who really know the score and fully realize the importance of its relationship to a film. Hitch was in on every musical note of *Marnie*, starting with conferences long before the picture began." . . . However, according to Herrmann, most producers today . . . think that a hit title tune over the screen credits automatically means a hit picture. "That's as wrong as a busted adding machine," snaps Herrmann. "In my 24 years in Hollywood the standard of movie music has gone down, down."
>
> He claims he's not in the business of writing a smash title tune that will sell platters like hotcakes, but not movies.[25]

Herrmann was more amiable during what would be the highest-profile appearance he made in his years with Hitchcock. That July, the Canadian Broadcasting Corporation aired a profile of the director as part of its series *Telescope*. At Hitchcock's request, Herrmann appeared on the program in a solo interview. Benny appears smiling and relaxed, as he speaks of his closeness with Hitchcock. But even here, he could not help undermining himself.

As an example of the "freedom with which Hitch thinks about music," he recounted how the director had asked for no music during *Psycho*'s shower scene. "However, I differed with Hitch about this, and felt that music was needed." He goes on to describe in detail Hitchcock's reversal after hearing "The Murder," making himself the rescuer of the sequence. "But you were against it," he recalls telling Hitchcock. He then shares Hitchcock's reply: "Oh no, all I made was a poor suggestion."[26]

The anecdote may seem innocuous. But for Hitchcock, who took pains to present himself as a fully-in-control auteur, Herrmann's remarks on national TV were almost certainly infuriating. Benny's message—*I was right, he was wrong*—must have felt like a betrayal to the director, especially after Hitchcock's decision to put a spotlight on Herrmann.

On June 1, *Marnie* was previewed for members of the Directors Guild of America. Response was positive. A week later, Hitchcock learned that the film had received an "X" (Adults Only) rating in Great Britain—a potential selling point for a movie Hitch described, like a naughty boy, as "a *sex* mystery." At first, reviews were promising. "Thanks to the craft of Hitchcock, the picture hypnotically arouses suspense and builds beautifully to the explosive climax," wrote the industry paper *Motion Picture Daily*. *Film Daily* was more succinct: "Nerve tingling. Good box office prospects. Smart cast."[27]

Then *Marnie* premiered in London on July 8—and like the title character, critics saw red. "Whatever has happened to Alfred Hitchcock?" asked the *Evening News*' reviewer. "Has he been paddling too long in the shallow water of TV films, or has high-brow praise in *Les Cahiers du Cinema* gone to his head?"[28] (Apparently, Hitchcock was now both too common and too sophisticated.) Observed *The Daily Telegraph*, "Without a single surprise or deepening of the interest, the film proceed[s] deliberately without variation of pace as if marching to a metronome."[29]

But their barbs were mere warmups for the punches thrown by American critics. With each, Hitchcock's increasingly fragile ego must have felt a crack.

> *A mélange of banal dialogue, obtrusively phony process shots, and a plot that congeals more often than it thickens.* —Time Magazine[30]
> *Pathetically old fashioned and dismally naïve.* —New York Herald Tribune[31]
> *The master's most disappointing film in years.* —New York Times[32]
> *Nothing less than a disaster.* —Newsweek[33]

Contrary to popular belief, Tippi Hedren was not savaged by the press—she was damned with faint praise. "It's a difficult assignment which she fills satisfactorily," wrote *Variety*.[34] Hedren "zips through some 32 costume

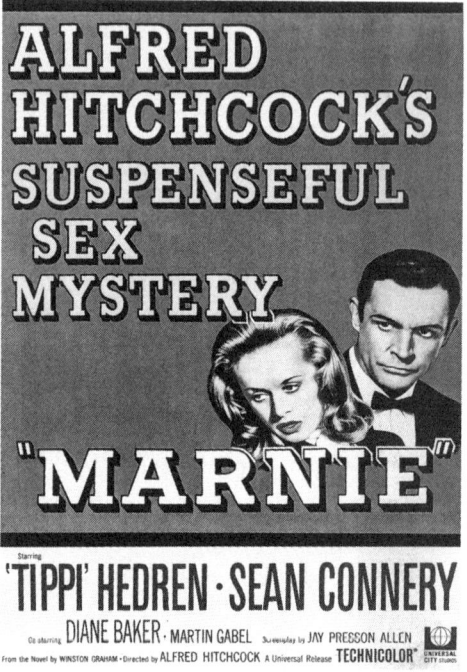

Example 12.4 *Marnie* poster (1964)

changes without seriously ruffling her composure," yawned *Time*.[35] "Miss Hedren and Mr. Connery [are] forced into roles that cry for the talents of Grace Kelly and Cary Grant," observed the *New York Times*. "Both work commendably and well—but their inexperience shows."[36] Connery would have to settle for starring in 1964's top-grossing film—not *Marnie*, but *Goldfinger*.

As for Nat King Cole's recording, it came and went like the mist in its lyrics. In February 1965, Cole died of cancer at the tragically young age of forty-five.

Thanks to Hitchcock's fame and Connery's popularity, *Marnie* made a profit, grossing $7 million against a cost of $3 million. But never in four decades had its maker been so pilloried. As painful as critics' dislike of the film was a running theme in their reviews: Hitchcock was self-indulgent. Old-fashioned. Boring.

The same disparaging words he applied to others' failures were now being hurled at him. "I am convinced that Hitchcock was never the same after

Marnie," Truffaut wrote in 1983, "and that its failure cost him a considerable amount of his self-confidence."[37]

Whispers that Hitchcock was past his prime were heightened by the vitality of his box office rivals. They included Stanley Kubrick's *Dr. Strangelove*, with its brilliant swings from *MAD* magazine satire to cold-sweat nuclear menace; Richard Lester's *A Hard Day's Night*, an intoxicating, semi-improvised showcase for the Beatles; and Tony Richardson's *Tom Jones*, which reimagined the eighteenth-century novel as madcap youth rebellion. *Marnie*'s fox hunt relied on subpar rear projection, filmed on the Universal backlot. *Tom Jones*'s depiction of a hunt was immersive and riotous, thanks to its hand-held camera and real locations, until the blood of whipped horses and a slaughtered stag darkened the tone.

The stench of *Marnie*'s failure led to finger-pointing. Hitchcock blamed Hedren. Jay Presson Allen blamed herself. And Universal . . . well, the studio was not about to blame its most important filmmaker, who also produced and starred in a still-running, hit TV series.

But from Universal's music department to its top executive offices, another individual became a target for criticism.

Surely Hitch could find a less old-fashioned composer.

13

The Curtain Falls

Part 1

March 1964. Alfred Hitchcock sits in his wide office chair across from Canadian interviewer Fletcher Markle and a small camera crew. The director is enjoying himself, recounting career highlights to a sophisticated, admiring interviewer. Hitch never mentions by name his behind-the-camera film collaborators—with one exception.

MARKLE: *Obviously you think very highly of the work of Bernard Herrmann.*
HITCH: *I certainly do.*
MARKLE: *How do you and Mr. Herrmann go about examining the contribution of music to a film?*
HITCH, SMILING: *Well, I don't know, as far as I'm concerned he does as he likes.*

CUT to Bernard Herrmann in close-up. He doesn't smile, and his nasal voice is hardly musical. But his mood is confident, almost self-satisfied.

HERRMANN: *I'm brought in at the beginning of a film. And by the time it's gone through all its stages of being written and re-written, and the final stages of photographing it, I'm so much part of the whole thing that we've all begun to think one way.*[1]

Two years to the month after that interview, Hitchcock and Herrmann were no longer speaking. The director had lowered a wall between him and his former friend, erasing him from his life. It was as if he and Herrmann had never met.

For eleven years, the pair had barely needed words to achieve a shared vision. In March 1966 that partnership was shattered irrevocably.

The reasons are complex. As the CBC program illustrated, each man had a healthy ego. "Hitchcock was a very strong personality," recalled John

Williams, who knew both. "He might not have liked the idea that his pictures were not as good without Herrmann's music. It may also have been possible that as their relationship got closer, Benny overstepped his line. He might have been too critical about some of the things Hitch did. Hitch may not have objected straight away, but let it build up. They were two men whose characters may have permitted a lot of irritating things to have gone unnoticed longer than they should."[2]

By 1964, Herrmann believed that his friend was changing. After Hitch moved to Universal, "He became a different man. They made him very rich, and they recalled it to him."[3] Benny later told editor Paul Hirsch that "Hitchcock got carried away with himself. Hitch thought he didn't need a cameraman or composer. He got carried away with his own publicity and didn't listen to anyone."[4]

On that last point, Herrmann was mistaken. With Hitchcock's self-confidence at a low after *Marnie*'s failure, he could not ignore the advice of Lew Wasserman and his team. "I am a slave to MCA," Hitch joked in the 1950s.[5] By 1964, it was almost a statement of fact.

"Wasserman had a hatchet man named Edd Henry, who was the liaison to Hitchcock," Norman Lloyd remembered. "Edd talked like a bookie and was the tough guy. He would intrude into Hitch's office without even knocking. When I complained about this to Hitch, he said, 'How can I stop him unless I lock the door?'"[6] Recalled John Houseman, "Hitch was always in a curious state of arrogance, but saying 'Yassah, yassah' to MCA."[7]

After *Marnie*, Wasserman felt it necessary to help guide what he hoped would be a major comeback for Hitch. Among the topics the men discussed was music. Weeks before *Marnie* premiered, the Beatles released the soundtrack album for *A Hard Day's Night*. It sold 5.4 million copies, outgrossing the film. With Decca Records now part of MCA, "There was great pressure on Hitchcock not to hire Benny Herrmann," recalled Lloyd. "That pressure came from the front office of Universal. The reason given was that Herrmann couldn't write a hit song."[8]

Perhaps not—but Herrmann had championed the Beatles to Decca five years earlier. Had they taken his advice, Decca/Universal could have controlled a music catalog valued in 2020 at over a billion dollars.

In 1964, MCA was happy to use Herrmann's talent, but only for TV programs. Shows like *Rawhide*, *Chrysler Theater*, and *The Alfred Hitchcock*

Hour were the composer's main avenue of employment. Herrmann believed that Wasserman was the cause. Recalled Norman Lloyd, "Benny disliked people in the Tower[9] who he felt got between him and everybody else."[10]

Herrmann and Wasserman's occasional interactions had grown tense by 1964. Recalled David Raksin, "One time Benny turned down a job at Universal. Wasserman got mad at him. He said, 'All right, Benny, when you get hungry you'll come to see me.' Benny said, 'Lew, when I get hungry, I go to Chasen's.'"[11] It was a nervy attitude to take with the executive who not only ran a studio, but had become an advisor to President Lyndon B. Johnson. Wasserman grew close to Johnson after JFK's death, and reportedly declined a cabinet position in his government.[12] In January 1965, Lew oversaw Johnson's inaugural ball luncheon. Its master of ceremonies was Alfred Hitchcock.

For much of 1964 Hitch's office simmered with tension. *Marnie* haunted him in the form of paychecks to Tippi Hedren, still under exclusive contract but never to work for him again. Instead, he met with writer Jay Presson Allen, who briefly cheered him with her adaptation of *Mary Rose*. J. M. Barrie's supernatural play had enchanted Hitchcock in 1920, and influenced the look and sound of *Vertigo*. He decided that *Mary Rose* would be his next film—"*A Ghost Story by Alfred Hitchcock*," he purred, "that'll get 'em"[13]—until Universal convinced him to scrap the ethereal drama. Matte artist Albert Whitlock, then at work on *Mary Rose*, asked his boss why he didn't fight harder. "'They believe it isn't what audiences expect of me,' Hitchcock explained. 'Not the kind of picture they expect from me,' he repeated."[14]*

To soften the blow, Universal revised Hitchcock's contract that August, raising his salary to what was rumored to be an industry high. They also gave him part-ownership of the studio. In exchange for precious assets—his TV series and the Paramount films he owned, including *Psycho*—he received 150,000 shares of MCA stock, making him the company's third-highest stockholder.[15] The multimillionaire was all smiles for the press. Privately he "complained that he had been robbed of his golden opportunity to make

---

* Universal's reservations are more understandable when one reads Allen's script, a talkfest more static than the play it's based on. But the supernatural moments in Barrie's original evoke a poetic beauty worthy of Michael Powell and Emeric Pressburger. With just two settings—a British country home, and a haunted island where Mary Rose disappears—it would have made a perfect episode of the *Hitchcock Hour*, especially with a Herrmann score à la *Vertigo* or *The Ghost and Mrs. Muir*.

Mary Rose," biographer Patrick McGilligan wrote.[16] Most offensive to Alma was another detail in the contract. Universal would own "future marketing of the name 'Alfred Hitchcock.'" It's likely that Herrmann saw a parallel: just as Jabez Stone sold his soul in *All That Money Can Buy*, Alfred Hitchcock had sold "Alfred Hitchcock" for the largest pot of gold in Hollywood.

"They've done a great job to strangle Hitchcock and other artists," Herrmann later said of MCA, "all in the name of 'doing their thing.' 'Doing their thing' means that they don't know what the hell they're doing and they hope it'll turn out all right."[17]

On November 20, 1964, George Tomasini stopped by Hitch's office to say goodbye; he was leaving for a weekend fishing trip. But the director was in a foul mood, and George waited two and a half hours outside his door before departing. He was too happy to be upset: in days he would start editing Otto Preminger's World War II epic *In Harm's Way*.

That Sunday, Tomasini was enjoying the air of the High Sierras with his friends. Suddenly he felt tired, and returned to his tent—where he died of a massive heart attack. The most genial member of Hitchcock's circle was fifty-five years old. Days before the trip, Tomasini's doctor told him that his cholesterol was dangerously high. George promised to change his diet. "It was a real tragedy," Peggy Robertson said. Hitchcock "really loved George."[18] Added Sue Gauthier, "Hitch was very full of remorse. But it was too late. He should have at least shook his hand or something, because George idolized him."[19]

Hitchcock's regrets that year were many. But thanks to Alma's devotion, most of his woes were professional. For Herrmann, 1964 was a year of nearly all-consuming misery. After Lucy's departure and divorce filing, he found some refuge conducting in Britain and writing TV scores for Hitchcock. In May he tried through his lawyer, David Licht, to reject Lucy's divorce suit, and begged her to change her mind. She refused.

Only one movie assignment came his way. MGM's *Joy in the Morning* was a bland tale of young love in the 1920s starring Richard Chamberlain, TV's *Dr. Kildare*, and Yvette Mimieux. Produced by Henry Weinstein (*Tender Is the Night*), it gave Benny his final chance to score a conventional Hollywood drama. This time he acquiesced when told to incorporate Sammy Fain and Paul Francis Webster's title song throughout his score. "Herrmann was very grateful to get the assignment," music editor Ralph Ives recalled. "He was down in the mouth."[20]

Channeling young romantic passion in music was an ironic task for a man filled with rage at the woman who had left him, and vitriol for the world in general. And while Herrmann's score is attractive, it strayed close at times to the themes and feel of *Marnie* (the orchestrations are nearly identical). The films had another similarity: During the recording of *Marnie*, Lucy left her husband. During the recording of *Joy in the Morning*, their divorce decree became final.[21]

Benny gave Lucy their home on Bluebell Avenue. He then leased it back from her, unwilling to move out despite the loneliness that consumed him in it. Friends who once loved his passionate curiosity and expansive conversations now avoided him. "He was consumed with rage and envy and malice and hatred," John Houseman said. "You couldn't spend an evening with Benny without him spending half of it in a terrible diatribe about one of the young musicians who'd gotten a job. It was boring, unbearable."[22]

Professionally, he continued to commit destructive acts that seemed designed to prove that no one could be trusted. For seven years he had worked happily on the fantasy films of Ray Harryhausen and producer Charles Schneer. Approached to score their latest, *First Men in the Moon*, "He gave us a price twice what he'd asked for before," Schneer recalled. "I said, 'We haven't got the money.' He came into my office, threw the script on the waiting room chair, and slammed the door without saying a word."[23] The trio never worked together again.

HITCH: *Anger. It was always oxygen to you—but now it took over. Why were you so angry? With the world? No, not with the world, with yourself? Were you frightened that you couldn't create if you were happy? Couldn't make work unless you had an enemy to vanquish? . . . You let your anger overwhelm you—and your music.*
BENNY: *I'd rather have an excess of emotion than a lack of it.*
　　　　　　—Andrew McCaldon, "Benny & Hitch" (BBC Radio 3)

By 1965, the only director who would work with Herrmann was feeling desperate. Nine months had passed since *Marnie*'s release, and Hitchcock was still searching for the story that would redeem him as a filmmaker. When he wasn't screening competitors' movies, including films by Truffaut and Antonioni, he was meeting with Wasserman and Edd Henry, pitching them projects. His spirits rose when Lew showed interest in an idea Hitch first considered in 1951. That year, two top British diplomats, Guy Burgess and Donald Maclean, fled the UK for Russia, after British security identified them as Soviet spies.

What, Hitchcock wondered, did Mrs. Maclean feel about it all? Did she know the truth about her husband? If not, did she suspect it? Many of Hitch's best films took a woman's point of view. Here was such an opportunity—one that could be paired with scenes of "real" spycraft, unlike the James Bond franchise, which had turned cartoonish by 1965.

On the latter point, leaning into reality, Wasserman was less encouraging. He advised Hitchcock to develop the story in the vein of his Paramount movies: beautiful people, beautiful scenery.[24] With that dictum, Hitch's creative decisions on what became his next film, *Torn Curtain*, began to flounder.

His best projects started with unhurried sessions with a writer, as they dissected ideas for weeks or months. Such was not the case with the writer MCA recommended. Irish-born author Brian Moore had an impressive résumé, most notably the poignant novel *The Lonely Passion of Judith Hearne*. For *Torn Curtain*, Moore's task was to develop the story of a prominent US physicist who seemingly defects to the Russians. His fiancée, also a scientist, is stunned by his action, and follows him to East Germany. There she discovers that he is actually on a spy mission for the United States. When his cover is blown, the pair spend the rest of the story fleeing their Soviet pursuers.

Moore found Hitchcock superficially charming, but soon realized "we were in for trouble. I found that he had absolutely no concept of character. . . . He kept switching from the woman's to the man's point of view, and the original story idea began to shift and fade uncontrollably."[25] According to Moore, the sixty-five-year-old director who wanted to be *au courant* couldn't resist falling back on familiar story tropes. When Moore told Hitch that "if it were a book I were writing, I'd scrap it, or do a complete rewrite," he was relieved to be given a ticket home.[26] But unlike *Vertigo*, which took a full year and multiple writers to develop, Hitchcock suddenly found himself out of time. The reason—an actor's schedule—was especially galling to the man who saw himself as the true star of his pictures.

The problem came wrapped in a golden envelope. Wasserman had convinced Hitch to cast two of the industry's most coveted stars: Paul Newman and Julie Andrews. Lew's instincts were not without merit. In Andrews's second film, 1964's *The Americanization of Emily*, she proved in a smoldering love scene that she had the makings of a Hitchcock blonde. But the director couldn't see beyond the two musicals that made her famous: her screen debut, *Mary Poppins*, and the just-released blockbuster *The Sound of Music*. Hitch didn't believe that audiences would accept Andrews as a scientist.[27] He also resented that the start of production would be dictated by her availability, which came sooner than a finished script.

As for Paul Newman, he too was a sensitive actor who could project intelligence along with sex appeal. Newman went into the project respecting Hitchcock and eager to collaborate. But his method-actor reputation unsettled the director from the start. When Newman sent him three pages of script suggestions, Hitchcock saw it not as an attempt to improve the work but as an affront to his abilities as a storyteller.[28] According to Brian Moore, the director became "inhibited" by the two stars foisted on him, and grumbled about their salaries—$1.8 million, half of the total budget.[29]

At least Moore's writing replacements were promising. The young British team of Keith Waterhouse and Willis Hall had penned stage and film hits (*Billy Liar* was both) that combined wit, cynicism, and emotion. But they joined *Torn Curtain* just days before shooting began. And while they too found their time with Hitch an "education and a joy,"[30] they could not dissuade him from including situations and dialogue that Waterhouse considered "immortally bad."[31] When the director campaigned to get them screen credit, the writers hadn't the heart to tell him that they were fighting to keep their names off the film. (They succeeded.)

Hitch's fears deepened when Robert Burks told him that he would not be his cinematographer. The reason given was mental exhaustion—Burks was a sensitive man prone to intense stress while working. But some believed he had another reason for exiting. *Torn Curtain* would be shot on the Universal backlot, not in West Germany as Hitchcock had wanted. Burks was disappointed by the look of *Marnie*—its phony sets and process work, its shabby painted backgrounds. Insiders said that Burks couldn't stomach another embarrassment.[32]

The three-and-a-half-month shoot of *Torn Curtain* began on October 18, 1965. It proved as miserable as Hitchcock expected. But the fault was partly his own. To Andrews he was cordial but aloof; to Newman he was dismissive. Unusually he lost his temper on the set, berating bit players rather than the actual causes of his anger.[33] Robert Burks's replacement, John F. Warren, had shot eighty episodes of Hitch's TV series; but according to Peggy Robertson,

Example 13.1 A glum assignment: Hitch, Julie Andrews, and Paul Newman on the set of *Torn Curtain*, 1965.

Example 13.2 Hitch and Newman agree at least to shrug, 1965.

he couldn't capture the nuances of light and color Hitchcock asked for. As a result, the director "got very depressed and just went through the motions," observed *Vertigo* writer and friend Samuel Taylor. One day, shortly before cameras were to roll, Hitchcock turned to Albert Whitlock and said, "You can do this, Al. You don't need me." He then left the set, leaving Paul Newman to be directed by the movie's matte artist.[34] Newman was angry but not surprised: "We all knew we had a loser on our hands."[35]

Rewrites continued throughout shooting, a practice Hitchcock abhorred. Equally painful were his reviews of the edit-in-progress with Bud Hoffman, George Tomasini's former assistant. Hitch had promoted Hoffman to be editor of *Torn Curtain*, mostly out of guilt after George's death. Peggy Robertson considered Hoffman's hiring a mistake: his only credit as solo editor was the children's TV series *Captain Fathom*. But Robertson could only express enthusiasm to Hitchcock, whose every anxiety she felt as if it were her own.

She wasn't alone in worrying. Wasserman and his staff were determined to prevent the studio's most important director from failing twice. Amid reports of unhappy cast and crew, they looked ahead to the film's commercial exploitation. And they implored Hitchcock to follow their advice. "They did not want Bernard Herrmann to write the score," wrote Hitch's authorized biographer.[36]

It can be argued that Wasserman and company were right in encouraging Hitchcock to change musical horses. John Barry's jazzy scores for the James Bond series proved that catchy pop themes and exciting orchestral scoring could go hand in hand. The same was true of Henry Mancini's tuneful music for *Charade*, a stylish Hitchcock imitation right down to the casting of Cary Grant. *Torn Curtain* aimed for a similar escapist tone. So it isn't surprising that "Universal was talking about getting Mancini for *Torn Curtain*," according to Norman Lloyd. "But that wasn't Hitchcock. Despite this pressure, Hitch felt comfortable with Benny, since Benny had done all the previous pictures and made enormous contributions."[37]

One of those enormous contributions echoed Hitch's current problem. The director had hated *Psycho*'s rough cut, until Herrmann's music electrified the footage, and helped to make it his biggest hit.

And yet . . . Nearly six years had passed since *Psycho*, and Benny was not the same man. Hitch had long tolerated his friend's eccentricities. But Herrmann's increasingly belligerent tone, and his diatribes against MCA, made the conflict-averse director shudder. Hitch also was angered after screening *Joy in the Morning*. It was bad enough that Benny's music sounded familiar. It was almost unforgivable that it sounded like *Marnie*. Feeling pressure from Wasserman, and worried that Herrmann was repeating himself, Hitch had ample reason to choose another composer.

Instead, he remained loyal to Benny.

After three weeks of filming on *Torn Curtain*, Hitchcock gave his decision to Lew and Edd Henry. It was likely accompanied by assurances that he would make Herrmann understand that he must deliver fresh, audience-friendly music.

That message was first delivered to Benny via Peggy Robertson.[38] Then Hitchcock stepped in. On November 4, 1965, he dictated a lengthy telegram to Herrmann, who was in London. Knowing how resistant Benny was to things he did not want to hear, Hitch tried to be as blunt and clear as possible.

DEAR BENNY

TO FOLLOW UP PEGGY'S CONVERSATION WITH YOU LET ME SAY AT FIRST I AM VERY ANXIOUS FOR YOU TO DO THE MUSIC ON TORN CURTAIN. HOWEVER I AM PARTICULARLY CONCERNED WITH THE NEED TO BREAK AWAY FROM THE OLD-FASHIONED CUED-IN TYPE OF MUSIC THAT WE HAVE BEEN USING FOR SO LONG. I WAS EXTREMELY DISAPPOINTED WHEN I HEARD THE SCORE OF JOY IN THE MORNING. NOT ONLY DID I FIND IT CONFORMING TO THE OLD PATTERN BUT EXTREMELY REMINISCENT OF THE MARNIE MUSIC. IN FACT, THE THEME WAS ALMOST THE SAME. UNFORTUNATELY FOR WE ARTISTS, WE DO NOT HAVE THE FREEDOM THAT WE WOULD LIKE TO HAVE, BECAUSE WE ARE CATERING TO AN AUDIENCE AND THAT IS WHY YOU GET YOUR MONEY AND I GET MINE. THIS AUDIENCE IS VERY DIFFERENT FROM THE ONE TO WHICH WE USED TO CATER. IT IS YOUNG, VIGOROUS AND DEMANDING. IT IS THIS FACT THAT HAS BEEN RECOGNIZED BY ALMOST ALL OF THE EUROPEAN FILM MAKERS WHERE THEY HAVE SOUGHT TO INTRODUCE A BEAT AND A RHYTHM THAT IS MORE IN TUNE WITH THE REQUIREMENTS OF THE AFORESAID AUDIENCE. THIS IS WHY I AM ASKING YOU TO APPROACH THIS PROBLEM WITH A RECEPTIVE AND IF POSSIBLE ENTHUSIASTIC MIND. IF YOU CANNOT DO THIS THEN I AM THE LOSER. I HAVE MADE UP MY MIND THAT THIS APPROACH TO THE MUSIC IS EXTREMELY ESSENTIAL. I ALSO HAVE VERY DEFINITE IDEAS

AS TO WHERE THE MUSIC SHOULD GO IN THE PICTURE AND THERE IS NOT TOO MUCH. SO OFTEN HAVE I BEEN ASKED, FOR EXAMPLE BY TIOMKIN, TO COME AND LISTEN TO A SCORE AND WHEN I EXPRESS MY DISAPPROVAL HIS HANDS WERE THROWN UP AND WITH THE CRY OF "BUT YOU CAN'T CHANGE ANYTHING NOW, IT HAS ALL BEEN ORCHESTRATED." IT IS THIS KIND OF FRUSTRATION THAT I AM RATHER TIRED OF. BY THAT I MEAN GETTING MUSIC SCORED ON A TAKE IT OR LEAVE IT BASIS. ANOTHER PROBLEM: THIS MUSIC HAS GOT TO BE SKETCHED IN, IN ADVANCE, BECAUSE WE HAVE AN URGENT PROBLEM OF MEETING A TAX DATE. WE WILL NOT FINISH SHOOTING UNTIL THE MIDDLE OF JANUARY AT THE EARLIEST AND TECHNICOLOR REQUIRES THE COMPLETED PICTURE BY FEBRUARY FIRST.
SINCERELY,
HITCH
cc: Edd Henry (Tower Bldg.)

One sentence was deleted from the first draft of the cable: "WILL YOU PLEASE COOPERATE AND DO NOT BULLY ME."

Herrmann would later claim that he turned down the assignment, saying that Hitchcock "wanted pop stuff. And I said, 'No, I'm not interested.'"[39] Correspondence tells a different story. The composer replied to Hitch's telegram with a cable of his own.

DELIGHTED TO COMPOSE A VIGOROUS BEAT SCORE FOR TORN CURTAIN. ALWAYS PLEASED [TO] HAVE YOUR VIEWS REGARDING MUSIC FOR THE FILM. PLEASE SEND SCRIPT INDICATING WHERE YOU DESIRE MUSIC. I CAN THEN BEGIN COMPOSING MUSIC HERE. WILL BE READY TO RECORD A WEEK AFTER YOUR FINAL SHOOT DATE. GOOD LUCK.

For the first time, Herrmann would be writing a score for Hitchcock without seeing the film. He would be unable to assess the performances, their strengths and weaknesses, or the look and rhythm of the film. And unlike their previous teamings, *Torn Curtain*'s script was being rewritten daily. At best he could only have an approximate sense of what the final movie would be like. No doubt he thought that his cable was cooperative—but Hitchcock realized that the message he intended to send was not understood.

> November 15, 1965
> Dear Benny:
> Delighted to hear you will again be associated with Hitch on his current production "Torn Curtain."
> We are preparing a contract on the basis of 10 weeks at $17,500.00 and pro rata with the start date of December 10. I will forward contract and Hitch's marked script hopefully within the next few days.
> Benny, there is one point that Hitch asked me to stress and that is the fact that you should not refer to his "views" toward the score, but rather his requirements for vigorous rhythm and a change from what he calls "the old pattern."
> If these terms meet with your approval, please write or cable me upon receipt of this letter....
> Sincerely,
> Paul C. Donnelly [production associate]
> bcc: Alfred Hitchcock

Although Herrmann had strived to sound upbeat in his message, in fact he was plunging deeper into depression. 1965 had been the most unproductive year of his career. No conducting invitations. The release of one unmemorable film, *Joy in the Morning*. The music he wrote that year consisted mostly of short TV cues whose chief purpose was to set a mood—usually a dark one.

Take his score for the *Hitchcock Hour*'s "An Unlocked Window." Heard within the episode, it masterfully conveys a sense of claustrophobia and doom. Heard as pure music, the low, muddy color of trombones and double basses is almost unbearably oppressive. It is as if Herrmann were scoring his own feelings—a plunge into blackness.

The coming year of 1966 held promise. Herrmann had decided to record, at his own expense, his opera *Wuthering Heights*, still unperformed after fifteen years. He had also accepted an offer from François Truffaut to score *Fahrenheit 451*, based on the novel by Ray Bradbury, a friend. In November 1965, Truffaut recounted his meeting with Benny in a letter to Hitch. "We had a long talk together about you and I feel that, in him, you have a great and genuine friend."[40]

Also an anxious one. That November, apprehension gnawed at Herrmann, as he waited in his flat near London's Regent's Park to hear from California.

November 18, 1965
Dear Peggy:
Nearly two weeks ago I replied to Hitch's cable. . . . As of today, I have not received the script and am anxious to have it as it will allow me to get down to work on it. I would also like to have Hitch indicate where he wishes music and also his ideas about the kind of music for each cue. If he could describe these in the same manner as he does when he gives the sound dept. his notes on sound. However, if he is too busy to do this now—could you at least send me the script as soon as possible.

Also, bear in mind that I can quickly compose the score so as not to be too far behind Hitch's shooting. When would he like me to return to begin on the film? I could start on <u>December 27 (Monday)</u> and be ready to <u>record on 19th of January</u>—which gives us the week of <u>January 24th for dubbing</u> and therefore making the Technicolor date of February 1st. This plan allows me 3½ weeks for composing. 2 or 3 days for the orchestra scoring—and a full week for dubbing. . . .

Please let me know how the above plans meet with Hitch's plans and approval. The above plan makes it possible for me to be neck to neck with Hitch's final shooting date. . . .

I have been asked to do Truffaut's new film next May or June. I am certain that this is because of Hitch and I thank him for it. . . .

I send all my greetings and all the best for the TORN CURTAIN. Indeed I feel certain it will be one of Hitch's greatest films. I just know it will be so.
Love,
Benny

Not until November 24, five weeks into filming, was Peggy able to send him a script of *Torn Curtain*. Her accompanying note reflected their shared love and concern for the director whose career was now in jeopardy.

Dear Benny . . .
The film is going to be absolutely sensational!
Hitch is tremendously busy, as you can imagine, and I don't think he will get a chance to do his music notes at present; he has been working every weekend so far. . . .

Please keep in touch, Bennie; it was certainly good to hear from you again....

Love,

Peggy

The disconnect between their messages and their actual feelings diverged further when Herrmann read the script. Although he sent an effusive letter to Peggy, he found the characters of Professor Michael Armstrong (Newman) and his fiancée Sarah (Andrews) flat, and the story uncompelling. He was further distressed by his inability to see the film. "I could never work from a script when scoring a Hitchcock film," he admitted in 1975. "It's Hitch's timing that creates the suspense. You can't guess his requirements ahead of time."[41] On *Torn Curtain*, that was exactly what he was expected to do.

Benny, Peggy, and Hitch continued to hide behind platitudes in their correspondence. "Was so glad to get your letter and reactions," Peggy wrote him. "Am really looking forward to the time when you screen the film which is really and truly marvelous—I think it will be Hitch's greatest. I read your letter to him and he was most pleased, as you can imagine."

At around the same time, Hitchcock was telling Al Whitlock to direct Paul Newman without him.

ANDREW MCCALDON, PLAYWRIGHT: *Why, if Hitch found Benny so difficult, didn't he cut the cord after* Marnie? *In my play, "Benny & Hitch," Hitch says, "Because you were my friend." That may seem sentimental or simplistic, but I think that is the heart of it. Hitch communicated by telegram partially to avoid conflict, but also because he knew deep down if they talked about things, he'd be firing Herrmann far sooner. He was lost and hoping for a miracle. Hitch could be ruthless. But he resisted with Benny, because the love and respect was still there.*[42]

On Monday, December 27, Herrmann finally was where he wanted to be: on the set of an Alfred Hitchcock film. Benny wasted no time after returning to Los Angeles to see Hitch, during week eight of the shooting of *Torn Curtain*. Also on set was Ray Bradbury, who posed with Benny and Hitch for photos. All three men wear coats and ties; Herrmann alone has a light vest, which covers a stomach almost as round as Hitch's. Benny and Ray beam with authentic smiles. Hitchcock's mouth also has an upward curve,

Example 13.3 Two admirers and a wary director: Ray Bradbury, Hitchcock, and Herrmann on the set of *Torn Curtain*, 1965.

but his smile seems tentative. One can only guess if the photo was taken before or after Hitchcock again described to Herrmann what he did and did not want in the score.

"We were in the midst of production and we had to rush," Peggy Robertson recalled. "Hitch said . . . to Benny, 'There's a spot in Reel One, right at the beginning, where we're talking about the cold weather, where there's an opportunity for humor. [Scientists on a boat to Copenhagen are freezing—the vessel's heater is broken.] I want a light and humorous score there.' Benny said, 'Okay.'"[43]

Hitchcock gave more details of the conversation to his biographer, John Russell Taylor. "He made clear to Herrmann . . . exactly what he wanted: nothing too heavy, not obvious thriller music, and particularly so in the rather light-hearted opening. Herrmann played him sketches, which he felt were a bit on the heavy side. But Herrmann said he could fix it.'"[44] Benny probably played his ideas on a piano, a scenario that in the past satisfied few of his directors. Recalled Philip Dunne, "There was always a secondary stage when he would be at the piano, saying, 'This is the theme. What do you think of it?' I would say, 'Well, how can I tell? You play it so badly!' Then he'd get mad."[45]

No fewer than four times, Hitchcock had told Herrmann what he did and did not want. The frequency reflects how concerned Hitch was in hiring his friend. He expected Benny to support him fully—his professional future was at stake. No less crucially, he needed to prove to Lew Wasserman that his faith in Herrmann was not misplaced.

Benny had been given ample chance to exit the project. A more prudent composer might have politely declined, as Robert Burks had done. Then, after the movie's failure, he could return to Hitchcock's fold doubly welcome, seen as a necessary ingredient for success.

It's unlikely that such a thought ever crossed Herrmann's mind. He needed the work for his own sanity. He also believed that he knew how to save his friend's movie. After all, he'd done it before on *Psycho*. And if saving the film meant ignoring Hitch's instructions—hadn't Benny shown that he knew best, with the shower scene?

Thus it was, with the very best of intentions, that Herrmann steered himself, and the director he loved most, toward disaster.

14

The Curtain Falls

Part 2

On Thursday, February 24, 1966, a group of old friends stepped out into the chilly, 55-degree night and into the warmth of Chasen's Restaurant in Beverly Hills. Alfred and Alma Hitchcock, Norman Lloyd, and the evening's host, Bernard Herrmann, had gathered to celebrate the end of shooting on *Torn Curtain* eight days earlier. Three months had passed since Benny received the script. The following morning he would see the movie for the first time.

But the night was shadowed by yet another unsettling loss. James Allardice, writer of Hitch's TV host wraps as well as his public speeches, died of a heart attack nine days earlier. He was forty-six. For Hitchcock, one of the TV series' greatest pleasures was enacting Allardice's outrageous concepts, like putting him in a Beatles wig or having him chat via split screen with his mustachioed twin brother George. Allardice was the voice of Hitch's public persona. As with George Tomasini and Robert Burks, the director never found a replacement of his caliber.

Hitchcock also seethed about *Torn Curtain*. After seeing the film's final cut, he wrote a memo to Edd Henry that was stunning in its sarcasm. "[A]t the end of our picture ... a further card requests the audience to visit and tour the Universal Studios. I am rather concerned about this card, because should the film not succeed, the request to tour the place where this bad picture was made could elicit raspberries from their mouths. Yours sneeringly, H."[1]

Hitchcock's contempt for the film made him all the more desperate in his hope that music might rescue it. If so, Benny had little time. The movie's shoot had run over schedule, reducing Herrmann's time to write its score. Two and a half days of recording were to start on March 24, giving him barely a month to finish and orchestrate the music he had begun without seeing the film.

Not until February 15 did Hitchcock provide the "Music Notes" Herrmann begged for in early December. Nearly all of the document listed simple in-and-out points for the music, without the commentary from Hitch that Benny asked for indicating "the kind of music for each cue."[2] Only once was the director specific. "I feel that the Main Title should be an exciting, arresting and rhythmic piece of music whose function would be to immediately rivet the audience's attention. Irrespective of the abstract designing of the titles and their background, the music could be, and should be, written before this is achieved."

Those who had seen the film agreed that its high point was the murder of an East German agent, Gromek, by Michael (Newman) and a female ally in a farmhouse. Neither Michael nor his helper can use a gun—another Soviet agent stands outside. Instead, they try strangulation, then stabbing Gromek in the chest with a butcher knife. Finally they succeed, in an echo of the Final Solution, by pushing Gromek's head in a gas oven. The sequence was prime Hitchcock: eight almost wordless minutes of carefully blocked action, as he showed through 138 edits "that it was very difficult, very painful, and it takes a very long time to kill a man."[3] Hitchcock included the murder in his list of scenes to be scored, but it's likely that he considered music backup insurance. Without a score, Gromek's murder felt realistic, brutal, and agonizingly long in the best possible way.

Since Hitchcock hadn't given specific directions for each music cue, Herrmann felt emboldened to follow his own instincts—instincts that

Example 14.1 *Torn Curtain*'s highlight: the killing of Gromek.

differed radically from the instructions he'd been given. Although he had agreed to write a score that was light and energetic, privately he imagined a very different approach.

On previous films, Hitchcock had said little about the style of a score before Benny started writing. Herrmann was convinced that the mandate for a "beat score" came not from Hitch, but from MCA—and no executive was going to tell Herrmann what a movie needed. "I wouldn't sell myself to that MCA boardroom nonsense. I knew they were wrong," he later said.[4] "What *Torn Curtain* needed was music that didn't make these people into ludicrous TV characters, but into reality. . . . I'd never cheapen a piece because somebody said that's what they want. That to me is where you separate the composers from the frauds."[5]

NICHOLAS MEYER, FILMMAKER: *With Herrmann, if you hired him, you had to just get out of the way and give this guy free rein to his very considerable intuitions and instincts. As long as Hitchcock was prepared to do that, he was going to get some form of gold. It's interesting—I've spent all my life riding horses, and I learned from experience: you cannot stop a runaway horse by pulling back on the reins. It just doesn't work. If you want to stop them, you're going to have to pull one rein and lead them gently. Getting Herrmann to write something different from his initial instincts. . . . The seed would have to be planted early. It was probably very hard to pull a different rein.*[6]

The Score

On February 26, with barely three weeks left before orchestra parts were needed for the recording, Benny began to write in earnest. First came his choice of orchestration. *Torn Curtain*'s interiors had the same TV-backlot look as *Marnie*, only worse. The movie conveyed little sense of entrapment in a Soviet country. Herrmann believed he could add that missing atmosphere of danger through another unorthodox ensemble.

Alarm bells should have rung in the Hitchcock office on March 4, when Peggy Robertson reported in a memo that "The orchestra will comprise the following: 12 Flutes, 16 Horns, 9 Trombones, 2 Tubas, 2 Players of Kettle Drums, A large group of Cellos and Basses."[7] No violins, and no modern instruments like guitars, saxophones, or keyboards. Instead, many of the lowest-pitched instruments in an orchestra would be augmented by—twelve flutes?

Herrmann had decided that East Berlin would be represented by a wall of muted brass. In contrast to this sound of force, flutes would be played in their highest register, to suggest a chilling whisper or shrieks of fear. "The sound of all those flutes," he told composer Laurie Johnson, "will be *terrifying*."[8]

Hitchcock had asked for music with "a beat and a rhythm . . . young, vigorous." In two of his best scores for Hitch, *North by Northwest* and *Psycho*, Herrmann had done just that. His Oscar-winning music for *All That Money Can Buy* is energetic, witty, and tuneful. And in past years, he didn't have to be told to think out of the box. He loved creating new sounds, like the electronic instruments in *The Day the Earth Stood Still*. But by 1966, Herrmann heard a different sound and tempo in his head. It was dark, tragic, and crawled in slow tone clusters like a building storm. His music for *Torn Curtain* would follow that style, versus Hitch's vaguely worded "beat score." "A 'beat score' in a picture," Herrmann later said, was "primitive music that suits the inarticulateness of the story itself. . . . It has nothing to do with the higher level of intellectual or emotional feeling."[9]

But were Herrmann's creative instincts right, or was he simply falling back on the familiar, incapable of delivering what Hitchcock wanted?

Contemporary listeners disagree.

JOHN MORGAN: *I think Herrmann failed completely with the score. He ruined it by using this outlandish orchestra. And other than the blast of music in his "Prelude" (Main Title), there's no theme you can remember and carry through the film. Really Mancini would have been the ideal choice.*

WILLIAM STROMBERG: *I think he just went overboard in the wrong kind of arrangement. The mood of the score is perfect for that slow, cold picture. I think it would have worked with a different orchestration. If he had scored the main title with five saxes playing the tune, and put a little beat behind it, Hitchcock would have said thank you, I love you. That could also have been a theme for Andrews or Newman if you played it with a sax or a flute, more lyrically. But he shot himself in the foot by using this gigantic, stupid orchestra with 16 horns and 12 flutes and all that. It's just nonsense, because the film didn't require that. He over-wrote.*

MORGAN: North by Northwest *feels like a chamber piece compared to this orchestration!*

Hitchcock had asked for light music for the film's first sequence, to heighten the comically social awkwardness of scientists freezing on a ship. Herrmann ignored him. Instead, he wrote music that makes the viewer *feel* the cold, with slowly shifting, unresolved chords, their color dominated by ethereal flutes. Levity is absent, replaced by eerie, glacial stasis. When Michael lies to Sarah about a telegram he received, low strings and high flutes engage in slow, menacing interplay without resolution. "The Radiogram," like many cues that follow, is moody and ideal for a generic music library. But it could not be more opposite from what Herrmann had agreed to deliver.

MORGAN: *These slow patterns don't pull the movie along. They don't really do anything. Does this music make people feel "real," as Herrmann said? Of course not!*

WILLIAM V. MALPEDE, COMPOSER: *The use of the flutes is great, that monochromatic sound. But the film needed energy and some lightness. And the energy is not there in Herrmann's score. It becomes a much more serious movie with his music.*

MICHAEL MCGEHEE, CONDUCTOR: *Herrmann was trying to portray the oppressiveness of a totalitarian society. He uses these Ivesian tone clusters that create a tight, oppressive feeling. In the film you don't actually see the totalitarian nature of the world. I think that's part of the reason that Benny was piling it on. The flute choir is brilliant and terrifying, and sounds different than any other score I know. But too much of the score is just "tick-tock" music, the standard Herrmann syncopations.*

LAURENT BOUZEREAU, FILMMAKER: *I love the score independently, but it does not match the movie at all. It's dark. It's slow. There's enormous pathos, there's beauty. But the movie is one of Hitchcock's most superficial—it's fluff.*

One may admire Herrmann's courage in doing what he felt would best serve the film. But when it came to scoring *Torn Curtain*'s finest sequence, Gromek's murder, his music sailed past creative differences toward artistic suicide. Hitchcock had accused him of reusing his "Marnie" theme in *Joy in the Morning*. The message was clear: do not repeat yourself. Yet Herrmann's "The Killing" is a repeat of his main theme for a *Hitchcock Hour* episode, "Behind the Locked Door." Did he think that Hitchcock wouldn't remember it? Did he believe that the music served *Torn Curtain* so well that Hitch wouldn't mind? Or was his reuse of the theme, with its pummeling blows of brass and percussion, a musical *Screw you* to the philistines at MCA?

MCGEHEE: *Hitchcock said he wanted "beat music." Herrmann gave him "beat over the head" music! But I do think his cue for the killing scene is brilliant.*

ANDREW MCCALDON, PLAYWRIGHT: *I think that Benny did his best work from a position of conflict. He was a fighter—that was his default position in a way. On* Torn Curtain, *I think he knew it was going to be a fight, and he sort of went in with battle armor.*

In Hitchcock's leather appointment diary for 1966, the date of Thursday, March 24, was filled with activity. Lunch with Samuel Taylor and Hitch's agent, Herman Citron. A 5:10 screening of *Torn Curtain* with Alma and Sam. A 7:30 dinner with Taylor and his wife at Perino's. But the event Hitch most looked forward to would happen at 2:20 p.m. "To: Scoring at Goldwyn Studios."

Peggy Robertson would be at the scoring stage an hour earlier, keeping track of what cues Benny recorded before Hitch arrived. At Goldwyn she

Example 14.2 Before the fall: December 1965.

found Herrmann full of adrenaline. Two years had passed since he last stood before an orchestra conducting a film score for Alfred Hitchcock. He was thrilled to be back. Outtakes from the session capture him in high spirits: he praises his musicians, and at one point jokes about needing to find himself "a shiksa" (non-Jewish girl). That Herrmann could jest about being single, just minutes into a score's first recording session, shows his level of confidence about the day ahead.

He began by conducting the "Prelude," *Torn Curtain*'s most rhythmically exciting cue. In it, Herrmann again showed his gift for grabbing the listener. Like the firing of a bullet, the thump of kettle drums introduces a fast, downward-falling ostinato for flutes—a musical conjuring of running feet—as horns proclaim a leaping perfect-fourth interval, evoking a lockstep army. Herrmann demanded maximum emotion from his players, especially the horns, and the four takes he recorded of the "Prelude" were draining and exhilarating. "We were all just overwhelmed by it," horn player James Decker recalled.[10]

Not everyone was impressed. Eleanor Slatkin, an exquisite cellist, sighed with boredom as the orchestra recorded "The Ship," "The Radiogram," and other slow cues. The music "was nothing but waves of sound, up and down. I couldn't believe it, because I knew what he was capable of."[11]

Slatkin's opinion didn't matter, but Peggy Robertson's did. And as she listened, she knew they were in trouble. "It was funereal, dirge-like music, where Hitch had wanted the light music. I was horrified and I didn't know what to do. And Benny said, 'How is it? How do you like it?' And I said, 'Well, Benny . . .' And just at that moment the doors opened and Hitch walked in. He came up to me and he said, 'How is it?' So I said, 'Well . . .'"[12]

Hitchcock turned to Herrmann and told him to play the cues for Reel One. "Don't hear Reel One, Hitch," Benny said. "Reel Two is the important one." Hitchcock replied, "No. I want to hear Reel One."

Three takes of the "Prelude," conducted at different tempos, were played. Still full of enthusiasm, Benny cited the first take as his favorite. Hitchcock remarked tersely that he preferred take three.[13] "Hitch was unhappy," Robertson recalled, "but Herrmann said, 'Wait 'til you hear the next cut.'" Hitch then instructed Benny to play "The Ship," the cue for the opening scene of traveling scientists—music Hitchcock had repeatedly stressed should be light.

It took ten bars of music, less than a minute in length, for the director to make his decision. His authorized biographer recounted what followed. "It was just what Hitch had said he did not want. Hitch was furious. He felt he had been betrayed."[14]

The room fell silent as his anger became apparent. Recalled Robertson, "It was the first time I've ever known him to do it.... He stopped [the session]. He said, 'That's enough. I've heard enough. I don't want to hear anymore.' And Benny said, 'Don't you love it?' Hitch said, 'No. I asked for light music there, Benny, and I don't want to talk about it anymore.'"[15]

The two men moved away from the orchestra, as Herrmann finally realized how dire the situation was. Hitchcock then canceled the session. Benny began to plead. The day was already paid for—couldn't he keep recording, and Hitch could listen to it later? The director, almost speechless with anger, said no—the recording was canceled. "I said finished, no other way, finished, goodbye."[16]

Herrmann was in psychological freefall. And as Hitchcock was driven back to Universal, the director no doubt dreaded his next, unscheduled appointment.

At 4:00, he walked into Edd Henry's office and apologized. He and Lew had been right. Herrmann had failed them. And he was willing to pay Mr. Herrmann's salary himself.[17]

Most of the musicians at Goldwyn left the stage quickly. One who remained was Alan Robinson, a Herrmann friend. Robinson drove Benny back to Bluebell Avenue. There, as they tried to process what happened, the phone rang. Herrmann answered, then covered the receiver. "It's Hitchcock," he told Alan. "I want you to hear this conversation."[18]

By his own telling, Robinson was the only person to hear the last professional exchange between the pair. "Benny told Hitchcock that he wrote a certain type of music, and he wouldn't by any means write anything he didn't feel. [The call was] about 15 minutes. And there was yelling. Hitchcock was raising his voice."[19] According to Herrmann, "Hitch said he was entitled to a great pop tune. I said, 'Look, Hitch, you can't outjump your own shadow. And you don't make pop pictures.'"[20]

While MCA wanted a popular song linked to the film, nowhere in any surviving papers does Hitchcock ask Herrmann for a song. Indeed, after

Benny's failure to write one for *Vertigo, North by Northwest*, and *Marnie*, it's likely that Hitch would have expected any song to be written by others. But by 1966, Herrmann considered the views of MCA and Hitchcock one and the same.

After eleven years, the relationship that had begun with a handshake, then expressions of love, ended in a yelling match and slammed phone receivers. And as Herrmann rejoined Alan Robinson, a thought must have dawned on him.

He had nowhere to turn.

"I was sitting in my office," Norman Lloyd recalled, "and the phone rings. Benny had elected to call me. He was a very dogmatic and abrasive man, but he was shattered. He said, 'I've got to see you immediately.' I said, 'Well, come over here.' He said, 'It would be very bad if I go on the lot.'

> So we met in a little hamburger joint on Ventura Boulevard. It was a sunny day. To sit in a hamburger joint on Ventura Boulevard in the afternoon, on a sunny day in California, was like being relegated to a corner of Dante's Hell. It just had nothing to do with the good things happening in the world.
>
> Benny arrived and I met him. And he told me this story as we sat in this deserted hamburger joint. That day I saw Benny as an almost totally destroyed human being. He was absolutely shattered. His relationship with Hitchcock and his history with Orson Welles were the two greatest things in his life. He considered himself a very good friend of Hitch's, and he felt that it was over.
>
> So we debated the issue—was there anything that could be done?
>
> There was no way that Hitch was going to listen to another note of the score. So one just held Benny's hand. The situation was one of total destruction.[21]

As supportive as Lloyd remained to the end of Herrmann's life, he did not agree with the composer's version of what led to the split. "I can see how Benny could say that [Lew] was the cause of the breakup. But I don't think that was it. It was just a factor. Hitch simply felt that Benny had disregarded his cable. Hitch felt that Benny had betrayed him. And he took the violation as a personal insult, because he had been so specific, so careful to lay out his instructions. Then you must realize that he had hired Benny over the objections of the front office. From his point of view, he'd been terribly let

Example 14.3 Norman Lloyd, one of Herrmann's last supporters at Universal.

down. I could understand this. In Hitchcock's mind, Benny had just gone his own way and ignored him. Therefore he didn't want to see him. The irony of the *Torn Curtain* situation was that Benny finally got what he had been giving, and he couldn't believe it."[22]

> "It wasn't Hitchcock's fault.... He's a good man, but they were just putting too much pressure on him."

Friends could hardly believe that such a statement could come from Herrmann, just days after his now-notorious firing.[23] Yet Benny defended Hitch again and again, to colleagues and later to interviewers. He could not accept that Hitchcock disliked his music, any more than he could accept that he himself played a role in the collapse of their relationship.

He also refused to believe that the break was permanent.

Los Angeles, 2019. Mary Ramos, music coordinator for director Quentin Tarantino, explains to Variety *reporter Chris Willman why Tarantino was* eager to use two cues from Herrmann's *Torn Curtain* score in Tarantino's latest epic, *Once Upon a Time . . . in Hollywood*. "Herrmann was the premier film composer of the time—real Hollywood royalty."[24] Using Herrmann's 1966 recording session, and Elmer Bernstein's 1978 record of the unused score, Tarantino and Ramos choose Herrmann's "The Killing" (of Gromek) for their movie's climax, in which Leonardo DiCaprio incinerates an attacker with a blow torch. Earlier in their film, Herrmann's "The Radiogram" underscores a tense scene with Brad Pitt. *Once Upon a Time . . . in Hollywood* will earn over $378 million worldwide.

Three hours after Herrmann's firing, Alfred Hitchcock sat across from Stanley Wilson, who oversaw the director's television music. The topic was urgent: what major composer was available . . . right now . . . to re-score *Torn Curtain*?

The question was painful for Wilson, who valued Herrmann's talent and had encouraged reluctant producers to hire him. Wilson even sent a studio memo at Herrmann's request: "Benny felt he should have been able to complete recording the score—Hitch to hear it in dubbing room and then anything Hitch didn't like, Benny would change."[25] It was a brave act, considering that the mention of Herrmann's name was likely to raise Hitchcock's blood pressure.

But Wilson knew that his duty now was to help the director find a new composer. After follow-up meetings with Wilson and Edd Henry, Hitchcock made his decision. Five days later, on March 29, he met with forty-six-year-old Englishman John Addison.

Accounts of *Torn Curtain*'s scoring usually end here. But what happened next is as fascinating, and telling, as the events preceding it.

Born in Surrey in 1920, John Addison studied composition at the Royal College of Music. After serving as a tank officer in World War II, he won notice as a composer writing for the stage, including Laurence Olivier's 1957 production of John Osborne's *The Entertainer*. His score was used in the acclaimed film version. In 1964, the well-liked composer known as "Jock" won the Academy Award for scoring 1963's Best Picture winner, *Tom Jones*. That music made his career, with its sardonic blend of Georgian harpsichord and jazz-style sax, united by a whimsical light orchestra. A similar approach brought Addison even more success twenty years later, with the theme for TV's *Murder, She Wrote*.

If Addison's work often sounded like musical cake frosting, it also could be delightful. And Jock had a deserved reputation for being even-tempered and collaborative. Apprised of the *Torn Curtain* crisis by Stanley Wilson, he set out to give Hitchcock the score he wanted.

Since writing his original "Music Notes," the director had reconsidered where he wanted score. The little he heard of Herrmann's music helped him be specific with Addison. "I found him absolutely clear," the composer said in 1977. "He would not profess to be any kind of musician, he doesn't know the technical terms, but certainly he knew what he wanted the music to do in his picture."[26]

For Addison, the assignment had a familiar ring. On *Tom Jones*, director Tony Richardson had literally asked for a "pop score" despite the story's eighteenth-century setting. "If I had thought when he said 'pop' he meant rock guitars, then I would have come up with the wrong score." Instead, Addison realized that Richardson wanted something fresh and just slightly anachronistic. Hence the addition of an alto sax, "which theoretically was quite wrong for the period. That was the 'pop' side of it."

Eager to satisfy Hitchcock, and to defuse the gloom suffusing the project, Addison tackled *Torn Curtain* with an emphasis on clear communication. For Hitch, rehashing its musical needs held little appeal. But Addison "was most anxious to work in my usual way, that is, closely with the director. He would remain in his office and I would run each reel as many times as I liked in his viewing room . . . and if there was anything I had a query about, I would just wander along the passage and say, 'Would you come and look at this with me?'"

By the time Addison finished his score, Hitchcock was in London, promoting the soon-to-be-released film with as much enthusiasm as he could fake. Back in L.A., Addison wanted Hitch's blessing on each cue before it was orchestrated and recorded. A costly long-distance phone call was arranged. Addison played his cues on the piano, then took notes on Hitchcock's reactions.

Addison's final score checked every box the director asked for. And when recording the music that May at Goldwyn Studios, he turned to the director for final approval.

So after all his exhaustive efforts to please, what was Hitchcock's verdict?

"Most of the time, he would just say, 'Right.' We became friends, and in fact he did many kind things for [my wife and me] . . . even having us stay at his wonderful house in Santa Cruz. But he never asked me to work with him again."

Hitchcock had gotten exactly what he asked for, and felt nothing. Besides the emotional wreckage he was still processing after eleven years with Benny, he was forced to acknowledge that nothing could save *Torn Curtain*. As for Addison's score, it has its admirers. But for many, it works too hard to compensate for the movie's weakness. Take Addison's love theme, a lightly pleasing waltz. In the early bedroom scene, as Newman and Andrews frolic under covers, the theme is introduced by swoony, vibrato-heavy violins, answered by "gay figures for the wood wind," per Addison's notes to Hitch.[27] Herrmann's icy twelve flutes have been replaced by chirping woodwinds that suggest cartoon bluebirds.

A song arrangement of Addison's theme was commissioned for a soundtrack album. The assignment fell to Jay Livingston and Ray Evans, who in happier times wrote "Que Será, Será." Their new product, "Green Years," was an embarrassment. One can imagine Hitchcock inside the sound booth at Goldwyn, his face showing only fatigue, as the Johnny Mann Singers croon

Example 14.4 Sheet music for *Torn Curtain*'s attempt at a song hit.

lyrics that artificial intelligence might have generated: *"Green years, laughter and tears, pleasures and fears and hopes and dreams...."*

Weeks later, MCA Music shipped a record of the song to radio stations, with a photo of Hitchcock looking severe. For a decade, his ad campaigns had been sophisticated and witty. The caption accompanying this photo reflected new management. "They're playing my favorite tune! *Hitch* your turntable to a hit!"

By then, the director viewed all things *Torn Curtain* with barely concealed disgust. Asked to approve the album's liner notes, he deleted just one sentence: "Hitchcock chose John Addison because he thought the music in the film, *Tom Jones*, contributed '33 1/3%' to keeping the picture moving."[28] No reference to his feelings about Addison remained in the notes.

When sent the final disc, he ignored it, leaving Peggy Robertson to pen an awkward reply. "I have just played it through and love it. I am sure Mr. Hitchcock would wish me to convey his thanks for his copy of the album."[29]

Far from restoring its director's reputation, *Torn Curtain* sank it further. Its two stars, plus Hitchcock's name, ensured a modest profit; but if *Marnie*'s reviews were a stomach-punch, those for *Torn Curta*in were lead bullets. Worst was the *New York Times*, which observed that it "looks no more novel or sensational than grandma's old knitted shawl."[30] Reading that, did Hitchcock see the image of another shawled figure—the skeletal corpse of Mrs. Bates? Six years earlier, he believed that *Psycho* had opened a new door, launching what would be the most creative time in his career. Now, all seemed lost.

Summer, 1966. A heavy-set man in glasses sits alone in a darkened movie theater. On the screen, two men struggle to the death in an East German farmhouse. The eight-minute scene is nearly silent, but the man in the audience can hear music all the same. His music. An hour later, the film is over. Lights in the auditorium are raised, but the man is in no hurry. He has nowhere to go.

15
Coda

Hitchcock's Secret

A somber autumnal day. The city is covered with a cloak of weariness and bleakness. The wind brings in its trail the smells of the first winter's snow. The city seems prepared to greet it with a melancholy song of despair and desolation. The mist fills the dark alleys and is a shroud for the dead trees. In its embers one smells the odor of decay and futility.

—Herrmann, age nineteen, 1930 diary entry

At the end of François Truffaut's *Fahrenheit 451*, the protagonist, Montag—a former book-burner, in a dictatorship that has banned reading—joins a group of outlaws in the forest. There, each man and woman has memorized a book. They repeat the texts aloud as they walk, to ensure they are not forgotten.

In the film's last minutes, the recitals of the book people are joined by a new sound: a lyrical, ascending phrase for strings. In long lines of melody, Bernard Herrmann's score becomes a musical poem. This cue, "The Road," came from its composer's heart, at a time when he too felt himself banished into a wilderness.

Like the hopeful mission of the book people, the scoring of *Fahrenheit 451* channeled Herrmann's energies in a positive direction. "Truffaut gave Benny a second life with *Fahrenheit 451*," observed John Williams.[1]

Herrmann was happiest in London, the city where the movie was scored. Friends urged him to move there. "You are a genuine eccentric," his American friend Kathryn Corwin told him, "and we don't appreciate that in our country. In England, they'll love you."[2]

Benny's devotion to his pets kept him from fully settling in London until 1972 (animals had to be put in a long quarantine). But he spent as much time as possible in the British capital. It was there, on New Year's Eve 1966, that he met the woman who would be his third wife. Twenty-six-year-old Norma

CODA 259

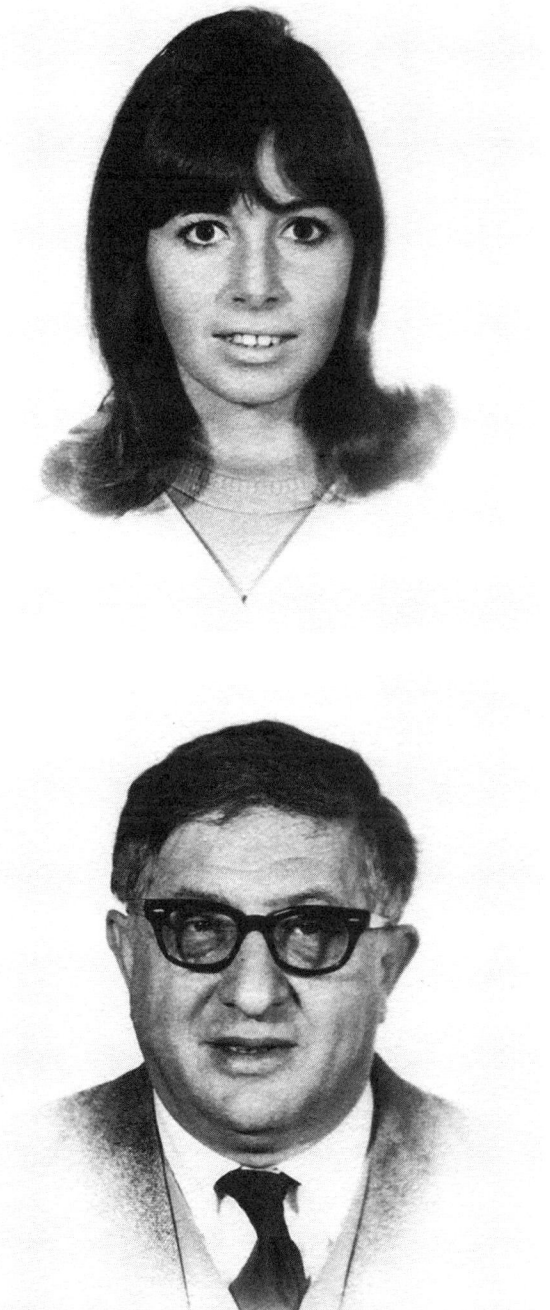

Examples 15.1 and 15.2 1968 passport photos for Norma Herrmann and Benny.

Herrmann was a beautiful, well-read producer for the BBC. She had many admirers. But despite her twenty-nine-year age gap with Benny, the two fell in love and married in 1967.

The pain of his rift with Hitchcock still weighed on him. "He and Hitch had been great friends," recalled Norma. "I think Benny missed that as much as he missed doing the films with him. And he deeply, deeply wished that they could get back together again."[3] Herrmann took every opportunity when speaking in public to praise his former friend. "I've been extraordinarily lucky in my career working with men like Hitchcock," he told the *Los Angeles Times*. The article addressed the *Torn Curtain* split, followed by the statement, "He hopes one day to be working again with Hitchcock."[4]

In early 1968, with Herrmann dividing his time between L.A. and London, Benny took a bolder step toward rapprochement. Two years before, he had recorded *Wuthering Heights*. With the excuse of introducing Norma to Hitch, and giving him a copy of the opera recording, Benny drove onto the Universal lot. "We approached Hitch's office," Norma later said.

> It was a miserable little place, and Benny said, "This is terrible." There was a space for about three cars. Benny stood there and said, "Hitch used to have an empire here. And look at this pathetic place they've given him, when he used to have an empire." He was really sorry about it.
>
> We went up some steps to the door. Benny had the record—and Hitch came to the door. I think he came to the door because Peggy Robertson wasn't in. She always got rid of people. Hitchcock looked a bit shocked and didn't ask us in. Benny said, "This is my record." And Hitch must have known about *Wuthering Heights* being written. Everybody knew about that. Benny said, "And this is my new bride."
>
> I got a nod from Hitchcock. He was ice cold, no smile. Nothing. And the whole thing lasted seconds rather than minutes.
>
> We left, and that was it. But Benny then got a note from Hitch, which he showed me. It said, "Thank you for the copy of your record. I haven't heard it yet, but I know that I'm going to hear something very special." And Benny was thrilled to get that.
>
> But that was the end of it. Whether he listened to the opera or not, we don't know. After that, Benny went twice again to Hitchcock's office. He went once to take the book that Truffaut had written about Hitchcock, and asked Hitch to autograph it. He went once again to pick it up. He didn't see Hitchcock, just Peggy. Whether Hitch was in, I don't know.[5]

At least the director's inscription in Herrmann's copy of *Hitchcock/Truffaut* was gracious. He filled a blank front page with a drawing of his self-caricature. Above it he wrote, "For Benny with my fondest wishes, Hitch."[6]

That same year of 1968, Herrmann took another step toward reconciliation. For Decca Records he recorded *The Great Movie Thrillers*, the first album of music from his scores for Hitchcock. *Psycho*, *Vertigo*, *North by Northwest*, *Marnie*, and *The Trouble with Harry* were represented, accompanied by liner notes by Benny praising Hitchcock. The record was a surprise bestseller, and reviews were raves. Wrote critic Howard Klein, "I [now] realize how much a debt Hitch owed to his composer.... Herrmann represents the serious American composer working effectively, often brilliantly, in film."[7]

But acclaim for those scores did nothing to change Hitchcock's mind. Indeed, the attention focused on Herrmann's contribution may have further alienated him. There would be no further interaction between the two.

If Herrmann was building a new life for himself, revitalized in Norma's company and conducting best-selling albums of his film scores, Hitchcock enjoyed few such pleasures in the late 1960s.

In 1967, he again tried to convince Universal to greenlight a risky project. *Kaleidoscope,* aka *Frenzy,* would be an avant-garde thriller about a necrophiliac serial killer. For the first time, a Hitchcock movie would have explicit violence, nudity, and a hand-held-camera aesthetic. Clouzot's *Diabolique* had influenced *Psycho*; now it was Antonioni's *Blow-Up* that Hitchcock emulated. "These Italian directors are a century ahead of me in terms of technique," he told screenwriter Howard Fast.[8]

The director even shot test footage to sell his concept. Universal executives were appalled. According to Fast, they "belittled Hitchcock's attempt to do precisely what they had been urging him to do—to attempt something different, to catch up with the swiftly moving times."[9]

A year later, on April 10, 1968, the Academy of Motion Picture Arts and Sciences gave Hitchcock the Irving G. Thalberg Memorial Award—his only Oscar. For its recipient, it seemed inadequate. His televised acceptance speech was two words: "Thank you."[10]

The most painful incident in 1968 was personal. On the night of May 11, the home of cinematographer Robert Burks and his wife Elizabeth was consumed in flames. They were unable to escape. Burks was fifty-eight years old.

Two years had passed since Hitchcock directed a film. Eager to work, he agreed to do a project MCA liked: a movie of novelist Leon Uris's political thriller *Topaz*. Hitchcock barely hid his lack of enthusiasm. "He was no longer the great brain that sat in the chair watching," recalled star John Forsythe. "He would go away for fifteen or twenty minutes, and lie down if he could, and it was sad to see." Dozing during takes, he would awake to ask, "Well, how was it?"[11]

Only once, with 1972's *Frenzy* (a different project from *Kaleidoscope/Frenzy*), did he connect again with critics and audiences. *Frenzy* also marked a turning point in the feelings of his former composer. "You know what?" Herrmann said to an interviewer. "Hitchcock told Ron Goodwin . . . that he thought his was the greatest score ever written."[12] With that, Benny gave up defending his friend, or trying to reconcile. Hitchcock, he told author Royal S. Brown, "only finishes a picture 60%. I have to finish it for him."[13] When asked how many directors he worked with "knew anything at all about music, even how to communicate on a simple level with composers," Herrmann snapped, "With the exception of Orson Welles, none of them knew anything."[14]

The omission of Hitchcock was impossible to miss.

When the director was asked about Herrmann, his replies confirmed that Benny would never be forgiven. "He is a very good composer, but a very difficult man. . . . Let me tell you how composers work. When we got to the end of [*Psycho*], the man rushes in with a knife. No screaming violins. I said, 'What happened?' We had screaming violins in the first two murders, and in the last one nothing. . . . You're crazy. Re-do [it] and make them all the same. That's musicians for you."[15]

Hitchcock conveniently forgot that it was Herrmann who overrode the director's instructions to write no music for the shower murder. Instead, Benny ignored him, writing the landmark composition that Hitch now complained he wanted more of.

The same year as *Frenzy*, a seemingly minor event in Herrmann's life laid the groundwork for an extraordinary comeback. Ironically, it was partly thanks to Hitchcock.

In the summer of 1972, twenty-six-year-old editor Paul Hirsch sat in a Manhattan cutting room. He had been hired by thirty-one-year-old director Brian De Palma, a relative novice, to edit *Sisters*, a low-budget Hitchcockian pastiche involving identical twins and murder. Shooting had begun before the movie's full budget had been raised. Hirsch's current task was to assemble the film's goriest murder scene to show potential investors. To make sure the scene was charged with emotion, Hirsch needed music.

Coincidentally, *Psycho* ran on TV that night. And as Marion Crane fled Phoenix by car, trailed by a policeman, Hirsch "realized that the extreme mental duress I was experiencing was due almost entirely to the music."[16] The next morning, he walked to Colony Records and ordered *The Great Movie Thrillers*. "I had to spell Herrmann's name for the clerk, two *r*'s, two *n*'s." When *Sisters*' murder scene was screened to the sound of *Psycho*'s shower music, "the small audience was riveted, and [we] got the money."[17]

De Palma was stunned by the power Herrmann's music added to his shocker. Tracking Benny down in London, he asked him to score *Sisters*.

In the years after *Fahrenheit 451*, Herrmann's film offers had been few. Physically, years of confrontation had taken their toll. Sixty-one years old and overweight, his hair now gray, he looked a decade older. But Herrmann's forcefulness remained. Meeting De Palma in New York, Benny launched into a cane-waving tirade whenever the director made a suggestion. But the afternoon ended with Herrmann cheerfully regaling his mesmerized listeners with tales about his youth, and working with Hitch. He agreed to score De Palma's film.[18]

Released in March of 1973, *Sisters* was a critical and commercial hit. Reviews lauded Herrmann, whose energetic, terrifying score blended wailing Moog synthesizers with clanging percussion and orchestral screams. "Herrmann, a composer of many great scores for Hitchcock, has contributed a textbook example of film music," *Variety*'s critic wrote. "Herrmann is one of the many rarely utilized musicians whose screen work is sorely missed."[19]

De Palma's circle of friends, including Spielberg, Lucas, and Scorsese, all paid attention. And seemingly overnight, Herrmann was "running with the kids now," to quote Lionel Newman's dismissive remark to Benny in 1962. After the success of *Sisters*, Newman called Herrmann in London and offered him a major film at Fox. "Sorry, Lionel," Herrmann replied, "*but I'm running with the kids now!*" SLAM went the receiver, as Benny chortled with glee.[20]

In the fall of 1975, after scoring De Palma's thriller *Obsession*, Herrmann began work on a drama that unsettled even him: *Taxi Driver*. "It makes *Sisters* look like a Sunday picnic," he told Paul Hirsch.[21] But after a decade of rejection, Benny connected deeply to Travis Bickle's isolation and loneliness.

The film's sense of dread also struck a chord, for a man whose internal tempo was slowing due to heart disease, and whose blood pressure was dangerously high. Said his close friend, composer Laurie Johnson, "Benny was living on borrowed time."[22]

As the sixty-four-year-old Herrmann worked on *Taxi Driver* from his London flat, Alfred Hitchcock, seventy-six, was on the Universal lot, overseeing editing on what would be his final film: *Family Plot*. Hitch also was in failing health, but he hadn't lost his humor. During the filming of a street scene that showed a garage door, co-star Bruce Dern suggested to Hitch that the door should have some graffiti. Hitchcock smiled and replied, "I know what we should write: *Fuck MCA*."[23]

To score *Family Plot*, Universal executive Harry Garfield made a savvy recommendation.[24] Forty-three-year-old John Williams had become a household name that summer thanks to *Jaws*. He also may have been the most considerate composer in the business. "When I first went to interview about *Family Plot*, I said, 'Mr. Hitchcock, wouldn't the film world be thrilled if Benny Herrmann and you worked together again?' Hitchcock said, 'No. Put that out of your mind. I want you to do the score. Mr. Herrmann and

Example 15.3 Editor Paul Hirsch, Benny, director Brian De Palma, and producer George Litto recording *Obsession*, August 1975. Courtesy of Paul Hirsch.

I won't work together again, so you should have no feelings of delicacy about doing the picture.'"25 Williams scored *Family Plot* with Benny's encouragement. Herrmann would not live to hear the result.

On December 23, after *Taxi Driver*'s last recording session, Benny and Norma joined director Larry Cohen and his wife to watch Cohen's latest thriller, which Benny had agreed to score. The low-budget *God Told Me To* was the least impressive of Herrmann's upcoming projects. Among the titles he looked forward to scoring were Brian De Palma's *Carrie* and the stylish Sherlock Homes adventure *The Seven-Per-Cent Solution*. The latter was written by Nicholas Meyer, adapting his own novel "about how Holmes meets Sigmund Freud. I wrote on the first page of the screenplay, 'The music is by Bernard Herrmann.' And [director] Herb Ross was wonderful. He went out and hired Bernard Herrmann."26

On the night of the 23rd, the Cohens drove the Herrmanns back to the Sheraton Universal. Norma slept late. She was surprised the next morning to see Benny, an early riser, still beside her. "I started running around getting dressed, and said, 'Come on, aren't you ever going to wake up?' I was just talking to myself. And then I suddenly thought...

"I just touched him with one finger. And I knew. I looked at his face. And his face was—fantastic. It was his doctor who said to me if you look at the face of a dead person, you know exactly what kind of death they had. And his face was lovely. It was really happy and peaceful. He just didn't wake up."27

Released on February 8, 1976, *Taxi Driver* ended with a title card:

OUR GRATITUDE AND RESPECT TO
BERNARD HERRMANN
JUNE 29, 1911–DECEMBER 24, 1975

Death may have come too soon for Herrmann, but at least it claimed him gently. Hitchcock was less fortunate. During the 1970s, Alma suffered a series of strokes, leaving her incapacitated. Hitch was terrified of losing her. He "couldn't cope," recalled his secretary, Sue Gauthier, "and he started drinking to excess. It ended up so terribly, with him being spoon-fed because he was so drunk."28

By 1978 the thought of death obsessed him. "When do you think I'll go? When?" he asked Peggy Robertson. When Ingrid Bergman visited, "he took both my hands, and tears streamed down his face. And he said, 'Ingrid, I'm going to die.'" When actor Hume Cronyn came by, the two men simply sat, holding hands, and wept.29

Example 15.4 Hitchcock receives the AFI Lifetime Achievement Award, 1979. © American Film Institute.

In 1978, Hitchcock's office at Universal closed.

Two years later, in January 1980, he returned to the studio that had brought him both grief and riches. The occasion should have been joyous: at Universal he received an honorary knighthood, bestowed by Queen Elizabeth and presented by the local British Consulate-General. But it came too late; the honoree could barely move. Four months later, on the morning of April 29, 1980, Alfred Hitchcock died of renal failure, in bed at his Bel Air home. He was eighty years old.

On July 6, 1982, Alma followed him, at the age of eighty-two.

The end of Hitchcock's career coincided with a new era at MCA-Universal. After two decades of success in TV, but mostly mediocre film releases, the studio became a big-screen powerhouse. Much of that boom was thanks to Steven Spielberg, whose gift for visual storytelling made him the closest thing to Hitchcock's successor. It was Spielberg who gave Universal *Jaws*, *E.T.*, *Schindler's List*, and the *Jurassic Park* series.

Well into his eighties, Lew Wasserman remained one of Hollywood's and Washington's most respected figures. By 1994, after Universal's sale to the Japanese corporation Matsushita Electric, Lew's net worth was

$450 million.[30] But nothing lasts forever. In 1995, Universal was sold again, to liquor giant Seagram. At age eighty-two, Wasserman was pushed out of the studio he had revitalized forty years earlier. Along with him went the studio's name. For years, the logo on its releases read "Universal—An MCA Company." Seagram dropped the MCA, rebranding their acquisition as Universal Studios, Inc.

In 2002, Lew Wasserman died at the age of eighty-nine.

It is a sign of genius if an artist has been able to create a world by which the force of his imagination and gifts he compels us to recognize as peculiarly his own. This is not necessarily greatness but argues a high degree of individuality—one of the most precious of creative gifts.
        —Text handwritten by Herrmann at Bluebell Avenue, 1950s

In 1965, Herrmann had asked François Truffaut why the director wanted him to score *Fahrenheit 451*. After all, Truffaut was friends with many avant-garde composers. The director replied, "You don't understand. They'll give me the music of the twentieth century. But you'll give me the twenty-first."[31]

A quarter into that twenty-first century, Truffaut has been proven right. In the 1960s, Herrmann's music was considered valueless by studio executives. Today, it is the most enduring and popular of his generation. "He is the most imitated composer," Martin Scorsese stated, "because his work is universal. It has deep psychological power, and it doesn't matter what language you speak. It affects you."[32]

Composer Atticus Ross discovered Herrmann in his youth, long before he joined the industrial rock band Nine Inch Nails, or won an Oscar for co-scoring David Fincher's *The Social Network*. Among 1990s musicians "Herrmann was someone we all knew. If you listen to a Radiohead album, there's no possible way that they haven't spent time listening to Mr. Herrmann. He's become a 'must-know' in the same way as the Beatles. He was an agent of change, moving from the idea of a tune to a psychological space. The kind of modular, cell-based, incredibly precise music he created . . . the instinctive emotion that inhabits every one of his scores. . . . That's why he's had this lasting effect, and why he has such a huge influence across so many genres of music."[33]

Most of his scores remain familiar—the Welles and Harryhausen films, *The Day the Earth Stood Still*, *Cape Fear*, to name just a few. But for the public it is his work with Hitchcock that towers above the rest. In January 2024, the New York Philharmonic sold out three concerts of *Vertigo*, with the score played live to picture. *North by Northwest* and *Psycho* are also regularly shown in symphony halls, accompanied by live score. Literally every day their partnership is discussed in articles, blogs, and podcasts around the world. The music from their films is repurposed—by moviemakers, pop divas, parodists, and advertisers. There is even a "Bernard Herrmann Composer Toolkit," a computer program that helps musicians embellish their work with effects in the style of Herrmann. The concept of a device that helps composers copy his style would have angered, or perhaps amused, the man who liked to quote Tolstoy: "Sparrows fly in flocks, but eagles fly alone."[34]

In 2016, celebrated choreographer Sir Matthew Bourne used Herrmann's music to create a two-hour ballet, based on the film *The Red Shoes*. Bourne had first toyed with the idea of a ballet about Hitch and Benny—an idea he realized was less visually attractive.

"Herrmann's music is synonymous with the films that I loved," Bourne told the author. "The music appealed to me dramatically. And a lot of his music does feel very danceable—he uses dance rhythms a lot. I think his music elevates the films to works of art. Herrmann was certainly one of the best at taking you inside the mind of a character. The music in these films becomes very much like the script, because you get very long sequences where you've got no dialogue. You're guided through by the music. And you almost take a deep breath at the end of those sequences when someone says something."[35]

Words were equally unnecessary for most of the years Hitchcock and Herrmann collaborated. "We had great composers," Peggy Robertson reflected in the 1990s. "We had John Williams. Maurice Jarre. We had all those people. But it just seemed that [Benny] had the feel of Hitch."[36]

Or as Stephen Sondheim put it, "Bernard Herrmann *is* Alfred Hitchcock."[37]

Like the doppelgangers that fill Hitch's cinema—Norman Bates and his mother, Madeleine and Judy, Roger Thornhill and the imaginary George Kaplan—director and composer seem destined to travel together in time. The painful last chapter of their story is famous only because their work remains so vital, the harmony between its creators so profound. Intuitively, Hitchcock and Herrmann understood what Benny's friend, Norman Corwin, called "the elemental passions of love, death, anxiety, pathos."[38]

They also were masters in the use of irresolution—which makes it fitting that one piece in the jigsaw puzzle of their story is likely never to be found.

"Benny always told me that he knew Hitchcock's secret," Norma Herrmann said. "What made Hitchcock tick. Everything that decided what he was. I tried for years to get Benny to tell me what it was, and he wouldn't. And I know there was something. I know there was something. And he said, 'I wouldn't tell anybody while he's alive. I'll tell you after he's dead.' I think it was some fact in Hitch's life. To this day I wonder what it was."[39]

Was the secret something Hitchcock shared with others? To writer Jay Presson Allen, he confided that he was "functionally impotent."[40] He also told her of a recurring dream in which his penis was made of crystal, and he had to conceal this from a cook. (Allen believed that the dream represented Hitch's need to keep his talent "separate and safe" from Alma, a formidable creator herself.)[41]

The secret may have been Hitchcock's admission to writer Rodney Ackland that, had he not met Alma, he might have "become a poof."[42] Homosexual characters abound in his work.

But perhaps, far from Hollywood, over drinks at the Berlin Hilton, during the week they spent together working on *The Birds* . . . perhaps Hitchcock shared something truly private, in a moment of vulnerability. Was it a more complex reason for his fear of the law? An infraction never punished? An incident that explained his ambivalent treatment of women?

Whatever the secret was, Herrmann took it to the grave. Which may have been intentional: after losing the director's trust and friendship, perhaps Benny wished to keep a piece of Hitch to himself. As to how revealing that secret may have been, a quote from Herrmann's first movie comes to mind. "Maybe Rosebud was something he couldn't get, or something he lost. Anyway, it wouldn't have explained anything. I don't think any word can explain a man's life."

The truth of Hitchcock's inner self, and that of Bernard Herrmann, is anything but secret. It is revealed in the pull of a shower curtain, as a woman's final screams are matched by shrieking violins. In the embrace of a man who reclaims his dead love, their kisses accompanied by an orchestral rhapsody.

The precariousness of life. Its fleeting moments of ecstasy. For Hitch and Benny, these ideas became obsessions. Obsessions became art, and the wellspring of friendship.

The art lives on. It unites us in the darkness.

*For Benny
with my fondest
wishes.*

Hitch

Acknowledgments

The bond between Alfred Hitchcock and Bernard Herrmann lasted eleven years. Writing this book, I've been fortunate to draw on four decades of friendships, along with shorter but memorable meetings with many of the people in these pages.

In 1983, while studying journalism and music at USC, I was disappointed to learn that there was no biography of Bernard Herrmann. My brother, Wayne Bryan, suggested that I write one. Two of Benny's friends taught at USC: composer David Raksin and writer-producer Norman Corwin. They encouraged me to write the biography and connected me with dozens who knew Herrmann. If they hadn't, my life might have taken a very different path.

Revisiting interviews conducted for my 1991 book, *A Heart at Fire's Center: The Life and Music of Bernard Herrmann*, I was reunited with friends who still had much to tell me long after their passing. Foremost was Lucille Fletcher, who shared the joys of being the first Mrs. Herrmann, the still-painful details of their breakup, and their conversations during the years that this book covers. During the 1980s, her cousin, Lucy Anderson, continued to process the trauma of her marriage to Benny. Ultimately, the warm, still-beautiful Lucy volunteered many stories of their years together. "I struggled very hard after my divorce from Benny to seek a new identity and to find some degree of peace of mind," she told me. "You have helped me to feel comfortable with my memories and talk about them."

Like Lucille and Lucy, most of those I interviewed are no longer with us. I'm gratified to include in this book recollections by Lady Evelyn Barbirolli, Elmer Bernstein, Ray Bradbury, Don Christlieb, Larry Cohen, Max and Sarah Cohn, Kathryn Corwin, Norman Corwin, Guy Della Cioppa, Philip Dunne, Len Engel, William Froug, Sue Gauthier, Charles Gerhardt, Alan Gleghorn, Diane Gleghorn, Morton Gould, John Green, Joan and Henry Greenwood, Ray Harryhausen, Jack Hayes, Buck Houghton, John Houseman, Marsha Hunt, Laurie Johnson, Louis and Annette Kaufman, Dorothy Kirsten, Ernest Lehman, Elliott Lewis, David Licht, Norman Lloyd, Lyn Murray, Lionel Newman, Christopher Palmer, Abraham Polonsky, Martha Ragland, David

Raksin, Alastair Reid, Miklós Rózsa, Charles Schneer, Eleanor Slatkin, Stephen Sondheim, Fred and Shirley Steiner, James G. Stewart, Ursula Vaughan Williams, and Robert Wise. My thanks to other interviewees for the first book who I hope enjoy this sequel: Howard Blake, Edward Johnson, Martin Scorsese, John Williams, and Leslie T. Zador.

New interviewees offered contemporary perspective on Hitchcock and Herrmann, or filled in missing details from Benny's life. My thanks to Keith Addis, Sir Matthew Bourne, Laurent Bouzereau, Andrew McCaldon, Ronnie Lang, Nicholas Meyer, Jill Meyers, David Newman, Michael Phillips, Alex Ross, Atticus Ross, Carolyn Schurmann, Chris Soldo, Oliver Patrice Weder, and John Wilson.

Laurent Bouzereau's in-depth documentaries on Hitchcock's films, which accompany their video releases, include dozens of interviews with the director's collaborators. These were invaluable. I also benefited from interviews conducted by Sandra Berg, Jon Burlingame, Bruce Crawford, James Curtis, Stephen DeRosa, Dennis McDougal, Howard Prouty, and Craig Reardon. Before he became a noted makeup artist, Craig interviewed many Herrmann associates shortly after the composer's death. I'm grateful once again for Craig's sharing of those conversations.

Over the last four decades, Dorothy Herrmann has been unfailingly generous in providing stories and answering my questions about her father, mother, stepmother, and family friends. Her contribution to this book is enormous.

Norma Herrmann merits a category of her own. Not long after we met in a BBC TV lobby in 1984, Benny's widow gave me full access to Herrmann material in her possession at the time. (His papers can now be found at the University of California, Santa Barbara, under the stewardship of David Seubert.) For the last forty years, Norma has enlightened and entertained me with stories that Benny told her about his childhood, his time with Hitch, and countless other topics.

It felt crucial to include the perspective of musicians who have performed Herrmann's work. Kudos to a quintet of experts who articulated the composer's process: William T. Stromberg and Anna Bonn Stromberg, the late and greatly missed John W. Morgan, William V. Malpede, and Michael McGehee. I urge readers to seek out the Strombergs' award-winning re-recordings of Herrmann scores.

RCA music producer Thomas Yotka has devoted years to researching Herrmann's music and the making of *Psycho*. His generosity in sharing his findings and his analyses was a gift. So was the beautiful BBC-3 radio play "Benny & Hitch," which dramatized its subjects with compassion and respect for accuracy. Thank you, Andrew McCaldon, for allowing me to quote from your play, and for your insights shared in conversation. (Readers: check online to see if "Benny & Hitch" is available for listening.)

Thanks to the late Patricia Hitchcock O'Connell, and to UCLA Library Special Collections, holder of primary documents from Herrmann's RKO years, including music papers for *Citizen Kane* and *All That Money Can Buy*. And a *fortissimo* fanfare to the Margaret Herrick Library, whose staff is deservedly famous for helping authors. This branch of the Academy of Motion Picture Arts and Sciences, and home of Alfred Hitchcock's papers, has been fortunate to have such exceptional representatives as Howard Prouty, Warren Sherk, Louise Hilton, Kristen Ray, Jeanie Braun, Genevieve Maxwell, Meg de Waal, Christina Ha, and Elizabeth Youle.

Wayne Bryan and R. Lee Procter gave indispensable notes on my early drafts. Thanks also to Shari Berman, Rudy Behlmer, Ned Comstock, Paul Farrar, Diana Friedberg, Gary Giddins, Tracey Goessel, Joel Gunz, Randy Haberkamp, Mike Hamilburg, Mona Huntzig, Leonard Maltin, Eddie Muller, David Pierce, Nick Redman, Libby Rice, Phillip Sametz, Clancy Sigal, Philip Skerry, Carolyn and Elwayne Smith, Mark Wanamaker, and Glen West.

The team at Oxford University Press has been a source of constant support. Much gratitude to Norm Hirschy, Egle Zigaite, Ganga Balaji, Timothy DeWerff, and Leslie Johnson.

The life and career of my literary agent, Georges Borchardt, would constitute a book as compelling as the Pulitzer and Nobel Prize winners he has shepherded into existence. My thanks to Georges and to Cora Markowitz for all they do.

Lastly, I thank my wife, Michelle Guy, whose love, support, and insight into human behavior informed the pages you have read.

Steven C. Smith
April 2025

Notes

Prelude

1. "Taxi Driver / Music Timing," Martin Scorsese Papers, AFI Los Angeles.
2. Details of the December 23, 1975, recording session are from author interviews with Don Christlieb, Dominic Fera, Jack Hayes, Norma Herrmann, Ronnie Lang, Jill Meyers, Michael Phillips, Uan Rasey, Alan Robinson, Martin Scorsese, Eleanor Slatkin, and Chris Soldo.
3. Phillips to author, July 12, 2023.
4. Scorsese to author, February 23, 1989. All Scorsese quotes in the Prelude are from this interview.
5. Soldo to author, November 22, 2022.
6. Williams to author, September 6, 1984.
7. Slatkin to author, August 28, 1984.
8. Meyers to author, September 28, 2022.
9. Lloyd to Howard Prouty, 1987.
10. William Rothman, *Hitchcock: The Murderous Gaze* (Cambridge, MA: Harvard University Press, 1984), 281.
11. BH, album notes, *The Great Movie Thrillers*, Decca, 1968.
12. Procter to author, February 24, 2024.
13. "Benny & Hitch," BBC Radio 3, aired December 25, 2022. Used with permission of Andrew McCaldon.
14. Patrick McGilligan, *Alfred Hitchcock: A Life in Darkness and Light* (New York: HarperCollins, 2003), 666.
15. BH, John Player Lecture, National Film Theatre, London, June 11, 1972.
16. Mark Eden Horowitz, *Sondheim on Music* (Lanham, MD: Rowman & Littlefield, 2019), 72.

Chapter 1

1. Details on Lew Wasserman and MCA are drawn principally from: Dennis McDougal, *The Last Mogul: Lew Wasserman, MCA, and the Hidden History of Hollywood* (Boston: Da Capo Press, 2001); Kathleen Sharp, *Mr. & Mrs. Hollywood: Edie and Lew Wasserman and Their Entertainment Empire* (New York: Carroll & Graf, 2003).
2. Details on AH and Selznick, and Transatlantic Pictures, are drawn principally from: Peter Ackroyd, *Alfred Hitchcock: A Brief Life* (New York: Talese/Doubleday, 2015); McGilligan, *Alfred Hitchcock*; John Russell Taylor, *Hitch: The Life and Times of Alfred Hitchcock* (New York: Pantheon, 1978).
3. Ackroyd, *Alfred Hitchcock*, 118.
4. Dan E. Moldea, *Dark Victory: Ronald Reagan, MCA, and the Mob* (New York: Viking, 1986), 16.
5. McGilligan, *Alfred Hitchcock*, 475.
6. Details on AH's contract with Paramount are drawn principally from: Dan Auiler, *Vertigo: The Making of a Hitchcock Classic* (New York: St. Martin's Press, 1998); McDougal, *The Last Mogul*; McGilligan, *Alfred Hitchcock*.
7. Charles Champlin, "Alma Reville Hitchcock, the Unsung Partner," *Los Angeles Times*, July 29, 1982.
8. McGilligan, *Alfred Hitchcock*, 494.
9. McDougal, *The Last Mogul*, 152–156.
10. Ibid., 122.
11. Ibid., 136.
12. Patrick Goldstein, "Ex-Secretary Recalls Memories of Hitchcock," *Los Angeles Times*, November 14, 1983.
13. Adriano, "Hitchcock on Film Music and Bernard Herrmann," September 26, 1972, http://adrianomusic.com/adriano-s-four-conversations.html.
14. Sidney Gottlieb, ed., *Hitchcock on Hitchcock*, Vol. 2 (Oakland: University of California Press, 2014), 142.

15. Nathan Platte, *Making Music in Selznick's Hollywood* (New York: Oxford University Press, 2017), 96.
16. Adriano, "Hitchcock on Film Music and Bernard Herrmann."
17. Waxman also scored Hitchcock's *Suspicion* for RKO.
18. From interviews between AH and François Truffaut, beginning in 1962 (later collected in François Truffaut, *Hitchcock/Truffaut*, rev. ed. (New York: Simon & Schuster, 1983).
19. Rudy Behlmer, ed., *Memo from David O. Selznick* (New York: Viking, 1972), 265.
20. Platte, *Making Music in Selznick's Hollywood*, 239. This book is the principal source for discussion of BH-Selznick interactions in this chapter.
21. Jerome Moross to Craig Reardon, 1979.
22. Charles Gerhardt to author, June 4, 2024.
23. Moross to Reardon, 1979.
24. Details on Herrmann family history and their life in New York City are drawn primarily from author interviews with Lucille Fletcher, Morton Gould, Dorothy Herrmann, Norma Herrmann, Laurie Johnson, and Martin Silver; interviews by Craig Reardon with Louis Herrmann and Jerome Moross; interview by Wayne Bryan with Max and Sarah Cohn; and family records of Steven E. Rivkin.
25. Norma Herrmann to author, February 16, 1985.
26. Norma Herrmann to author, November 1, 2022.
27. Cohn to Wayne Bryan, September 12, 1984.
28. Dorothy Herrmann to author, March 26, 1986.
29. John Green to author, June 23, 1984.
30. Lucille Fletcher to author, January 11, 1988.
31. Hector Berlioz, program notes, *Symphonie fantastique*, premiere date December 5, 1830.
32. BBC Radio interview, March 12, 1972. Also see BH chapter in Vivian Perlis, ed., *Charles Ives Remembered: An Oral History* (New Haven, CT: Yale University Press, 1974).
33. All Herrmann diaries quoted in the book were provided by Norma Herrmann in 1985.
34. Gould to author, July 19, 1984.
35. Gershwin details and quotes told by BH, BBC Radio interview, March 12, 1971.
36. Norma Herrmann to author, November 1, 2022.
37. BBC Radio interview, early 1970s.
38. For a detailed account of BH's pre-AH work, see: Steven C. Smith, *A Heart at Fire's Center: The Life and Music of Bernard Herrmann* (Berkeley: University of California Press, 1991).
39. John Houseman, *Run-Through: A Memoir* (New York: Simon & Schuster, 1972), 366.
40. Ted Gilling, "The Colour of Music: An Interview with Bernard Herrmann," *Sight & Sound* (Winter 1971–1972).
41. Ibid.
42. Stewart to author, March 28, 1984.
43. Wise to author, February 21, 1984.
44. Wilson to author, November 2, 2022.
45. Quoted by syndicated columnist Mildred Norton, 1946.
46. BH to Fletcher, December 7, 1942.
47. Fletcher to author, January 14, 1988.

Chapter 2

1. Herbert Coleman, *The Man Who Knew Hitchcock* (Lanham, MD: Scarecrow Press, 2007), 204.
2. Ibid., 193.
3. Ibid.
4. Ibid., 194, and McGilligan, *Alfred Hitchcock*, 502–503.
5. McGilligan, *Alfred Hitchcock*, 504.
6. Ibid., 503.
7. Coleman, *The Man Who Knew Hitchcock*, 200.
8. AH-Truffaut interviews, 1962.
9. Douglas Bell, "An Interview with C. O. Erickson," 2006, 105 and 136, Margaret Herrick Library.
10. Ackroyd, *Alfred Hitchcock*, 88.
11. Stephen Rebello, *Alfred Hitchcock and the Making of Psycho* (New York: Soft Skull, 1990), 113.
12. Coleman, *The Man Who Knew Hitchcock*, 181.
13. Murray to author, March 1, 1984.
14. Norma Herrmann to author, November 1, 2022.

15. Coleman, *The Man Who Knew Hitchcock*, 208.
16. BH, album notes, *The Great Movie Thrillers*.
17. Kevin Thomas, "Film Composer Settles a Score," *Los Angeles Times*, February 4, 1968.
18. Michael Ratcliffe, "Composing the 'Emotional Scenery' for the Screen," *Sheffield Telegraph*, March 25, 1961.
19. BH letter to *Musical Times*, January 1959, 24.
20. BH, "Musical England," *New York Herald Tribune*, December 1946.
21. Barbirolli to author, February 4, 1985.
22. Morris Hastings, "Bernard Herrmann: A CBS Institution," CBS press release, 1944.
23. BH letter to *Musical Times*, January 1959, 24.
24. Zanuck to Newman, December 11, 1953, provided by Norma Herrmann, 1985.
25. Paramount interoffice memo, December 7, 1954.
26. Coleman, *The Man Who Knew Hitchcock*, 208.
27. Paramount interoffice memo, December 7, 1954.
28. Details about BH's home and guests are drawn primarily from author interviews with Lucy Anderson, Lady Evelyn Barbirolli, Elsa Clay, Kathryn Corwin, Oliver Daniel, Guy Della Cioppa, Margaret Della Cioppa, Dorothy Herrmann, Norma Herrmann, Marsha Hunt, Louis and Annette Kaufman, Norman Lloyd, Lyn Murray, Robert Presnell Jr., David Raksin, Alan Robinson, and Fred Steiner.
29. Dorothy Herrmann to author, July 4, 2022.
30. Dorothy Herrmann to author, March 26, 1986.
31. Royal S. Brown, "An Interview with Bernard Herrmann," *High Fidelity*, September 1976.
32. Dorothy Herrmann to author, March 26, 1986.
33. BH writing in ink was described in author interviews with Elmer Bernstein and Laurie Johnson.
34. Brown, "An Interview with Bernard Herrmann."
35. BH, album notes, *The Great Movie Thrillers*.
36. The score of *The Trouble with Harry*, and other AH-BH scores, can be reviewed at University of California Santa Barbara Library, Department of Special Research Collections.
37. Gilling, "The Colour of Music."
38. Quotes from Laurent Bouzereau, Michael McGehee, Nicholas Meyer, John Morgan, William Stromberg, and John Wilson in this chapter are from author interviews conducted in 2022 and 2023.
39. Fletcher to author, January 12, 1988.
40. Christlieb to author, July 11, 1984.
41. Carolyn Schurmann to author, August 4, 2023.
42. BH, "From Sound Track to Disc," *Saturday Review*, September 27, 1947.
43. Irving Kolodin, "The Wide Screen World of Bernard Herrmann," *Saturday Review*, March 6, 1976.
44. Studio Orchestra Manager's Daily Report, Paramount, May 11, 1955.
45. Christlieb to author, July 11, 1984.
46. Lyn Murray diary, shared with author March 1, 1984.
47. Lewis to author, June 26, 1984.
48. Bernstein to author, November 14, 1984.
49. Lyn Murray diary, shared with author March 1, 1984.
50. Coleman, *The Man Who Knew Hitchcock*, 208.
51. Dorothy Herrmann to author, March 26, 1986.
52. Adriano, "Hitchcock on Film Music and Bernard Herrmann."

Chapter 3

1. Taylor, *Hitch*, 228.
2. Martin Grams Jr. and Patrik Wikstrom, *The Alfred Hitchcock Presents Companion* (Churchville, MD: OTR, 2001), 19.
3. Rebello, *Alfred Hitchcock and the Making of Psycho*, 43.
4. Taylor, *Hitch*, 230–231.
5. Coleman, *The Man Who Knew Hitchcock*, 174.
6. Bell, "An Interview with C. O. Erickson," 4.
7. Rebello, *Alfred Hitchcock and the Making of Psycho*, 33.
8. Gauthier to author, October 30, 1984.
9. Norma Herrmann to author, November 1, 2022.

10. Diane Gleghorn to author, July 4, 1984.
11. Engel to author, July 17, 1984.
12. Pat Hitchcock O'Connell and Laurent Bouzereau, *Alma Hitchcock: The Woman behind the Man* (New York: Berkley, 2003), 193.
13. Norma Herrmann to author, February 16, 1985.
14. Guy Della Cioppa to author, July 25, 1984.
15. Steiner to author, March 3, 1984.
16. Dorothy Herrmann to author, July 29, 2022.
17. Anderson to author, 2001.
18. Taylor, *Hitch*, 233.
19. For a detailed account of this film's production, as well as later AH-BH films, see McGilligan, *Alfred Hitchcock*; Taylor, *Hitch*; and Ackroyd, *Alfred Hitchcock*.
20. AH to Sidney Bernstein, July 25, 1955, AH Papers, Margaret Herrick Library.
21. The piece's official name depends on your source. Benjamin's score calls it "The Storm Clouds." The 1956 film credits identify it as "Storm Cloud Cantata"—but within the film, a poster is shown advertising "Cantata Storm Clouds." For consistency I've chosen "Storm Clouds."
22. Gilling, "The Colour of Music."
23. Alan Gelb, *The Doris Day Scrapbook* (New York: Grosset & Dunlap, 1977), 88–90.
24. Newman to author, July 16, 1984.
25. Dorothy Herrmann to author, July 29, 2022.
26. Gilling, "The Colour of Music."
27. BH Radio interview with Mischa Donat, February 1973.
28. Benjamin to Paramount Pictures Corp., May 24, 1955.
29. Coleman, *The Man Who Knew Hitchcock*, 219.
30. Hayes took his quest for solo credit to the Writers Guild of America and won.
31. Coleman, *The Man Who Knew Hitchcock*, 220.
32. Screenplay, AH Papers, Herrick Library.
33. "English Audiences Keenly Interested in Modern Music," *Musical Courier*, 1946.
34. *Variety*, December 4, 1946.
35. Dorothy Herrmann to author, July 29, 2022.
36. Daniel to Craig Reardon, March 18, 1979.
37. *New York Times*, July 29, 1947.
38. Fletcher to author, January 12, 1988.
39. Ross to author, August 30, 2023.
40. Steiner to author, March 3, 1984.
41. Gerhardt to author, June 4, 1984.
42. Raksin to author, January 25, 1984.
43. Farrell to Craig Reardon, January 24, 1977.
44. Diane Gleghorn to author, July 4, 1984.
45. Steiner to author, March 3, 1984.
46. Louis Herrmann to Craig Reardon, June 4, 1979.
47. For details on the film's production schedule, see AH Papers, Herrick Library.
48. Greenwood to author, May 13, 1985.
49. Ibid.
50. AH Papers, Herrick Library.
51. McGilligan, *Alfred Hitchcock*, 519–520.
52. Ackroyd, *Alfred Hitchcock*, 88.
53. Quotes from John Morgan, Alex Ross, William Stromberg, and John Wilson in this chapter are from author interviews conducted in 2022 and 2023.
54. Stewart repeated this anecdote throughout the 1970s and 1980s, including in his speech at the AFI Lifetime Achievement Award ceremony honoring Hitchcock on March 7, 1979.
55. "Bernard Herrmann on Film Music," Eastman College lecture, 1973.
56. Coleman, *The Man Who Knew Hitchcock*, 221.
57. McCaldon to author, April 5, 2023.

Chapter 4

1. BH interview with Leslie Zador and Greg Rose, September 26, 1970.
2. Steiner to author, March 3, 1984.
3. Lloyd to author, May 11, 1984.

4. Palmer to author, May 1985.
5. Houseman to author, April 20, 1984.
6. Greenwood to author, May 13, 1985.
7. Ackroyd, *Alfred Hitchcock*, 176–177.
8. Ibid.
9. Rebello, *Alfred Hitchcock and the Making of Psycho*, 229–230.
10. Norma Herrmann to author, November 1, 1922.
11. AH acceptance speech, AFI Lifetime Achievement Award, March 7, 1979.
12. Goldstein, "Ex-Secretary Recalls Memories of Hitchcock."
13. McGilligan, *Alfred Hitchcock*, 382–383.
14. Coleman, *The Man Who Knew Hitchcock*, 227.
15. Ibid.
16. Bell, "An Interview with C. O. Erickson," 105.
17. Scott Eyman, *Hank and Jim: The Fifty-Year Friendship of Henry Fonda and James Stewart* (New York: Simon & Schuster, 2017), 227.
18. Lloyd to Howard Prouty, 1987.
19. Coleman to BH, December 1, 1956.
20. Kolodin, "The Wide Screen World of Bernard Herrmann."
21. Louis Herrmann to Craig Reardon, June 4, 1979.
22. "An Oral History with Peggy Robertson," interview by Barbara Hall, 2002, 101, Herrick Library.
23. Coleman to BH, January 25, 1956.
24. Coleman telegram to BH, January 30, 1956.
25. Quotes from Fletcher in this chapter are from interview with author, January 11, 1988.
26. Sondheim to author, April 16, 1986.
27. BH, John Player Lecture.
28. Bernstein to author, November 14, 1984.
29. Quotes from William V. Malpede, John Morgan, Alex Ross, Atticus Ross, and William Stromberg in this chapter are from author interviews conducted in 2022 and 2023.
30. "Bernard Herrmann on Film Music."
31. Ibid.
32. Coleman, *The Man Who Knew Hitchcock*, 232.
33. Roger Ebert, "Scorsese Learns from Those Who Went before Him," *Chicago Sun-Times*, January 11, 1998.
34. BH letter to AH, February 21, 1958.

Chapter 5

1. Auiler, *Vertigo*, 52.
2. Ackroyd, *Alfred Hitchcock*, 184.
3. "Mary Rose, Riverside Studios," *Fourth Wall Magazine*, April 4, 2012.
4. Ackroyd, *Alfred Hitchcock*, 84.
5. Rebello, *Alfred Hitchcock and the Making of Psycho*, 131.
6. Ackroyd, *Alfred Hitchcock*, 215.
7. BH quoted in *Newsweek*, May 12, 1980.
8. Coleman, *The Man Who Knew Hitchcock*, 223.
9. Martha Ragland to author, November 29, 1984.
10. Bernstein to author, November 14, 1984.
11. Williams to author, September 6, 1984.
12. Fletcher quotes in this chapter are from author interviews, January 11 to 14, 1988.
13. BH to LA, 1948. Letters from BH to LA shared by LA with author.
14. Steiner to author, March 3, 1984.
15. Houseman to author, April 20, 1984.
16. Herrmann to author, July 29, 2022.
17. Fletcher to author, January 13, 1988.
18. Coleman, *The Man Who Knew Hitchcock*, 247.
19. Auiler, *Vertigo*, 45–47. Auiler's book is the most thorough account of *Vertigo*'s making.
20. Coleman, *The Man Who Knew Hitchcock*, 254.
21. Auiler, *Vertigo*, 49.
22. Ibid.
23. McGilligan, *Alfred Hitchcock*, 546.

24. Auiler, *Vertigo*, 25.
25. BH, John Player Lecture.
26. McGilligan, *Alfred Hitchcock*, 553.
27. Auiler, *Vertigo*, 179.
28. AH Papers, Herrick Library cutting notes, February 6, 1958.
29. Details regarding BH's hiring, schedule, and meetings with AH on this and later films, as well as AH "Musical Suggestions" and "Sound Notes," are in AH Papers, Herrick Library.
30. Brown, "An Interview with Bernard Herrmann."
31. Quotes from Laurent Bouzereau, Norma Herrmann, William V. Malpede, Nicholas Meyer, John Morgan, Alex Ross, Anna Bonn Stromberg, and William Stromberg in this chapter are from author interviews conducted in 2022 and 2023.
32. Brown, "An Interview with Bernard Herrmann."
33. Ibid.
34. Gerhardt to author, June 4, 1984.
35. Palmer to author, May 1985.
36. Scorsese, *Title Sequence Seminar*, 1995 booklet, Herrick Library.
37. Aylin Zafar, "Deconstructing Lady Gaga's 'Born This Way' Video," *The Atlantic*, March 2, 2011.
38. "Best Songs of 2011," MTV News, December 14, 2011.
39. Coleman, *The Man Who Knew Hitchcock*, 259.
40. BH, John Player Lecture.
41. The habanera originated in Cuba in the nineteenth century; its name means "from Havana."

Chapter 6

1. Quotes from Laurent Bouzereau, Norma Herrmann, William V. Malpede, Nicholas Meyer, John Morgan, Alex Ross, Anna Bonn Stromberg, William Stromberg, and John Wilson in this chapter are from author interviews conducted in 2022 and 2023.
2. AH, "Musical Suggestions," AH Papers, *Vertigo*, Herrick Library.
3. Coleman, *The Man Who Knew Hitchcock*, 247.
4. "Jessye Norman Sings Richard Wagner's Liebestod from Tristan und Isolde," *The Solari Report*, February 21, 2020.
5. Kevin Mulhall, album notes, *Vertigo*, conducted by Joel McNeely/Royal Scottish National Orchestra, Varèse Sarabande, 1996.
6. Auiler, *Vertigo*, 53.
7. Hunt to author, March 13, 1984.
8. Norma Herrmann to author, November 1, 2022.
9. AH-Truffaut interviews, 1962.
10. BH, album notes, *The Great Movie Thrillers*.
11. Gilling, "The Colour of Music."
12. "Bernard Herrmann on Film Music." In the film, "Scene d'amour" lasts five minutes. Herrmann's 1968 re-recording is five and a half minutes.
13. Gregg Kilday, "Kim Novak Cries 'Rape' over 'The Artist's' Use of Music," *Hollywood Reporter*, January 9, 2012.
14. Coleman, *The Man Who Knew Hitchcock*, 259.
15. Ibid., 260. Herrmann's politics were complex. His conservatism was libertarian in nature, as demonstrated by his contempt for the union rules that impacted *Vertigo*.
16. Ibid.
17. Ibid.
18. Ibid., 261.
19. Ibid.
20. The Vienna sessions were not recorded in stereo.
21. Ibid.
22. Steve Harris, "An Afternoon with Bernard Herrmann," publication unknown, 1970s. Courtesy of Craig Reardon.
23. Coleman, *The Man Who Knew Hitchcock*, 262.
24. Froug to author, March 6, 1984.
25. Raksin to author, July 11, 1984.
26. Coleman, *The Man Who Knew Hitchcock*, 263.
27. Ibid., 264.
28. Ibid., 264–265.

29. Auiler, *Vertigo*, 164.
30. Taylor, *Hitch*, 245.
31. Ackroyd, *Alfred Hitchcock*, 192.
32. Ibid.
33. O'Connell and Bouzereau, *Alma Hitchcock*, 177.
34. *Vertigo* review, *Hollywood Reporter*, May 12, 1958.
35. *Vertigo* review, *Time*, June 16, 1958.
36. Ratcliffe, "Composing the Emotional Scenery for the Screen," *Sheffield Telegraph*, May 25, 1961.
37. Rebello, *Alfred Hitchcock and the Making of Psycho*, 72.
38. McDougal, *The Last Mogul*, 244.

Chapter 7

1. Mary Brian, widow of George Tomasini, to James Curtis. Curtis to SCS, 2022.
2. Robinson to author, June 13, 1984.
3. Coleman, *The Man Who Knew Hitchcock*, 259.
4. Compiled from incidents shared with author by William Froug, Charles Gerhardt, Joan and Henry Greenwood, Dorothy Herrmann, Louis and Annette Kaufman, Lyn Murray, David Raksin, Miklos Rozsa, Fred and Shirley Steiner, and from BH interview with Leslie Zador and Greg Rose.
5. Lehman to author, March 5, 1984.
6. Ackroyd, *Alfred Hitchcock*, 193.
7. Ibid., 191.
8. McGilligan, *Alfred Hitchcock*, 496.
9. Ibid., 566.
10. Ibid., 570.
11. Coleman, *The Man Who Knew Hitchcock*, 285.
12. All dates of AH-BH meetings cited in this book are from AH appointment diaries, AH Papers, Herrick Library.
13. "An Oral History with Peggy Robertson," 176.
14. BH Radio interview with Mischa Donat, February 1973.
15. Christopher Husted, album notes, *North by Northwest*, original soundtrack, Rhino, 1995.
16. Lewis to author, June 26, 1984.
17. Murray to author, March 1, 1984.
18. Quotes from Laurent Bouzereau, Michael McGehee, John Morgan, Anna Bonn Stromberg, and William Stromberg in this chapter are from author interviews conducted in 2022 and 2023.
19. Album notes, *North by Northwest*, original soundtrack, Intrada, 2012.
20. Don Wardell, "Music to Commit Murder By," *Soho Weekly News*, September 9, 1976.
21. MGM Studio Daily Report, April 23, 1959.
22. The movie was originally released in monophonic sound. Video releases and a 2024 theatrical restoration used the original tracks to mix it in stereo.
23. Ives to author, October 24, 1984.
24. Lloyd to author, May 11, 1984.
25. Lehman interview, *Creative Screenwriting* 7, no. 6 (November 1, 2000).
26. Ackroyd, *Alfred Hitchcock*, 195.
27. Scott Eyman, *Cary Grant: A Brilliant Disguise* (New York: Simon & Schuster, 2020), 329.
28. Ibid.
29. BH, handwritten note on telegram from Saint, July 17, 1959.
30. BH, album notes, *The Great Movie Thrillers*.
31. Tony Albarella, ed., *As Timeless as Infinity: The Complete Twilight Zone Scripts of Rod Serling*, Vol. 2 (Colorado Springs, CO: Gauntlet Press, 2005).
32. McDougal, *The Last Mogul*, 230. Also the chief source for discussion of MCA in this chapter.

Chapter 8

1. "Jerry 'Beaver' Mathers Helped Create the Mrs. Bates Skull in 'Psycho,'" *MeTV* website, August 9, 2017.
2. Rebello, *Alfred Hitchcock and the Making of Psycho*, 102.
3. "Jerry 'Beaver' Mathers Helped Create the Mrs. Bates Skull in 'Psycho.'"
4. Unless noted, details on the film's making are from Rebello, *Alfred Hitchcock and the Making of Psycho*.

5. Anthony Boucher, *New York Times Book Review*, April 19, 1959.
6. Coleman, *The Man Who Knew Hitchcock*, 287.
7. Rebello, *Alfred Hitchcock and the Making of Psycho*, 26.
8. Ibid., 57.
9. Ibid., 59.
10. Ibid.
11. Ibid., 61.
12. Ibid.
13. Ibid., 116.
14. "An Oral History with Peggy Robertson," 105–108.
15. Herrmann later erroneously said that the shower scene was shot in a day. He may have been recalling the original schedule, or the fact that the week he began scoring *Psycho*, Hitch was doing one pick-up day of shots for the shower scene.
16. Rebello, *Alfred Hitchcock and the Making of Psycho*, 134.
17. Ibid., 143.
18. Ibid., 160.
19. Philip J. Skerry, *Psycho in the Shower: The History of Cinema's Most Famous Scene* (New York: Continuum, 2009), 218.
20. Peggy Robertson to Frank Caffey, June 22, 1960.
21. Rebello, *Alfred Hitchcock and the Making of Psycho*, 177.
22. Dorothy Herrmann to author, July 29, 2022.
23. D'Amato to author, April 7, 1986.
24. AH to BH, December 11, 1959, AH Papers, *Psycho*, Herrick Library.
25. BBC Radio interview with Mischa Donat, February 1973.
26. Quoted in Brian De Palma, "Murder by Moog: Scoring the Chill," *Village Voice*, October 11, 1973.
27. BBC Radio interview with John Amis, early 1970s.
28. De Palma, "Murder by Moog."
29. Evan Cameron, ed., *Sound and the Cinema* (New York: Redgrave, 1980).
30. BH interview, "A Talk with Alfred Hitchcock," *Telescope*, CBC TV, 1964.
31. Wardell, "Music to Commit Murder By."
32. BH, album notes, *The Great Movie Thrillers*.
33. Gilling, "The Colour of Music."
34. Rebello, *Alfred Hitchcock and the Making of Psycho*, 180.
35. *The Trouble with Harry*, *The Man Who Knew Too Much*, and *The Wrong Man* used relatively small ensembles for their underscore, with the exception of the main title for *TMWKTM* and its cantata "Storm Clouds," not written by Herrmann and not part of the underscore.
36. Paramount Studio Daily Report, March 16, 1960.
37. Yotka to author, July 12, 2022.
38. Rebello, *Alfred Hitchcock and the Making of Psycho*, 181.
39. Steiner to author, March 3, 1984. Herrmann's original sketches show that he did experiment with adding a flute for one cue. Ultimately he used only strings.
40. Charles Gerhardt to author, 1985.
41. Cameron, *Sound and the Cinema*.
42. Quotes from Michael McGehee, John Morgan, Anna Bonn Stromberg, William Stromberg, and John Wilson in this chapter are from author interviews conducted in 2022 and 2023.
43. BBC Radio interview with John Amis.
44. Christopher Palmer, album notes, re-recording of *Psycho* conducted by BH, Unicorn, 1976.
45. One of the violinists, Sidney Sax, worked often with Herrmann on his recordings in London.
46. Paul McCartney, "Writing 'Eleanor Rigby,'" *New Yorker*, October 18, 2021.
47. *Revolver: Special Edition, 5CD (Remastered)*, Capitol, 2022.
48. BBC Radio interview with Mischa Donat, February 1973.
49. Palmer, album notes, *Psycho*.
50. Rebello, *Alfred Hitchcock and the Making of Psycho*, 175.
51. BBC Radio interview with Mischa Donat.
52. Paul Hirsch to author, March 21, 1984.
53. BBC Radio interview with Mischa Donat.
54. Gilling, "The Colour of Music."

Chapter 9

1. Charles Gerhardt to author, 1985.
2. Quotes from Andrew McCaldon, Michael McGehee, John Morgan, David Newman, Anna Bonn Stromberg, William Stromberg, and John Wilson in this chapter are from author interviews conducted in 2022 and 2023.
3. Williams to author, September 6, 1984.
4. Rebello, *Alfred Hitchcock and the Making of Psycho*, 143.
5. Howard Klein, "The Man Who Composed 'Citizen Kane,'" *New York Times*, June 27, 1971.
6. Johnson to author, June 4, 1984.
7. Cameron, *Sound and the Cinema*.
8. Wardell, "Music to Commit Murder By."
9. Palmer, album notes, *Psycho*.
10. Mark Eden Horowitz, *Sondheim on Music* (Lanham, MD: Rowman & Littlefield, 2019).
11. Herrmann would use the same "converging motion" concept in 1962's *Cape Fear*, in which Gregory Peck's and Robert Mitchum's characters are on a deadly collision course.
12. BH, "Recorded and Neglected Russian Music ('The Five')," publication unknown, 1940s.
13. Palmer, album notes, *Psycho*.
14. Skerry, *Psycho in the Shower*, 217.
15. Ibid., 182–183.
16. Cameron, *Sound and the Cinema*, 133.
17. Ibid.
18. Skerry, *Psycho in the Shower*, 185.
19. *78/52*, feature documentary, 2012.
20. Skerry, *Psycho in the Shower*, 59.
21. *The Making of Psycho*, Universal home video documentary, 1997.
22. Rebello, *Alfred Hitchcock and the Making of Psycho*, 185.
23. Schlom to James Curtis. Partially quoted in ibid., 185–186.
24. Ibid., 187
25. Ibid., 186.
26. Ibid., 192.
27. Ibid., 207.
28. Ibid.
29. Ibid., 209.
30. Ibid.
31. *78/52*. Also Ackroyd, *Alfred Hitchcock*, 206.
32. Rebello, *Alfred Hitchcock and the Making of Psycho*, 210.
33. Ibid., 231.
34. Ibid., 221.
35. Dorothy Herrmann to author, July 29, 2022.
36. Rebello, *Alfred Hitchcock and the Making of Psycho*, 181.
37. Ibid., 223.
38. Ibid., 181.
39. Jack Sullivan, *Hitchcock's Music* (New Haven, CT: Yale University Press, 2006).
40. Paramount's "Summary of Detail Picture Cost" lists $17,500 for "composer & conductor" and $17,000.51 for "under-score musicians, projection for music, music editors, rental & cartage of instruments." A "Production Budget" report dated July 5, 1960, after *Psycho*'s completion, lists final music costs as $38,175, indicating an overage of $3,674.
41. Dorothy Herrmann to author, March 26, 1986.
42. Newman to author, July 16, 1984.
43. Rebello, *Alfred Hitchcock and the Making of Psycho*, 207.

Chapter 10

1. Rózsa to author, June 20, 1984.
2. Ringo Starr replaced Best in 1962.
3. Lloyd to author, May 11, 1984.
4. BH interview with Leslie Zador and Greg Rose.
5. Lloyd to author, May 11, 1984.
6. Greenwood to author, May 13, 1985.

7. Murray to author, March 1, 1984.
8. Murray to Craig Reardon, April 27, 1977.
9. Robert P. Kolker and Nathan Abrams, *Kubrick: An Odyssey* (Berkeley, CA: Pegasus Books, 2024.).
10. Berres to author, August 1, 1984.
11. Bernstein to author, November 14, 1984.
12. Dorothy Herrmann to author, March 26, 1986.
13. Louis Herrmann to Craig Reardon, June 4, 1989.
14. Wally Trabing, "Seabird Invasion Hits Coastal Homes," *Santa Cruz Sentinel*, August 18, 1961.
15. "The Story behind Hitchcock's Crazed 'Birds,'" *Scripps Institution of Oceanography*, February 1, 2012.
16. Bradbury to author, December 14, 1984.
17. McDougal, *The Last Mogul*, 230–232.
18. Ibid., 284.
19. Taylor, John Russell, interviewed in *Reputations: Alfred Hitchcock*, BBC TV, 1999.
20. Rebello, *Alfred Hitchcock and the Making of Psycho*, 231–232.
21. "An Oral History with Peggy Robertson," 223.
22. McDougal, *The Last Mogul*, 296–300.
23. Author interviews with David Licht, Norman Lloyd, and David Raksin.
24. Tony Lee Moral, *The Making of The Birds* (Harpenden: Kamera Books, 2013), 39. Unless noted, details about the film's making are drawn primarily from this source.
25. Gassmann to AH, April 18, 1962, Gassmann Papers, Special Collections, University of California, Irvine. Unless noted, details on Gassmann and Oskar Sala's work comes from these papers.
26. Ibid.
27. Ibid.
28. Tom Ham, "Musical Silence," unknown publication, c. 1938. BH Papers, University of California, Santa Barbara.
29. BH's separate violin parts, and date of their recording, can be found in Music files, *All That Money Can Buy*, Charles E. Young Research Library, UCLA.
30. BH, John Player Lecture.
31. Ibid.
32. Ibid.
33. Stewart to author, March 28, 1984.
34. AH Papers, Herrick Library.
35. Correspondence between BH and Lucille Fletcher, shared with author by Fletcher, 1988.
36. AH-Truffaut interviews, 1962.
37. AH Papers, Herrick Library.
38. Schneer to author, February 11, 1985.
39. Reid to author, June 6, 1984.
40. Gassmann Papers, UC Irvine. Other cue sheet quotations come from this source.
41. AH Papers, Herrick Library.
42. Bay to author, May 9, 1984.
43. Corwin to author, May 16, 1984.
44. Anderson to author, 1984.
45. Dorothy Herrmann to author, July 29, 2022.

Chapter 11

1. Lloyd to Howard Prouty, 1987.
2. Jon Burlingame, *Music for Prime Time: A History of American Television Themes and Scoring* (New York: Oxford University Press, 2023), 13. The definitive source on the history of TV music.
3. Quoted by Kevin Brownlow, "Alfred Hitchcock," *Film Preservation Society* newsletter, February 1, 2023.
4. Burlingame, *Music for Prime Time*, 33.
5. Melinda Newman, "John Williams Honored with Namesake Award at BMI Film, TV & Visual Media Awards," *Billboard.com*, May 10, 2018.
6. Lloyd to author, May 11, 1984.
7. BH interview with Leslie Zador and Greg Rose.
8. Lloyd to author, May 11, 1984.

9. Details on the series' production and AH's involvement are drawn primarily from Howard Prouty's 1987 interviews with Norman Lloyd, this author's interview with Lloyd, and two books: John McCarty and Brian Kelleher, *Alfred Hitchcock Presents* (New York: St. Martin's Press, 1985), and Grams and Wikstrom, *The Alfred Hitchcock Presents Companion*.
10. Lloyd to Prouty, 1987.
11. Ibid.
12. Ibid.
13. Ibid.
14. Jon Burlingame, album notes, *The Alfred Hitchcock Hour: Volume Two*, Varèse Sarabande, 2011.
15. Quotes from John Morgan and William Stromberg are from author interviews in 2022.
16. Norman Lloyd never forgot Gish's arrival at Universal. "She said, 'You know, the last time I was on this lot was when we did [1915's] *The Birth of a Nation*.' I took a deep breath and said, 'Was a studio here?' She said, 'No, it was a big field!'" Lloyd to Prouty, 1987.
17. After a decade, Joan Harrison was ready to move on. She also wanted more personal time after marrying author Eric Ambler.
18. Christopher Husted, album notes, *Marnie*, conducted by Joel McNeely/Royal Scottish National Orchestra, Varèse Sarabande, 2000.
19. Lloyd to Prouty, 1987.
20. Stephen King, *Danse Macabre* (New York: Scribner, 2011). See also Bulingame, album notes, *The Alfred Hitchcock Hour: Volume Two*.
21. Reviews of "An Unlocked Window," imdb.com episode entry.
22. Herrmann also scored "You'll Be the Death of Me," "Nothing Ever Happens in Linvale," "Change of Address," "Water's Edge," "The McGregor Affair," "Misadventure," "Where the Woodbine Twineth," "Wally the Beard," and "Death Scene." "Linvale" is a comic riff on *Rear Window* voyeurism, wryly scored. "Water's Edge" is a tense find-the-stolen-money thriller, with showy roles for Ann Sothern and John Cassavetes. "Woodbine" laces provocative racial commentary into a tale of a Southern child with the doll of a black girl that may be more than an imaginary friend. The other episodes were mediocre, but Herrmann's music was always additive.
23. Lloyd to Prouty, 1987.
24. Ibid.

Chapter 12

1. Rózsa to author, June 20, 1984.
2. Greenwood to author, May 3, 1985.
3. Dorothy Herrmann to author, July 29, 2022.
4. Robert Presnell Jr. to author, March 13, 1984.
5. BH to LA Anderson, letter shared with author by Anderson.
6. BH to Arnold Weissberger, July 21, 1952.
7. McGilligan, *Alfred Hitchcock*, 622.
8. McDougal, *The Last Mogul*, 313.
9. Rebello, *Alfred Hitchcock and the Making of Psycho*, 235–236.
10. Dorothy Herrmann to author, July 4, 2022.
11. Donald Spoto, The Dark Side of Genius: The Life of Alfred Hitchcock (Boston: Little, Brown & Co., 1983), 483.
12. Norma Herrmann to author, May 2022.
13. Ackroyd, *Alfred Hitchcock*, 229.
14. Taylor, *Hitch*, 272.
15. Houghton to author, November 16, 1984.
16. Quotes from Laurent Bouzereau, William V. Malpede, John Morgan, William Stromberg, and John Wilson are from author interviews in 2022 and 2023.
17. Husted, album notes, *Marnie*.
18. Golding to Hitchcock, spring 1964, AH Papers, Herrick Library.
19. Craig Reardon interview notes, 1977.
20. Tony Lee Moral, *Hitchcock and the Making of Marnie* (Lanham, MD: Scarecrow Press, 2013), 117.
21. Martha Newman Ragland to author, November 29, 1984.
22. Diane Gleghorn to author, July 4, 1984.
23. Joan Greenwood to author, May 13, 1985.
24. Peggy Robertson to David Golding, July 7, 1964, AH Papers, Herrick Library.
25. "Herrmann Says Hollywood Tone Deaf to Film Scores," *Hollywood Reporter*, July 14, 1964.

26. "A Talk with Alfred Hitchcock."
27. *Motion Picture Daily*, June 9, 1964.
28. *Evening News*, July 9, 1964.
29. *Daily Telegraph*, July 10, 1964.
30. *Time*, July 31, 1964.
31. *New York Herald Tribune*, July 23, 1964.
32. *New York Times*, July 23, 1964.
33. *Newsweek*, July 31, 1964.
34. *Variety*, July 1964.
35. *Time*, July 31, 1964.
36. *New York Times*, July 23, 1964.
37. Truffaut, *Hitchcock/Truffaut*, 327.

Chapter 13

1. "A Talk with Alfred Hitchcock."
2. Williams to author, September 6, 1984.
3. Brown, "An Interview with Bernard Herrmann."
4. Hirsch to author, March 21, 1984.
5. McGilligan, *Alfred Hitchcock*, 515.
6. Lloyd to author, May 11, 1984.
7. Houseman to author, April 20, 1984.
8. Lloyd to author, May 11, 1984.
9. Universal's foreboding administration building was nicknamed the Black Tower.
10. Lloyd to Prouty, 1987.
11. Raksin to author, January 25, 1984.
12. McDougal, *The Last Mogul*, 330.
13. Moral, *Hitchcock and the Making of Marnie*, 208.
14. McGilligan, *Alfred Hitchcock*, 652.
15. Ibid., 653.
16. Ibid.
17. BH interview with Leslie Zador and Greg Rose.
18. "An Oral History with Peggy Robertson," 249–250.
19. Gauthier to author, October 30, 1984.
20. Ives to author, October 24, 1984.
21. Christopher Husted, album notes, *Joy in the Morning*, *Film Score Monthly*, 2007.
22. Houseman to author, April 20, 1984.
23. Schneer to author, February 11, 1985.
24. McGilligan, *Alfred Hitchcock*, 661.
25. Ackroyd, *Alfred Hitchcock*, 234.
26. McGilligan, *Alfred Hitchcock*, 668.
27. Ibid., 663.
28. Ibid., 672.
29. Ibid., 665.
30. Ibid., 670.
31. Ibid.
32. Moral, *Hitchcock and the Making of Marnie*, 228–239.
33. McGilligan, *Alfred Hitchcock*, 673.
34. Alexandra Brouwer and Thomas Lee Wright, eds., *Working in Hollywood* (New York: Avon, 1991), 254.
35. McGilligan, *Alfred Hitchcock*, 672.
36. Taylor, *Hitch*, 277.
37. Lloyd to Prouty, 1987.
38. Correspondence on *Torn Curtain* between BH, AH, and AH's office can be found in AH Papers, Herrick Library.
39. Brown, "An Interview with Bernard Herrmann."
40. *François Truffaut: Letters* (London: Faber & Faber, 1989), 290.
41. Wardell, "Music to Commit Murder By."
42. McCaldon to author, April 5, 2023.
43. "An Oral History with Peggy Robertson," 294.
44. Taylor, *Hitch*, 277.

45. Dunne to author, May 15, 1984.

Chapter 14

1. AH to Henry, March 18, 1966, AH Papers, Herrick Library.
2. Correspondence between BH and AH office, as well as AH Music Notes, AH Papers, Herrick Library.
3. Truffaut, *Hitchcock/Truffaut*, 311.
4. Wardell, "Music to Commit Murder By."
5. BH interview with Leslie Zador and Greg Rose.
6. Quotes from Laurent Bouzereau, William V. Malpede, Andrew McCaldon, Nicholas Meyer, Michael McGehee, John Morgan, Anna Bonn Stromberg, and William Stromberg are from author interviews in 2022 and 2023.
7. Robertson memo, March 4, 1966, AH Papers, Herrick Library.
8. Johnson to author, June 4, 1984.
9. BH interview with Zador and Rose.
10. Decker to author, June 13, 1984.
11. Slatkin to author, August 28, 1984.
12. "An Oral History with Peggy Robertson," 294–295. AH and BH quotes in these paragraphs come from this interview.
13. Robertson noted AH's and BH's take preferences. AH Papers, Herrick Library.
14. Taylor, *Hitch*, 278.
15. "An Oral History with Peggy Robertson," 294–295.
16. Adriano, "Hitchcock on Film Music and Bernard Herrmann."
17. Ibid.
18. Robinson to author, June 13, 1984.
19. Ibid.
20. Brown, "An Interview with Bernard Herrmann."
21. Lloyd to author, May 11, 1984.
22. Ibid.
23. William Froug, David Raksin and others to author, 1984–1985. BH made a similar remark to Gilling, "The Colour of Music."
24. Chris Willman, "Quentin Tarantino's 'Once Upon a Time . . . in Hollywood': Deconstructing the Soundtrack," *Variety*, July 25, 2019.
25. AH Papers, Herrick Library.
26. Elmer Bernstein, "A Conversation with John Addison," *Film Music Notebook* 3, no. 3 (1977): 30–31. Addison quotes in this chapter are from this article.
27. "John Addison's Music Notes for 'Torn Curtain,'" AH Papers, Herrick Library.
28. AH Papers, Herrick Library.
29. Ibid.
30. *New York Times*, July 28, 1966.

Chapter 15

1. Williams to author, September 6, 1984.
2. Corwin to author, May 16, 1984.
3. Norma Herrmann to author, November 1, 2022.
4. Thomas, "Film Composer Settles a Score."
5. Norma Herrmann to author, November 1, 2022.
6. Shared with author by Norma Herrmann, 1985.
7. Klein, "The Man Who Composed 'Citizen Kane.'"
8. Ackroyd, *Alfred Hitchcock*, 238.
9. Ibid.
10. It is unclear if he intended to say more. His pause after "Thank you," and audience laughter at his brevity, triggered play-out music as Hitchcock was guided offstage.
11. Ackroyd, *Alfred Hitchcock*, 239.
12. Brown, "An Interview with Bernard Herrmann."
13. Ibid.
14. Pat Gray, "Interview with Bernard Herrmann," in Irwin Bazelon, *Knowing the Score: Notes on Film Music* (New York: Van Nostrand Reinhold, 1975).

15. Adriano, "Hitchcock on Film Music and Bernard Herrmann."
16. Hirsch to author, March 21, 1984.
17. Ibid.
18. De Palma, "Murder by Moog."
19. *Variety*, December 31, 1972.
20. Norma Herrmann to author, November 1, 2022.
21. Hirsch to author, March 21, 1984.
22. Johnson to author, June 4, 1984.
23. Joseph McBride, "Hitchcock: A Defense and an Update," *Film Comment*, 1979.
24. "Plotting *Family Plot*," Laurent Bouzereau, producer, *Family Plot* home video release, 2001.
25. Williams to author, September 6, 1984.
26. Meyer to author, June 5, 2022.
27. Norma Herrmann to author, February 16, 1985.
28. Gauthier to author, October 30, 1984.
29. Ackroyd, *Alfred Hitchcock*, 259.
30. McDougal, *The Last Mogul*, 501.
31. BH, John Player Lecture.
32. Scorsese to author, February 23, 1989.
33. Ross to author, July 16, 2023.
34. Thomas, "Film Composer Settles a Score."
35. Bourne to author, April 7, 2023.
36. "An Oral History with Peggy Robertson."
37. Mark Eden Horowitz, *Sondheim on Music* (Lanham, MD: Rowman & Littlefield, 2019), 72.
38. Corwin to author, February 17, 1984.
39. Herrmann to author, May 2022.
40. McGilligan, *Alfred Hitchcock*, 177.
41. Ackroyd, *Alfred Hitchcock*, 227.
42. Ibid., 37.

Selected Bibliography

Books and Articles

Ackroyd, Peter. *Alfred Hitchcock: A Brief Life.* New York: Doubleday, 2015.
Auiler, Dan. *Vertigo: The Making of a Hitchcock Classic.* New York: St. Martin's Press, 1998.
Barrie, J. M. *Mary Rose: A Play in Three Acts.* London: Samuel French, 1924.
Brown, Royal S. "An Interview with Bernard Herrmann." *High Fidelity*, September 1976.
Brown, Royal S. *Overtones and Undertones: Reading Film Music.* Berkeley: University of California Press, 1994.
Burlingame, Jon. *Music for Prime Time: A History of American Television Themes and Scoring.* New York: Oxford University Press, 2023.
Burlingame, Jon. *Sound and Vision: 60 Years of Motion Picture Soundtracks.* New York: Billboard Books, 2000.
Christlieb, Don. *Recollections of a First Chair Bassoonist: 52 Years in the Hollywood Studio Orchestras.* Sherman Oaks, CA: Christlieb Products, 1996.
Coleman, Herbert. *The Man Who Knew Hitchcock.* Lanham, MD: Scarecrow Press, 2007.
Cooke, Mervyn. *A History of Film Music.* New York: Cambridge University Press, 2008.
Daniel, Oliver. "A Perspective of Herrmann." *Saturday Review*, July 13, 1968.
Darby, William, and Jack Du Bois. *American Film Music: Major Composers, Techniques, Trends, 1915–1990.* Jefferson, NC: McFarland, 1999.
DeRosa, Steven. *Writing with Hitchcock.* New York: Faber & Faber, 2001.
Gilling, Ted. "The Colour of Music: An Interview with Bernard Herrmann." *Sight & Sound*, Winter 1971–1972.
Herrmann, Bernard. "Bernard Herrmann: A John Player Lecture." *Pro Musica Sana*, Spring 1974, Summer 1974.
Herrmann, Bernard. "Music in Motion Pictures: A Reply to Mr. Leinsdorf." *New York Times*, June 24, 1945.
Houseman, John. *Front and Center.* New York: Simon & Schuster, 1979.
Isralowitz, Jason. *Nothing to Fear: Alfred Hitchcock and the Wrong Men.* Columbus, OH: Fayetteville Mafia Press, 2023.
Johnson, Edward. *Bernard Herrmann: Hollywood's Music-Dramatist.* London: Triad Press, 1977.
Karlin, Fred. *Listening to Movies: The Film Lover's Guide to Film Music.* New York: Schirmer Books, 1994.
Mauceri, John. *The War on Music: Reclaiming the Twentieth Century.* New Haven, CT: Yale University Press, 2022.
McDougal, Dennis. *The Last Mogul: Lew Wasserman, MCA, and the Hidden History of Hollywood.* Boston: Da Capo Press, 2001.
McGilligan, Patrick. *Alfred Hitchcock: A Life in Darkness and Light.* New York: HarperCollins, 2003.
Moral, Tony Lee. *Hitchcock and the Making of Marnie.* Lanham, MD: Scarecrow Press, 2013.
Moral, Tony Lee. *The Making of Hitchcock's The Birds.* Harpenden: Kamera Books, 2013.
Palmer, Christopher. *The Composer in Hollywood.* London: Marion Boyards, 2000.
Platte, Nathan. *Making Music in Selznick's Hollywood.* New York: Oxford University Press, 2018.
Rebello, Stephen. *Alfred Hitchcock and the Making of Psycho.* New York: Soft Skull Press, 1990.
Ross, Alex. *The Rest Is Noise: Listening to the Twentieth Century.* New York: Picador, 2007.

Ross, Alex. *Wagnerism: Art and Politics in the Shadow of Music.* New York: Macmillan, 2020.
Rothman, William. *Hitchcock: The Murderous Gaze.* Cambridge, MA: Harvard University Press, 1984.
Rózsa, Miklós. *Double Life.* New York: Hippocrene, 1982.
Skerry, Philip J. *Psycho in the Shower.* New York: Continuum, 2009.
Smith, Steven C. *A Heart at Fire's Center: The Life and Music of Bernard Herrmann.* Berkeley: University of California Press, 1991.
Smith, Steven C. *Music by Max Steiner: The Epic Life of Hollywood's Most Influential Composer.* New York: Oxford University Press, 2020.
Sullivan, Jack. *Hitchcock's Music.* New Haven, CT: Yale University Press, 2008.
Taylor, John Russell. *Hitch: The Life and Times of Alfred Hitchcock.* New York: Pantheon, 1978.
Thomas, Tony. *Film Score: The Art & Craft of Movie Music.* Burbank, CA: Riverwood Press, 1991.
Thomas, Tony. *Music for the Movies.* 2nd ed. Los Angeles: Silman-James, 1997.
Truffaut, Francois. *Hitchcock/Truffaut.* Rev. ed. New York: Simon & Schuster, 1983.
White, Edward. *The Twelve Lives of Alfred Hitchcock.* New York: W. W. Norton, 2021.
Zador, Leslie T., and Greg Rose. "A Conversation with Bernard Herrmann." In *Film Music 1*, edited by Clifford McCarty. New York: Garland, 1989.

Index

For the benefit of digital users, indexed terms that span two pages (e.g., 52–53) may, on occasion, appear on only one of those pages.

Figures are indicated by an italic *f* following the page number.

39 Steps, The, 17, 31, 139

Addison, John, 254–57
Alfred Hitchcock Hour, The (TV series), 197–211, 200*f*, 229–30, 244
  "Behind the Locked Door," 203–4, 248
  "Body in the Barn," 202–3, 285n.16
  "Consider Her Ways," 204–5
  "Home Away from Home, A," 200–2
  "Jar, The," 205–7, 206*f*
  "Life Work of Juan Diaz, The," 207–8
  "Terror at Northfield," 202
  "Unlocked Window, An," 208–11, 209*f*, 239
Alfred Hitchcock Presents (TV series), 55–56, 78, 80n.*, 100, 197, 198, 244
Allen, Jay Presson, 58, 219, 227, 230, 230n.*, 269
All That Money Can Buy, 30, 85, 189–91, 190*f*, 230–31
Anderson, Lucy
  divorce from Herrmann, 221–23, 231–32, 271
  falling in love with Herrmann, 97–99
  married life with Herrmann, 40, 41*f*, 120, 134–35, 195
  relationship with Hitchcocks, 58–59, 67, 132, 212–14
Andrews, Julie, 233–36, 235*f*, 241, 256
Artist, The, 122

Bass, Saul, 108–9, 109n.*, 126, 129*f*, 140, 160, 188
Beatles, The, 161, 180, 191, 227, 229, 244, 267
Benny & Hitch (radio play), 9–10, 85, 106, 132, 212, 217, 221, 232, 241
Bernstein, Elmer, 51, 71, 86, 96, 181, 182–83, 253–54
Bernstein, Leonard, 64, 135
Birds, The
  making of, 183–84, 184*f*, 186–88, 187*f*, 214–15
  response to, 214
  soundtrack of, 188–89, 191–94, 194*f*, 195*f*
Bloch, Robert, 149–50, 174–75, 200–1
Bourne, Sir Matthew, 268
Bouzereau, Laurent, 52, 54, 110, 143, 159, 219, 220, 248, 272
Boyle, Robert, 94, 137, 216–17
Bradbury, Ray, 183, 205–6, 206*f*, 207, 239, 241–42, 242*f*
Burks, Robert, 34–35, 82*f*, 82, 234, 261–62
  Vertigo, filming of, 102, 104, 117
Busta Rymes, 160

Cape Fear, 186, 210, 267–68, 283n.11
Carrie (film), 265
CBS Symphony, 29, 64, 66, 76, 97, 99
Citizen Kane, 22, 29–30, 29*f*, 31, 48, 50, 85, 182
Cohen, Larry, 265
Cole, Nat King, 223, 224, 226
Coleman, Herbert
  friendship with Herrmann, 37, 134
  Man Who Knew Too Much, The, 57*f*, 63, 75
  North by Northwest, 137
  Psycho, 149–50
  Trouble with Harry, The, 32–33, 34, 36, 51–52
  Vertigo, 100, 101, 112, 125–26, 127
  Wrong Man, The, 80–81, 83
Columbia Workshop, The (radio series), 28–29, 189
Connery, Sean, 219, 220, 225–26
Crime Classics (radio series), 52

Day, Doris, 59–61, 62*f*, 63, 67–69
Day the Earth Stood Still, The, 42–43, 191, 247, 267–68
Debussy, Claude, 49, 109, 120, 182
De Palma, Brian, 4–5, 105, 262–64, 264*f*, 265
Diaboliques, Les (novel and film), 95, 148–49, 261

Dudamel, Gustavo, 122

Erickson, C.O. "Doc", 34–35, 56, 57f, 82

Fahrenheit 451 (film), 89, 120, 201, 239, 258, 263, 267
Family Plot, 7, 264–65
Fletcher, Lucille
   courtship by Herrmann, 84–85
   friendship after divorce, 99, 196
   married life with Herrmann, 31, 96f
   separation and divorce from Herrmann, 97–98
   writing libretto of *Wuthering Heights*, 76–77
Fonda, Henry, 18, 80, 82f, 82–83
Forsythe, John, 34, 35f, 47, 262
Frenzy (1972), 262
Funeral March of a Marionette (composition), 198, 202

Gassman, Remi, 188–89, 191–93
Gauthier, Sue, 57, 79–80, 185–86, 231, 265
Gershwin, George, 28, 139
Ghost and Mrs. Muir, The, 38–39, 123, 230n.*
Goodwin, Ron, 262
Grant, Cary, 19, 33, 186–88, 225–26
   and *North by Northwest*, 137, 139, 140f, 141, 143f, 146

Hangover Square, 38–39, 85
Harrison, Joan, 56–57, 127, 197–98, 199, 200f, 285n.17
Harryhausen, Ray, 138–39, 181, 191, 193, 232, 267–68
Hayes, John Michael, 33, 62–63, 74, 99–100, 183–84
Hedren, Tippi, 187f, 188, 191–92, 215–17, 216f
Henry, Edd, 229, 232–33, 237, 238, 244, 251, 254
Herrmann, Bernard
   Anglophilia of, 37–38, 58, 147, 258
   childhood, 24–26
   composing process, 40–43
   composing style, 30, 43, 46, 49, 72, 85–86, 117, 169, 200, 247
   conducting style, 65–66, 77, 78f
   conflict with studios and producers, 30, 126–27, 135, 180–81, 182–83, 229–30, 246
   musical education of, 26–28
   romantic nature of, 95–97, 98–99, 105–6
   salary demands, 39, 43, 81, 83, 155
   scoring process with Hitchcock, 62, 104–5, 121, 155–56, 228, 238–39, 241
   socializing with Hitchcock, 58–59, 193, 244
Herrmann, Dorothy "Taffy," 40–42, 41f, 54, 64, 96f, 155, 177, 183, 196, 213, 215
Herrmann, Norma. *See* Norma Shepherd
Herrmann, Wendy, 40, 41f, 96f, 178
Hirsch, Paul, 229, 262–64, 264f
Hitchcock, Alfred
   anxieties and fears of, 35, 69, 79–80, 129–30, 155, 174, 216, 265
   breakdown of relationship with Herrmann, 228–29, 236–38, 241
   daily routine of, 56, 132
   early filmmaking work, 15–17
   financial dealings of, 12, 13–15, 55–56, 136, 147, 150–51, 177, 214–15, 230–31
   firing of Herrmann, 250–51
   first meetings with Herrmann, 30–31, 36–37
   music, feelings about, 19–22, 51–52, 61, 104–5, 237–38
Hitchcock, Alma Reville
   contribution to husband's work, 7, 15–17, 16f, 139, 230–31
   health issues and death of, 129–30, 265, 266
   married life with Hitchcock, 12, 16–12, 215, 231
   socializing with Herrmanns, 31, 58–59, 132, 212, 244
Hitchcock, Patricia "Pat," 17, 55–56, 94, 130
Houseman, John, 12, 29, 77, 98–99, 229, 232
Hunter, Evan, 183–84, 219

Ives, Charles, 26–27, 46, 64, 248

Jane Eyre (film), 38–39, 76, 77, 219
Journey to the Center of the Earth, 139
Joy in the Morning, 231–32, 236–38, 239

Kelly, Grace, 13f, 19, 33, 34, 94, 100, 215
King, Stephen, 205–6

Lady Gaga, 11, 110
Lehman, Ernest, 135–37, 139, 146, 183–84
Leigh, Janet, 152–53, 161–62, 166, 174, 176
Livingston, Jay & Evans, Ray, 61, 127, 128f, 256–57
Lloyd, Norman, 7, 77, 82, 129, 146, 180
   and Hitchcock TV series, 197–200, 205–7, 211, 216
   and *Torn Curtain*, 229–30, 236, 244, 252–53, 253f
Lolita (film), 182

London Symphony Orchestra, 66–67, 74, 75, 77–78

MacLaine, Shirley, 34, 35*f*
Magnificent Ambersons, The, 30, 31, 85
Malpede, William V., 90, 114, 120, 121, 218, 219, 248
Mancini, Henry, 181, 236, 247
Man Who Knew Too Much, The (1934) 17, 20–21, 59, 60–61, 62, 72–73
Man Who Knew Too Much, The (1956)
  Albert Hall sequence and scoring of film, 66–75, 111
  making of, 59–64
Marnie
  commercial exploitation of music, 223–25
  making of, 215–17
  reaction to film and score, 225–27
  scoring of, 217–21
Mary Rose, 15, 94–95, 101, 104, 117, 230–31, 230n.*
Mathieson, Muir, 125–26
MCA (aka Music Corporation of America)
  early years of, 8, 12, 13, 18–19
  Herrmann's antipathy toward, 214, 229–30, 231, 236–37, 246
  Hitchcock, involvement in career of, 13–15, 55–56, 150, 152, 185, 197, 198, 211, 214–15, 223, 229, 230–31, 257, 262
  last years of, 266–67
  purchase of Universal backlot and studio, 130–31, 185–86
  television shows, production of, 55, 147, 152, 214
McCaldon, Andrew, 75, 169, 241, 249. See also *Benny & Hitch*
McGehee, Michael, 44, 48, 52, 144, 162, 168, 248, 249
Meyer, Nicholas, 49, 105, 246, 265
Miles, Vera, 82–83, 100, 102, 152
Morgan, John W., 43
  on *Alfred Hitchcock Hour, The,* 203, 204, 205, 207, 210
  on *Man Who Knew Too Much, The,* 70, 71, 72
  on *North by Northwest,* 141, 142
  on *Psycho,* 160, 164, 166
  on *Torn Curtain,* 247–48
  on *Trouble with Harry, The,* 45, 47, 48, 49
  on *Vertigo,* 109, 110, 112, 113
  on *Wrong Man, The,* 87, 89, 90
Moross, Jerome, 23, 24, 28

Murray, Lyn
  conflict with Herrmann, 182
  friendship with Herrmann, 51, 141
  work with Hitchcock, 19, 36, 199

Newman, Alfred, 38–39, 46, 51, 96, 178
Newman, David, 166
Newman, Lionel, 61, 178, 182, 263
Newman, Paul, 55, 233–36, 235*f*, 241, 245, 245*f*, 256
New York Philharmonic, 23, 64–65, 267–68
North by Northwest, 150, 267–68
  making of, 136–39
  reaction to and influence of, 146
  scoring of, 139–46, 219
Novak, Kim, 100, 102, 103*f*, 104, 105, 108, 116*f*, 117, 122

Obsession (film), 105, 123, 263–64
Once Upon a Time. . .in Hollywood, 253–54
On Dangerous Ground, 144–45

Paradine Case, The, 22
Paramount Pictures
  contract with Hitchcock, 12, 14–15
  filming and scoring at, 35–36, 50–51, 60, 67–69, 75, 184–85
  history of, 14
  Hitchcock's departure from, 184–85, 230–31
  and *Psycho,* 148, 150, 175
  and *Vertigo,* 102, 124–25, 126–29
Perkins, Anthony, 151–52, 172*f*, 176
Pleasure Garden The, 15, 16*f*, 20–21
Psycho
  influence and legacy of, 7, 263, 267–68
  making of, 148–55, 151*f*, 154*f*, 175*f*
  reaction to, 174–78, 185
  scoring of, 155–63, 159*f*, 164–74, 262
  shower murder music (aka "The Murder"), 7, 155, 166–68, 173, 176, 178, 193–94, 224–25, 263
  Taxi Driver connection, 6

Raksin, David, 66, 127, 230, 271
Rear Window, 12, 13*f*, 18, 22, 33, 80, 94
Rebecca, 12, 22, 101
Rebello, Stephen, 56–57, 175, 177, 185
Robertson, Peggy, 56–57, 186*f*, 189, 194, 265, 268
  on Hitchcock, 83, 153, 185–86, 231
  Torn Curtain, 234–36, 237, 242, 246–47, 249–51, 257

Ross, Alex, 65, 71, 87
  on *Vertigo*, 106, 109, 110, 112, 113, 114, 120, 122, 123
Ross, Atticus, 92, 267
Rózsa, Miklós, 180, 212, 220

Saint, Eva Marie, 137, 140*f*, 143*f*, 146
Sala, Oskar, 188–89, 191–93, 194*f*
Scorsese, Martin, 1, 2–5, 6, 93, 108, 163, 263, 267
Selznick, David O., 12, 17–18, 21, 22, 31, 83
Seven-Per-Cent Solution, The, 265
Shadow of a Doubt, 17–18, 21, 31
Shepherd, Norma (aka Herrmann, Norma), 114
  on Herrmann's death, 265
  on Hitchcock & Herrmann, 57–58, 260, 269
  marriage to Herrmann, 258–60, 259*f*, 261
  Taxi Driver sessions, 5, 6
Sisters, 262–64
Snows of Kilimanjaro, The (film), 42–43, 92, 109
Sondheim, Stephen, 11, 85, 169, 203, 268
Spellbound, 22, 220
Spielberg, Steven, 4, 139, 263, 266
Star Wars, 165
Stefano, Joseph
  on Herrmann, 158, 174, 177, 178
  on Hitchcock, 79, 130
  writing for Hitchcock, 151–52, 155, 161–62, 176
Steiner, Fred, 59, 66, 158
Steiner, Max, 21, 43, 65, 181
Stewart, James, 13*f*
  Man Who Knew Too Much, The, 59–60, 61, 63, 71, 74
  and MCA, 18, 55
  Vertigo, 100, 101, 102, 103*f*, 104, 105, 108, 116*f*, 130
Stokowski, Leopold, 40, 77, 85
"Storm Clouds" Cantata, 60–61, 62, 66–67, 70, 72–75, 278n.21
Strangers on a Train, 19–20, 21, 34–35, 92
Stravinsky, Igor, 42, 64, 83
Stromberg, Anna Bonn, 43, 110, 121, 142, 160, 165
Stromberg, William T.,
  on *Alfred Hitchcock Hour, The*, 201, 204, 205, 207, 210
  on *Man Who Knew Too Much, The*, 70, 71, 72
  on *Marnie*, 210
  on *North by Northwest*, 141
  on *Psycho*, 160, 161, 162, 166, 169
  on *Torn Curtain*, 247
  on *Trouble with Harry, The* 43, 45, 46, 47

  on *Vertigo*, 108–9, 111, 112, 113, 115, 117, 120, 121, 123, 126
  on *Wrong Man, The*, 87, 88, 89, 90
Studio system, Hollywood, 8, 14, 18, 55, 124, 136, 149, 178, 185–86

Tarantino, Quentin, 11, 253–54
Taxi Driver, 1–6, 93, 263–64, 265
Taylor, Samuel, vi, 101, 102, 119, 234–36, 249
Tender is the Night, 181–82
Tiomkin, Dimitri, 21–22, 61, 87, 237–38
To Catch a Thief, 19, 33, 36, 82, 137
Tomasini, George, 56, 118, 132–34, 137–38, 186, 216–17
  Birds, The, 192, 193
  death of, 231, 236, 244
  Psycho, 150–51, 154–55, 162, 172–73
Topaz, 262
Torn Curtain, 235*f*, 242*f*, 245*f*, 249*f*, 253*f*, 256*f*
  making of, 232–36
  reaction to, 257
  scoring of, 236–43, 244–57
Toscanini, Arturo, 23–24, 29
Tristan und Isolde (opera), 98, 118, 121–22
Trouble with Harry, The, 8, 55, 56, 138, 148
  hiring of Herrmann, 36, 37, 39
  making of, 32–36
  scoring of, 44–54
Truffaut, Francois
  and Herrmann, 89, 239, 240, 258, 267
  influence on Hitchcock, 188, 232–33
  interviews with Hitchcock, 120, 192, 260–61
  remarks on Hitchcock, 69, 177, 214, 226–27
Twilight Zone, The, 120, 139, 146, 171, 196, 205, 217

Universal Studios
  Hitchcock's offices at, 185–86, 266
  music department, 198–99
  and *Psycho*, 7, 150, 153–54
  sale of backlot and studio to MCA, 130–31, 185–86

Vaughan Williams, Ralph, 38, 46, 48, 64, 65, 78, 204
Vertigo
  making of, 94–95, 99–104
  reaction to and legacy of, 127–30
  scoring of, 104–14, 115–27, 219

Warner Bros., 13–14, 21, 43, 80–81, 83, 92–93, 178

Wasserman, Lew, 8, 9*f*
   early life and career, 18–19
   and Herrmann, 221, 223, 229–30
   and Hitchcock, 12–14, 18, 100, 102, 136, 185–86
   and Hitchcock TV series, 55–56, 211
   last years, 266–67
   and *Psycho,* 150, 151, 152, 174, 175, 175*f,* 179
   and *Torn Curtain,* 232–34, 236–37, 243, 251
Waxman, Franz, 22, 42, 181
Welles, Orson, 31, 57–58, 199, 221, 252, 262
   radio and film work with Herrmann, 22, 29–30, 29*f*

Williams, John, 4, 122, 165, 198–99, 200, 228–29, 258, 264–65, 268
Williamsburg: The Story of a Patriot, 93
Wilson, John, 30, 46, 72, 108, 116, 121, 126, 160, 166, 171, 217
Wilson, Stanley, 141, 198–99, 254, 255
Wrong Man, The 82*f,* 89*f,* 100
   making of, 79–83
   scoring of, 83–84, 85–93
Wuthering Heights (opera), 76–77, 178, 197, 239, 260

Zanuck, Darryl F., 38–39, 178